KERRY BROWN is Professor of Chinese Studies and Director of the Lau China Institute at King's College London, and Associate Fellow specializing in Asia at Chatham House. With 20 years' experience of life in China, he has worked in education, business and government, including a term as First Secretary at the British Embassy in Beijing. He writes regularly for international media, and has authored over ten books on contemporary China, among them *The New Emperors* (I.B.Tauris, 2014), *Contemporary China* (2012) and *Struggling Giant: China in the 21st Century* (with Jonathan Fenby, 2007).

KERRY BROWN
CEO, CHINA
THE RISE OF XI JINPING

I.B. TAURIS
LONDON · NEW YORK

Published in 2016 by
I.B.Tauris & Co. Ltd
London • New York
www.ibtauris.com

ISBN: 978 1 78453 322 9
eISBN: 978 0 85772 961 3
ePDF: 978 0 85772 757 2

A full CIP record for this book is available from the British Library
A full CIP record is available from the Library of Congress
Library of Congress Catalog Card Number: available

Typeset by Tetragon, London
Printed and bound in Sweden by ScandBook AB

Dedicated to Jim O'Donoghue and Katherine Peters

CONTENTS

Master Tseng said, Every day I examine myself on these three points: in acting on behalf of others, have I always been loyal to their interests? In intercourse with my friends, have I always been true to my word? Have I failed to repeat the precepts that have been handed down to me?

Analects 1.4

ACKNOWLEDGEMENTS

I am grateful to Tomasz Hoskins and his colleagues at I.B.Tauris for their continuing support in commissioning this work, as well as to my former colleagues at the University of Sydney and Chatham House in London for all their insights, inspirations and assistance. I am also, as ever, grateful to my daughter Tanya Brown for her patience and forbearance while I wrote this in early 2015, and to Kalley Wu for her support. I am extremely grateful for the help of Emily Dunn, Simone van Nieuwenhuizen, Caroline Chong, Samuel Johnson and Haimin Huang for their work on correcting the text, and to Alexander Middleton for copy-editing it so well, Alex Billington at Tetragon for his work on the production, and Sarah Terry for her proofreading.

NOTE ON THE TEXT

All transliterations of Chinese into English are in Pinyin. The translations from Chinese to English in the text are my own, unless otherwise stated in the endnote references.

PREFACE

There is an occupational hazard for anyone who chooses to write about Chinese politics in the second decade of the twenty-first century. We may live in an age of openness and information, but the inner workings of the Chinese political system, and in particular the lives and thinking of its leaders, remain one of the few bastions of opacity. Those who choose to write about it, therefore, have to face two different kinds of criticism. From one side, there is the complaint often made from within China that anyone trying to work out its internal politics 'doesn't really understand' because he or she is an outsider. These people use dark phrases like 'you don't really know how China works'. The implication is that the system is so fiendishly complicated and successfully protective of its secrets that only those deep within can truly understand it – and of course, they are the last to say what they know. There are also many outside China who have a vested interest in maintaining this image of 'unknowability'. To them, years of observation and careful scrutiny of 'name lists' are the only legitimate pathway to understanding. Perhaps tellingly, one of the diplomats I worked with in the past combined professional interest in elite Chinese politics with collecting dead moths. He got a lot of things right, but spoke about China and the Chinese like they were taxidermy exhibits in a museum.

On the other side, there is the complaint that those who try to write with some sympathy, or attempt to understand internal Chinese politics too much on its own terms, are apologists, people who have 'gone native' and are guilty of producing external propaganda for an immoral system. The work of (the American) Robert Lawrence Kuhn is most representative here. His earlier biography of Jiang Zemin was one of very few based on meetings and first-hand encounters with China's then president, and his follow-up book on the new leadership in 2011 was similarly advantaged by excellent top-level access. Kuhn's writings, however, have been criticized for being over-respectful and fawning, presenting leaders like Xi in an uncritical light.[1] This accusation of partisanship is a common taunt against those who write about Chinese politics in a far more neutral tone than Kuhn's.

After almost a quarter of a century trying to work out what power means in China, how it is exercised and what makes Chinese elite leaders tick, something I have come to realize is that hybrid approaches work best, taking methods and insights from diverse areas and trying to link them to what one observes in China. It is a good idea too to treat Chinese political behaviour the way one would address political habits and modes of action anywhere. The United Kingdom and the United States both have peculiarities about their systems and the way people operate in them. But, broadly speaking, people strive for power and are motivated to acquire that power for very similar reasons no matter where they are. We are all part of one species, so there should be no shock about this. The important thing is to keep a sense of proportion between the unique features of specific systems and their shared attributes. Overstressing one and understressing the other are both mistaken.

Xi Jinping, who is the subject of this book, is the current leader of the People's Republic of China (PRC). His elevation to this position happened with little transparency, and with almost every observer and pundit who watched the process initially predicting that he would have much less influence and power than he has seemingly accrued since being made general secretary of the Chinese Communist Party (CCP) in November 2012. Since that time he has adorned himself with a host of titles and leadership positions. On paper, at least, in recent decades China has never before had such a powerful person. But as I will argue throughout this book, in China, more than most other places, power is a tricky thing. That is why choosing the right framework within which to understand power and in particular the kinds of power that someone like Xi, ostensibly at the top of the political system, exercises is so important. Chinese politics exists in an historical, cultural, social and intellectual context, from where it gains much of its specificity. And as we shall see, power in modern China is circumscribed by all sorts of boundaries and manifestations that give it its unique attributes and qualities. The issue then is one of interpretation and the level of emphasis placed on each factor. Overemphasizing the organization of the CCP, and not looking at its ideological or emotional basis, means we miss something crucial about what this entity is, and how people like Xi are able to direct it. Chinese politics, like politics anywhere, is very dynamic. Seeing the visible signs of that dynamism is not difficult. The question then becomes how to devise a way to capture this dynamism and strike a balance between general and particular features. Empirical observation plays a part in that, but so does imagination. It is, as I go out of my way to make clear many times throughout this book, not a precise science. But nor is it a modern version of alchemy.

Chinese politics has often been treated as something remote and mysterious, best left to specialists. This book is part of an attempt to change that, and encourage as wide an audience as possible to think about, and engage with, the political life of China. That gives some of what follows a sometimes quite personal tone. As the great sinologist Pierre Ryckmans (whose pen name was Simon Leys) once wrote, 'we cannot learn any foreign values if we do not accept the risk of being transformed by what we learn.'[2] In that sense, China, with its re-emergence to global economic and political prominence, is already transforming us. The simple polarities that sufficed in the past – 'they are Communists, we are democracies; they are bad, we are good!' – have eroded to the point where the boundaries between 'them' and 'us' are almost no longer visible, a bit like the tiny vestiges of the Great Wall of China in the far west of the country, which are not easy to see even if you stand beside them, let alone if you are trying to see them from the moon.[3]

I hope, therefore, that this book at least captures something of the dynamism of China's political culture and, in particular, of the current phase it is going through. Something that unites the chapters that follow is that they all in different ways address questions about power, largely through Xi Jinping, and the relationship he has to the political party he leads, the CCP. Where is power located in contemporary China? And how can we best find and then describe it? These are important issues, and ones that we all need to spend time answering, because the decisions made by Xi Jinping and the people around him are not remote from us. They have global consequences, and reach deep into our lives, no matter where we happen to be based. While it is often in the Party's interests to bask in secrecy, this is not something that external observers need to comply with. We do have a responsibility to try to understand as best we can what the Chinese leadership are doing, and where they are driving the immensely important country they are in charge of in the coming years. One issue that will therefore be coiled intimately around Xi and his personal power is how best to describe the CCP itself. What sort of thing is it? A hard-nosed, money-making machine that exists to enrich its key leaders (the claim of many critics)? Or the repository of political wisdom and ideological experience for the last six decades of PRC history, which has delivered staggering success (the view closest to that articulated by Xi himself)? Can it be both of these? This book's title implies that I do regard the Party as, in some senses, a business. But it is a business with values and objectives far more complex than any normal enterprise that exists inside or outside China, and one that does not just deal in producing GDP growth and economic success, but has to articulate a national vision that increasingly, as Xi shows, appeals to people's emotional allegiance and their hopes and fears. Just like a business it has to forge loyalty, look after its stakeholders and try to articulate and deliver its core aims. The Party is, in some senses, currently the world's most successful and complex enterprise. But Xi, as its CEO, is also trying to carry it towards a mission that is more akin to that of a religious or cultural organization. This book will plot the ways he is trying to achieve that, and what his chances of success might be.

I have commenced each chapter with a quotation from Confucius.[4] There is a simple reason for this. Unlike in the Maoist period, as I will explain later in this book, modern Chinese leaders – with Xi very prominently among them – have set the moral teaching of the philosopher from 2,500 years ago as the worthy standard to appeal to and seek legitimacy from. The quotes, therefore, are partly to create the right frame of mind in the reader so that he or she can start thinking about the historic and cultural context of authority and power in China, but they also act as a reminder of just how high Chinese modern leaders set their sights. I leave it to the reader to be the final judge of whether the CCP in the twenty-first century can truly claim to have successfully lived up to the ancient Confucian precepts and ideals of justice, harmony and righteous authority.

LIST OF ABBREVIATIONS

APEC	Asia-Pacific Economic Cooperation
BRICS	Brazil, Russia, India, China and South Africa
CCP	Chinese Communist Party
CDIC	Central Discipline and Inspection Commission
CMC	Central Military Commission
CNPC	China National Petroleum Corporation
CPPCC	Chinese People's Political Consultative Conference
DPRK	Democratic People's Republic of Korea
DRC	Development Research Centre of the State Council
GSK	GlaxoSmithKline
IMF	International Monetary Fund
MSS	Ministry of State Security
NPC	National People's Congress
OECD	Organization for Economic Cooperation and Development
PAP	People's Armed Police
PLA	People's Liberation Army
PRC	People's Republic of China
RMB	renminbi (the official currency of the PRC)
SEZ	Special Economic Zone
SCO	Shanghai Cooperation Organization
SOE	state-owned enterprise
WTO	World Trade Organization

KEY PEOPLE

BO XILAI (1949–)   Former Party secretary for Chongqing. Sentenced to life imprisonment in 2013 for corruption.

BO YIBO (1908–2007)   Father of Bo Xilai and one of the 'Eight Immortals' of the CCP.

CHEN XI (1953–)   Executive deputy head of the Organization Department of the CCP. Considered a close friend and mentor of Xi Jinping.

CHEN YUN (1905–95)   One of the 'Eight Immortals' and key contributor to China's economic strategy under Deng Xiaoping.

GENG BIAO (1909–2000)   Former minister of national defence for whom Xi worked as secretary in the 1980s.

HU JINTAO (1942–)   General secretary of the CCP from 2002 to 2012 and president of China from 2003 to 2013.

HU YAOBANG (1915–89)   General secretary of the CCP from 1982 to 1987. His death in 1989 sparked the Tiananmen protests.

JIANG QING (1914–91)   Mao Zedong's fourth wife and alleged ringleader of the Gang of Four.

JIANG ZEMIN (1926–)   General secretary of the CCP from 1989 to 2002 and President of the PRC from 1993 to 2003.

LI PENG (1928–)   Premier of the PRC from 1987 to 1998. Famous for advocating military intervention in the Tiananmen protests.

LI YUANCHAO (1950–)   Vice president of the PRC.

LIN BIAO (1907–71)   Vice chairman of the CCP from 1958 to his death in 1971. Died in a mysterious plane crash shortly after being accused of an assassination attempt against Mao Zedong.

LIU SHAOQI (1898–1969)   President of the PRC from 1959 to 1968. Was purged by Mao but posthumously rehabilitated in 1980.

LIU XIAOBO (1955–)   Chinese human-rights activist, and winner of the Nobel Peace Prize in 2010. Detained for involvement in the Charter 08 manifesto.

LIU YUNSHAN (1947–)   Member of the Standing Committee of the Politburo of the 18th Congress of the CCP, chairman of the CCP Central Guidance Commission for Building Spiritual Civilization and former head of the Propaganda Department.

MAO ZEDONG (1893–1976)   Revolutionary, poet, politician. Chairman of the CCP from 1949 to 1976.

PENG DEHUAI (1898–1974)   China's defence minister from 1954 to 1959. Purged for criticism of Mao's leadership.

WANG HUNING (1955–)   Director of CCP Policy Research Office from 2002 to 2012. Member of the 18th Party Congress Politburo. Regarded as China's chief foreign-policy thinker.

WANG QISHAN (1948–)   Member of the Politburo 18th Standing Committee and secretary of the Central Commission for Discipline Inspection.

WEN JIABAO (1942–)   Premier of the PRC from 2003 to 2013.

WU BANGGUO (1941–)   Chairman and Party secretary of the Standing Committee of the NPC from 2003 to 2013.

XI ZHONGXUN (1913–2002)   Xi Jinping's father and one of the 'Eight Immortals' of the CCP.

YU ZHENGSHENG (1945–)   Chairman of the CPPCC from 2013 and member of the Politburo Standing Committee of the 18th Congress of the CCP.

ZHANG DEJIANG (1946–)   Deputy head of the National Security Commission, chairman of the Standing Committee of the NPC and member of the Politburo Standing Committee of the 18th Congress of the CCP.

ZHOU YONGKANG (1942–)   Former secretary of the Central Political and Legal Affairs Commission and Politburo Standing Committee member from 2007 to 2012. Sentenced to life in prison for corruption and abuse of power in June 2015.

ZHU RONGJI (1928–)   Premier of the PRC from 1998 to 2003.

TIMELINE OF XI JINPING'S LIFE

(and key dates in post-1949 Chinese history)

1949	Founding of the PRC.
1950–3	Korean War, in which China fights on the side of North Korea.
1953	Xi is born in Beijing, the son of Xi Zhongxun and Qi Xin.
1956–7	Mao Zedong's Hundred Flowers Campaign, which turns into an anti-rightist campaign against his critics.
1958–61	The Great Leap Forward, an economic and social campaign intended to accelerate China's industrialization, leads to widespread famine.
1960–2	Sino-Soviet split.
1963	Xi Zhongxun is purged due to his support for a novel regarded as critical of Mao Zedong.
1964	China tests its first nuclear bomb.
1966	The start of the Cultural Revolution cuts Xi Jinping's schooling short. His father is expelled from Beijing to undertake hard labour.
1969–75	Xi Jinping is sent to the Shaanxi countryside in central China, becoming a 'sent-down youth'.
1972	Nixon makes his historic visit to China, signalling US–China rapprochement.
1974	Xi successfully applies to join the CCP after ten failed attempts.
1975	Xi returns to Beijing to begin studies at the faculty of chemical engineering at Qinghua University.
1976	Mao dies, and the Gang of Four are arrested.

1978	Xi Zhongxun is fully rehabilitated and appointed second secretary to Guangdong Province. Deng Xiaoping initiates the 'reform and opening-up' process.
1979	After graduation from Qinghua University, Xi Jinping begins work at the CMC as defence minister Geng Biao's secretary. Sino-Vietnamese War.
1982	Xi begins working in Zhengding village, Hebei Province, first as deputy secretary and then as secretary.
1985	Xi makes a visit to the United States, travelling to Iowa as part of an agricultural delegation. He moves to Xiamen, Fujian Province, where he becomes executive vice mayor.
1987	Xi marries his second wife, Peng Liyuan.
1988	Xi becomes Party secretary of Ningde, Fujian Province.
1989	Tiananmen Square protests. Xi Zhongxun opposes military intervention and moves to Shenzhen, where he lives until his death.
1990	Xi Jinping becomes Party secretary of Fuzhou, Fujian Province.
1992	Deng Xiaoping undertakes his 'Southern Tour', which includes Fuzhou, to reinvigorate the reform process.
1996	Xi is promoted to deputy governor of Fuzhou.
1997	Xi misses out on election to the Central Committee of the Party, coming 151st. The Asian financial crisis hits.
2000	Xi becomes governor of Fujian Province.
2001	China enters the WTO.
2002	Xi becomes Party secretary of Zhejiang Province; the same year his father Zhongxun dies. Hu Jintao succeeds Jiang Zemin as president of the PRC and chairman of the CCP.
2007	Xi is named Party secretary of Shanghai, and becomes a Politburo Standing Committee member. He also becomes president of the Central Party School.

2008	Xi chairs the coordinating committee for the Beijing Olympic Games. Riots break out in Lhasa, Tibet, four months before the start of the games. Wenchuan earthquake causes 80,000 deaths and significant damage in Sichuan Province. The Global Financial Crisis occurs.
2009	Sixtieth anniversary of the founding of the PRC and 50th of CCP control of Tibet. Protests break out in Xinjiang.
2010	Xi is named vice chairman of the CMC.
2012	At the 18th National Congress, Xi Jinping is named general secretary of the CCP Central Committee and chairman of the CMC.
2013	Xi is announced as president of the PRC.
2014	Hong Kong's 'umbrella revolution' and Taiwan's 'sunflower movement'. Bo Xilai is convicted of corruption and sentenced to life in prison.
2015	Zhou Yongkang, China's former security tsar, is sentenced to life in prison for corruption and abuse of power.

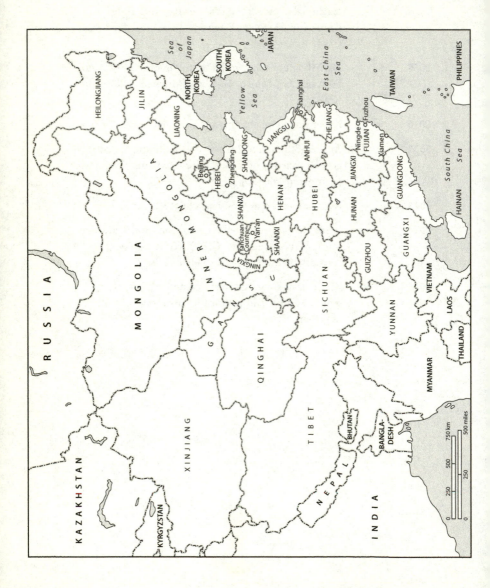

INTRODUCTION

In 2007, my work partially involved running an organization called the Liverpool–Shanghai Partnership. Partly by accident and partly by design, Liverpool and Shanghai had ended up being formally associated as sister cities in the 1990s. It has to be said that they were a somewhat odd couple. Shanghai, only a decade after being granted Special Economic Zone (SEZ) status in 1990 under the late reforms of the then paramount leader, Deng Xiaoping, was a city with more than 13 million people, redeveloping the vast Pudong area south of the Huangpu River and creating – where there had once been farmland and run-down warehouses – one of the great modernist skylines of the world. Skyscrapers were already being thrown up, with the iconic Oriental Pearl Tower mast staring across at the older Bund waterside buildings, almost as though it were laying down a challenge.

Liverpool may once have been the second city of the British Empire, a place of trade and success in the Victorian period, but it was only slowly emerging from its long decades of decline. The 1980s had been particularly nightmarish, with riots, urban decay and accelerated migration out of the city area to softer, more welcoming surrounding ones. Its main assets were mostly by then intangible ones – it was the home of Merseybeat and the Beatles, a cultural hotspot that had produced more than its fair share of writers, artists and thinkers. By the 2000s, the city had reacquired some of its old swagger. Large areas had been successfully regenerated, not least of them the world famous Three Graces buildings on the Mersey front. But it looked, and felt, a very different place to Shanghai, its streets often deserted in the evening, its population only gradually creeping back up and its economy undergoing a painful readjustment.

Shanghai and Liverpool did have one very solid connection, gifted to them by history. The ports of the two cities had links going back to the nineteenth century. This alone meant that Liverpool had one of the earliest, if not *the* earliest, Chinatowns anywhere in Europe through the arrival and settlement of sailors on ships coming there from China's Qing dynasty. Chinese people figured in the social and economic history of the city long before they started to appear elsewhere in Europe. Small, low-profile and somewhat shabby as it was by the first decade of the twenty-first century, the few streets of Liverpool's Chinatown, close to the Anglican cathedral, were authentic memorials of a long-standing, living bond between the two very different places.

Participating in Liverpool delegations to its sister city on the other side of the world was always a mind-stretching experience for delegates. Those who had never been to China and were unprepared were usually struck speechless gazing across at the Pudong evening skyline, with its glittering, neon-lit buildings hurling out Chinese and English slogans across a waterway thriving with cargo ships, passenger liners and small boats. The infectious energy of Shanghai is infamous. Economist Yasheng Huang refers to its mesmerizing impact on Indian business people and politicians who would come in the 1990s and 2000s and gaze at a place they aspired to make their own country look like.[1] After offering this vignette in his book, Huang goes on to give a somewhat more sobering critique of the city – a place that its disgraced former Party leader, Chen Liangyu, boasted in the mid-2000s was more than 85 per cent state-run, and where most of the land upon which the great new skyscrapers were constructed was acquired with scant compensation for farmers who were then shipped out to harder, more isolated lives away from the precious centre. This caused immense resentment. Shanghai, Huang states, is a monument to many things: modern Chinese entrepreneurialism, radicalism, openness. It is also a symbol of lawlessness and illegality.

In 2007, Shanghai was convulsed by a domestic political drama. The most powerful official running the local Party, and in effect the municipal government, Chen Liangyu – a local man educated briefly in the United Kingdom as a British-funded Chevening scholar – was felled after being accused of corruption. His was the most high-profile removal from power in a decade. Chen was not just a local politician, but a member of the full Politburo of the Chinese Communist Party (CCP) in the national government. He was a significant and important person, and one who had been associated with aggressively pro-Shanghai policies, raising the city's profile and striving to give it increasingly greater autonomy. Perhaps this had been the real reason for his fall. But the ostensive one was his siphoning of vast amounts of funds from a city pension pot, which, it was claimed, were going to his cronies and business associates. One committed suicide when the purge began. Others were taken into detention. Chen himself disappeared, to be sentenced a few months later to 16 years' detention.

This happened only a few months after the 17th National Congress, a major CCP meeting. Beijing was about to announce a new line-up of leaders who were likely to guide it into the second and third decades of the twenty-first century. Such drama and disruption raised tension at a time when tensions were already running high enough. The reason for this was very simple: leadership successions have never been relaxing affairs in China. Rules by which they are run are scant, and precedents for their conduct are rare. Previous attempts to designate a successor have all ended badly. Mao Zedong's choice, Lin Biao, ended up dead in a plane crash. Deng Xiaoping's first candidate, Hu Yaobang, was felled for mishandling protests before Deng had fully retired from politics and his second, Zhao Ziyang, was placed under long-term house arrest after the Tiananmen Square uprising in 1989. Hu Jintao's succession in 2001–2 had, up to a point, been smooth, although he had been dogged by claims that his predecessor Jiang Zemin was still extremely influential even after he took up office. For the so-called 'fifth-generation' leadership that was emerging, stability was crucial. Public political battles only months before a major change were deeply unwelcome.[2]

The resilience of the CCP and its ability to turn a crisis to good advantage are often overlooked. Sometimes, in fact, it almost seems to work best when there are calamities that force its hand. The immediate issue raised by Chen's hasty departure was that a temporary replacement had to be found to run the city for a few months. The person finally chosen was until that moment Party leader of the neighbouring Zhejiang Province. Prior to that, he had enjoyed a largely provincial career in the south of China. However, the one fact everyone seemed to know about him was that he was married to one of China's most popular and glamorous singers, Peng Liyuan. His name was Xi Jinping.

Xi's name had only recently started to figure in the lists of those who were in a good position to be elevated to the all-important Politburo Standing Committee in autumn 2007. In the 1990s he had barely scraped through to be elected onto the Central Committee elite. His provincial leadership record had been an unspectacular one. In the early 2000s, it was figures like the younger Li Keqiang or even Li Yuanchao who enjoyed positive speculation about their future.[3] When a Chinese journalist I was speaking to in London in 2007 handed me a biography of Xi issued in Hong Kong and told me to 'watch this man', I wondered what all the fuss was about.

I did have one chance to observe Xi close up when he was in Shanghai as Party secretary there. He had only been in his position for a few weeks when I arrived with my delegation of political and business leaders from Liverpool, visiting the city to re-energize the relationship. The usual lobbying had secured a meeting with the then mayor, a man called Han Zheng. But most people were aware that the real power lay in the hands of the Party boss, and that securing a meeting with him was unlikely. The local bureau of foreign affairs, who were looking after practical matters, went through the motions, advising his office and recommending a courtesy call. But there were low expectations. Seeing the mayor was enough.

To almost everyone's surprise, however, the news came back during the first day of our visit that Mr Xi *did* want to see us. This was so unusual that the junior local official charged with looking after us was unable to conceal his amazement that a group as relatively unimportant as ours was to be granted golden moments with someone who was expected, very soon, to become one of the most powerful people in the world. The only question about Xi in 2007 before the National Congress was whether he would become the first- or second-ranking leader in five years' time.

Meeting a high-level Chinese leader is always an event accompanied by theatre. As a diplomat years before for the British government based in Beijing, I had always been impressed by how well the Chinese managed to seduce visitors – with the venues, the choreography and the sheer drama – while meeting elite leaders. For business people from the United Kingdom, politicians, academics – however tough and down-to-earth they were – the frisson of excitement at being whisked in cavalcades of cars with flashing lights through Beijing traffic, down to the gateway of the Zhongnanhai government compound at the heart of the city, or to the grand steps of the Great Hall of the People gazing imperiously out over Tiananmen Square, always changed them, rendering them reflective at best, simpering and sycophantic at worst. The whole process never failed to have some sort of impact.

Meeting Mr Xi Jinping was like this. We were led by two black cars, with a third behind us, their blue lights flashing, clearing the way through the narrow streets of the city until we came to the environs of one of the government guest houses where these sorts of receptions were often held. Going through the gates was like passing from one realm of existence into another. The scrappy, bustling messiness of the everyday Shanghai world simply vanished. In its place, there were clear green lawns, isolation and an eerie sense of calmness. The cavalcade drew up to one of the most prominent buildings, and we were ushered first into a large waiting room with thick carpets and a heavy wooden screen. Then, when the time came, officials told us to follow them around the edge. There stood a rotund man at the head of a queue of other, mostly male, mostly besuited, officials. All of us in the delegation had to pass down this line, shaking the hand of each person. Mr Xi proved adept at simply moving people on, shaking hands while gently tugging them so that people did not linger, so the meeting could start and end promptly.

I remember almost nothing of what the future leader said. He sat, as usual, facing the leader of our delegation, a politician from Liverpool who, somewhat distressingly, thought it best to handle the meeting as though he were addressing a council chamber, raising his voice in oratorical style when something more conversational and intimate would have been better. Mr Xi, though, had the main facts to hand, and ran through them – volumes of trade between the two cities, the main sectors this trade was concentrated in, recent educational and cultural cooperation. One thing China proved at the time was that the technocrats who ruled it were people who knew how to use a brief. Xi did not put a foot wrong. The meeting ended punctually, and we were whisked away, us to our fate, he to his.

A few days after this meeting, we crowed about it to British journalists based in Shanghai, and they laughed. They had recently heard a story by another group who had had a similar experience – they had arrived in Shanghai on a low-profile business delegation, expected to only meet a deputy mayor, or, at best, the mayor himself, and then found themselves taken to meet Mr Xi. 'The speculation is that Xi needs to do the least risky, most fail-safe things at the moment,' one of the journalists said. 'Any edgy delegations or people who might challenge him at all, and he keeps away from them. But the minor stuff that carries no risk is fine. The last thing he wants to do is blot his copybook so close to getting final promotion.' Unflattering as it may have been, it sounded as good an explanation as any for our being gifted with this high-level attention. It also says something quite profound about how to get to the top in modern China.

While this is a book about the man we met that afternoon, Xi Jinping, it is, inevitably, also about the issue of power in modern China. This is a subject that I have spent a quarter of a century thinking about, since my first real encounter with modern Chinese history, language and culture in 1990, when I started learning Chinese characters while living in Japan. I visited China for the first time in May 1991, the same week Mao Zedong's wife, Jiang Qing, reportedly committed suicide in a Beijing jail by hanging herself with a pair of nylon tights. Her story illustrates some of the vagaries and complexities of power in modern China. A third-rate actress from the province of Shandong who in the 1930s had managed to make some inroads into the cinema industry then thriving in Shanghai, she had ended up in the revolutionary base of Yan'an, where her youth and spirit had attracted the CCP leader, Mao Zedong, and the two married. This, his fourth marriage, was not a welcome one for the rest of the Party leadership then, distracted by war and the fight for survival, but it was sanctioned on the condition that she not become involved in politics.

For the next two decades she stuck to the agreement, maintaining a low profile. But by the mid-1960s, Mao, ready to take on the very party he had brought to power, was willing to have her come back into the fold of activism. For the next decade, she became one of the most influential people in the country, pushing forward the devastating Cultural Revolution, promoting a virulent version of utopian Marxism on the surface, but all the while savagely settling scores and clearing away old enemies behind the scenes. Few dared to confront her directly. Those who did rarely fared well. Even President Nixon, during his visit to China in 1972, found her cold and unappealing.[4] But her power was not secure. Within a few weeks of Mao's death in 1976, she was arrested, and four years later she was given a suspended death sentence. Few could have fallen so precipitously and spectacularly. Her story is a cautionary one, and illustrates the almost unfathomable difference in China between power owned and power borrowed.

Xi Jinping's own career, as I will seek to show in what follows, offers a modern morality tale for what power is, how it is acquired and what its characteristics are, in the world's second-largest economy, most populous nation and fastest-growing major country. Keeping in mind the story of Jiang is worthwhile because of the illusory qualities that power has, and the ways in which what can seem like real influence may quickly dissolve. Xi himself has been exhaustively compared to figures like Jiang's husband, Mao Zedong, or Mao's successor Deng Xiaoping. President Obama praised him in late 2014 by saying that he had consolidated power more quickly than any other leader of modern China.[5] Exiled writer Yu Jie called him 'China's godfather' in a book published in Chinese in the United States and Hong Kong in 2014.[6] Others, more politely, say he is a 'strongman'.[7] A former Singaporean leader, the late Lee Kuan Yew, even went as far as to claim that Xi was 'Asia's Mandela' because of his rusticated past.[8] But all I briefly saw during the Shanghai meeting in 2007 was someone who looked, sounded and acted like any other official at that level in the CCP I had ever come across or seen on TV. If Xi has become as powerful as some believe (and I will offer evidence later in this book, once we know what we mean by power, that he has significant power, but that these powers might not be as dramatic as many think), then the question of how he achieved this is an important one. And we can never wholly dispel the suspicion that his power may disappear as quickly as it appeared.

POWER FROM THE GUN: THE LONG SHADOW OF CHAIRMAN MAO

The Maoist shadow is a long and deep one for China even today, almost four decades since the chairman died. If there is one individual who instinctively understood power, and knew where to find it and how to exercise it, then Mao is that man. Power oozed from his personality, to the extent that many found him unsettling and uncomfortable even physically to be around. For Mao, the costs of his acquisition and consolidation of power were borne by his family (a son killed in one of the wars his father engaged China in: the Korean War from 1950 to 1953; one wife executed for her links to Mao and his political party in the 1930s), his closest relationships (successors like Liu Shaoqi and Lin Biao were brutally removed when they were deemed a threat, with both subsequently perishing) and his own ideals (he himself was to claim his vast efforts had achieved little in truly reforming China towards the end of his life). But from the moment he assumed leadership of the CCP in the early 1940s to the day of his death in September 1976, not a single attempt to remove him or replace him succeeded.

The China of the twenty-first century might be purged of many of his statues. Walls might no longer be daubed with his sayings. And in the lives of young Chinese he figures more as a distant cultural icon, the man who stares down stolidly from portraits in Tiananmen Square and who is regarded as the founding father of the country they live in, rather than as a living political influence. But as the opening ceremony of the 2008 Beijing Olympics proved, even by attempts to exclude it the Mao brand is a contentious, often toxic one. His image there famously made a non-appearance, swamped by Confucius, a character he mandated vicious attacks on. Former premier Wen Jiabao was castigated by critics towards the end of his time in power for never mentioning the Chairman in his speeches, and showing disrespect towards his historic legacy. And yet Mao continues to re-emerge, whether through the solemn visit to his mausoleum in Beijing on the 120th anniversary of his birth in 2013, an event which all of China's current elite leaders attended to mark their respects, or through the ways in which he continues to crop up in speeches and Party statements. As though mocking the current Chinese hybrid capitalist system that tried to bury him, Mao appears on the banknotes that modern China is awash with, control over which has proved such a source of grief and contention as the country has grown richer.

Mao's exercise of power might be the envy of a modern Chinese politician, but it is a dangerous issue to play with. Bo Xilai, one of the most dazzling politicians of his generation, was accused of resurrecting revolutionary songs and propaganda from the period of late Maoism while in charge of Chongqing from 2007. According to his political peers, Bo, felled over his wife's involvement in the murder of British businessman Neil Heywood, was culpable above all for abusing the Chairman's legacy and name for his own divisive political ends. His career death knell was sounded by a curt statement in March 2012 in Beijing when the then premier Wen Jiabao, welling up in a rare display of feeling, said that China wished never to see a second Cultural Revolution.[9] Wen spoke with good cause. As I will show later in this book, the experience of this era for Xi and almost all of the people around him was a complex and often searing one. It would be shocking if they were to wish to see this period occur again.

But the Maoist approach to power retains its allure, long after Mao's death. His pursuit of idealistic ideological aims through deployment of a charismatic, highly manipulated persona, mass campaigning and shrewd propaganda reached deep into the hearts and minds of a great many Chinese and changed them for the rest of their lives. This sort of politics truly got under the skin of the Chinese people. This is why his style haunts China to this day, where it is half admired and half rejected. The issue of whether Xi is a 'Maoist' is a live one in China. It boils down to a simple question: does he believe that it is permissible to achieve political goals through ruthless promotion of personality cults, decimation of opponents and incitement of public passions and sentiments, in the same way the Chairman did? Since the late 1970s, the Party may have publicly said it has set itself against this mode of operation. But in a time of challenges and crises, when a great historic opportunity looms on the horizon for China once more to become a strong, rich, powerful nation, who can argue back to a leader who says that more Maoist strategies need to be pursued, at least for today, to bring about this desired objective?

The dark side of Maoism is better known now than ever. Early, courageous observers like the late Pierre Ryckmans (who wrote under the name Simon Leys) pointed out the dangers of this concentration of power in one person. But it was only with the rise of Deng in the late 1970s that a modest reappraisal of Mao was allowed. Over the next decades, evidence has mounted up of the costs of Maoism: the campaigns that broke families, destroyed intellectuals and divided society; the decimation of the countryside and mass starvation in the early 1960s; and the fearsome intra-elite conflicts throughout the final decade of the Chairman's life. Our moral intuitions are torn when we look at this legacy. As academic Mobo Gao, who grew up in China in the Cultural Revolution, rightly said, China was a country that lifted most of its developmental targets radically upwards during the post-1949 period, and which saw its economy improve yearly, but that also saw a series of epic tragedies, which may have accounted for 40 million deaths.[10] Do the achievements justify the means? Surely there were ways to avoid these calamities? For anyone studying modern Chinese history, the Maoist power template is a hard thing to deal with dispassionately, and yet it sits, entrenched and immovable, at the heart of what China has been and done, good and bad, in the last six decades, an unavoidable part of the whole.

Xi has made his position on this crystal clear: he is proud to live with the Maoist legacy. He has spoken often of marrying the pre- and post-1978 eras together, rather than regarding them as divided. He has linked Mao and Deng as two parts of one whole, leading the Party on a journey on which it has made great mistakes but has learned from them and become a better governance vehicle. The thrust of his argument, implicit rather than explicit, seems to be that when the moment arrives when China truly is once more a proud, strong, rich, rejuvenated country, then all the former mistakes and suffering will have been worth it. History may prove Xi right. If all goes well, then maybe everything that has gone before will indeed be forgiven. But this betrays more than just a commitment to Maoism by China's modern leader: it also indicates a strong faith in the teleology of history, and in perfect outcomes being realizable. Like Mao, Xi is looking increasingly like an idealist, someone who speaks about his belief in the fulfilment of dreams, and as in politics anywhere, such people are often worrying. 'All men are dreamers,' T. E. Lawrence said in his masterpiece *The Seven Pillars of Wisdom* (1922), but

> those who dream by night in the dusty recesses of their minds, wake in the day to find that it was vanity: but the dreamers of the day are dangerous men, for they may act on their dreams with open eyes, to make them possible.

Is Xi this kind of leader, a man who sees dreams in the day?

The structure of this book is straightforward. Chapter 1 will address the simple question of what power actually is in modern China: how it is manifested, its various channels, modes and forms, and how it is best understood. This chapter is based on my career of observing, and trying to make sense of, this thing called Chinese political power.

Chapter 2 will look at the career path and story of Xi himself. As I will argue in Chapter 1, one of the salient features of Xi's method of exercising power, and something that has not figured much in the armoury of any of his most immediate predecessors, is his deployment of a personal narrative, a life story, with which he appeals to the public in order to create a connection with the people he is speaking to. This stands in stark contrast to his immediate predecessor, Hu Jintao, who was resolutely faceless in his public statements, and seemed to have no 'backstory' at all.

Chapter 3 will look at the networks around Xi – starting with his family relationships, where the bonds are strongest, but then moving on to political ones, the allies and friends among whom he works – along with the ways in which he has developed them, and the loyalty that he has built up in those around him in the last few decades. I then consider some of his enemies and antagonists. This chapter will try to describe the world that Xi might see from his position at the centre, in Zhongnanhai – a world dominated by specific people who figure as his friends or his opponents.

Chapter 4 will look at one of the core sources of his power – his political programme. The assumption here is that one doesn't just want power for its own sake, but in order to exercise it and do something with it. The CCP issues no manifestos, and Xi did not need to spell out a policy platform when he came to power, the assumption being that he could drive for continuity, not disruption. But there is in fact a new policy platform, something we can see from the plenum meetings of 2013 and 2014, when the Party met collectively and set out its priorities for the next few years. Xi has helpfully added a personal explanatory note to the Third Plenum of 2013. In his own words, here are the core areas, the policy highlights, that he has associated his name with and that he has sponsored. We can describe this as his own political programme. These are the things he wants the government and Party he leads to achieve.

Chapter 5 will look at China's place in the world under Xi, the sort of relationship that Xi outlines for his country in the coming years, with its concentric circles of different diplomatic relationships around it. As with his personal relationships, in this chapter there will be a gradient leading from the highest-value links (the United States and the EU) to the slightly less important ones (Africa and the Middle East). But for a global power like China is now, there is nowhere that can truly be said not to be of interest; nor is there anywhere that can be said to be uninterested in China. In the final chapter, I will address the vision issue – the world according to Xi and his co-leaders in the coming two decades and what sort of place they want it to become. I will endeavour to map out the vision they have for their country based on what they are doing now, and how the most likely outcomes of these policies project into the future. This will show the ways in which Xi's vision promotes and solidifies the power of the Party.

At about the time that Xi was briefly meeting the Liverpool delegation I mentioned at the start of this chapter, he was also making his mark, albeit briefly, in China's most dynamic, giddy city. There were three striking things he did while there that help in some degree to provide a starting point for trying to understand him. The first was that he opposed the lavish supply of government goods and services to him as Party leader in the city. He asked for a smaller apartment than the one allocated to him, and also insisted that he did not need the fleet of cars that was at his call when in office. Secondly, he reportedly demanded that his family not become involved in business in the city while he was there, and made it clear that they could not call on his help if they went against this instruction. And thirdly, he met Ding Xuexiang, a competent private secretary who was to make a powerful enough impression on him to merit being subsequently summoned to Beijing some years after Xi was securely ensconced there. The nine fleeting months in a city that often acts like it has no memory or past, therefore, did have a deeper impact than anyone might have supposed. It made clear the sort of story that Xi wanted to tell the world, particularly in China: that he was able to resist the heady charms of a place even as intoxicated, and intoxicating, as Shanghai.

Xi does present his country and the world with something very different from his much more aloof and mysterious predecessor, Hu Jintao. He is a man who conveys the sense that he does actually believe and buy into a worldview that has arisen from his own experience rather than been handed to him or acquired through years of attending Party meetings. Prime among these convictions is the belief he articulates in China being once more within arm's reach of greatness, but only through the guidance and direction of the Party that he has worked for most of his life, and now leads. In this context, the personal power he has acquired is magnified because it figures and is justified as a means to that much greater, more epic end. This core belief in the Party and its fundamental importance as the guardian of national greatness gives his sponsorship of anti-corruption measures a particular piquancy. It almost seems as though he does take the venality and irresponsibility of some of his colleagues personally, and he has risked a great deal in order to confront them because they threaten this greater aim. Before he became leader, few saw the extent of this ambition. But with ambition on this scale comes danger. He lives in the most extraordinary and unusual world, one very divorced from normality, where restraint is hard to find, and honest counsel rare and precious. It is too early to say whether Xi's ambition will transform into something verging on megalomania. As of April 2016, the evidence is ambiguous. The most the outside world can say is that we are witnessing someone who still seems to be working for the interests of the organization he leads, or at least his vision of it, rather than for himself. But power is intoxicating and can fundamentally change people. This book will try to show both the nature and location of his power, but also the kinds of temptations that might lie ahead as Xi tries to guide his country towards its moment of destiny, as a modern, powerful and wealthy nation, its painful, often tragic century-long battle to modernize itself finally realized. Whatever the 'China Dream' might be, this must surely be Xi Jinping's vision, and it defines and marks his actions and worldview.

1

THE HUNT FOR POWER IN MODERN CHINA: DO WE KNOW WHAT WE ARE LOOKING FOR?

He who rules by moral force is like the Pole Star, which remains in its place while all the lesser stars do homage to it.

—Analects 2.1

WHERE IS POWER IN CHINA?

One of the most trite observations that anyone can make about China in the twenty-first century is that it is run by a single party of which Xi Jinping is the current leader, and which is interested solely in staying in office and cares only about power, and that one must assume therefore that if power is located anywhere, it must be there. This is as illuminating as saying that humans need food and want to live. The interesting question is what sort of power the Party wants and how it wishes to use it. What no one disputes, however, is that when talking about political power – the ability physically to organize people, and to control material resources – any discussion has to embrace and understand the CCP. It is in this entity that the real action happens, and it is here that we need to seek answers to the question of what political power is in modern China.

EVERYONE'S PARTY?

The CCP, which Xi leads, is one of the wonders of the modern world. Established in 1921 as an offshoot of the international Communist organization known as the Third International, or the Comintern, its first congress in July of that year was attended by a mere 13 people, two of whom were foreign observers. It managed to produce only a basic constitution, before reverting to underground activity, mostly in the middle provinces of Henan and Hunan during the Republican period. Being a Communist in this era was a tough existence. Sporadic loose coalitions with the ruling Nationalists, largely undertaken on the strength of imperious orders from Moscow, usually ended badly, at least for the CCP. In one bitter night in April 1927, more than 5,000 known Party activists were rounded up and murdered. From that moment, the CCP went even deeper underground, retreating to the countryside, violating Marxist orthodoxy by seeking support not from China's nascent and weak urban proletariat, but from rural people. A farmers' party emerged with the ultimate peasant emperor, Mao Zedong – son of a moderately wealthy landlord who had skirted around the edges of the Communist movement while a lowly librarian in Beijing, and then seized his chance to take an increasingly strong role in the leadership of the Party during its wilderness years. His progression to the top was not easy, and there were bitter challenges through the 1930s, not least from external war and internal dissent. But Mao's psychology was very particular. Personal trauma or some other root cause meant that he seemed capable of ruthless jettisoning of alliances and bonds when he felt that it served his and therefore the CCP's larger cause. The conflation of Mao's ambitions and those of the institution that he led meant that, in ensuing decades, Mao's and the Party's interests came to be seen seen as one.[1]

Whatever the idealistic, egalitarian principles of the Party were in its youth, Mao was its tutor in the use of hard-eyed tactics to get what it needed. There was nothing soft about his approach. Ranks of enemies were to learn the tough way, many paying with their lives, about just how focused Mao was on achieving his objectives. In his universe, violence, however messy its deployment, was justifiable as long as it got the right outcome. He had a point, inasmuch as the Party's opponents were willing to use horrific levels of brutality against it. Cao Yesun, one of the earliest martyrs to the cause, offers a sobering illustration of the price some had to pay. Abducted as an underground agent by Nationalist police in Hong Kong in 1931, he was taken back to Guangdong. His wife had already been slaughtered by Nationalists. His fate was harsher. Tortured horrifically for names of other allies in the CCP movement, he held out and betrayed no one. He was executed by having iron nails driven through his arms and legs so that he was pinned against a prison wall, and red-hot irons held against him. The CCP's period coming to power was the most bitter, harsh schooling in what power means, what happens to those who don't have it, and why once you get it you should never relinquish it without the fight of your life.

Xi Jinping and his generation, including figures like the academic Yu Keping, often point out that the Party existed in its youth as one of revolution and then became one of governance after victory in the 1946–9 Civil War.[2] Xi talks of the lessons that the Party learned during its first period trying to govern, as it made this journey. In this context, its achievement in creating the China the world sees today justifies the costs of epic social movements, famines and turmoil from 1949 to 1978. These were the years it was learning. Now it has internalized the lessons of that period, and is an effective governing force, directing China towards its mission – to be a great, rejuvenated country, restored to its central role in the world.

These are consoling narratives. But the Party's previous cultures of power and the methods in which it dispensed its forces of violence and coercion are not so comfortably compartmentalized. Mao's genius was, partially, to understand a particular form of brute power, and to accrue it with iron discipline. Those who challenged him invariably perished, however much they relented after their claimed displays of disloyalty. The culture of power in the Party was linked to its monopoly on the sources of violence, and to its almost total control over information and material resources. The state was in effect hostage to the Party, which provided the framework for everything from economic planning to news dissemination, people's work lives and movements, and military and foreign policy. China's internal workings were often regarded as complex and obscure in the Maoist era, but, paradoxically, the final source of power was one person. Underneath all of its mysteries, therefore, Mao's China was disarmingly simple, at least in this respect.

For Mao, power famously grew from the barrel of a gun. It was a gun he proved willing to pull the trigger of when he felt he needed to. But for reformist China since 1978, the gun has not been an easy option, even though it was used with bloody results in the 1989 uprising at Tiananmen Square. The fallout from the 1989 events, with China ostracized internationally for a number of years afterwards, and the Party losing much of its moral mantle, has meant that this use of violence as a political tool, one that stood it in such good stead in previous phases of its history, is less and less possible. Now the dominant official discourse is of peace, harmony and 'win–win'. Using weapons to forge this vision of peace and harmony tends – to say the least – to create confusion and resentment. The Party wants, under Xi, people to love it for its success, its links to China's traditional culture and its openness, not its ability to thwack down opponents as soon as they open their mouths, beat up opposition and slam dissidents into jail. Most of its Maoist and pre-Maoist history therefore is a problem when it tries to present itself in modern, reformed guise in the twenty-first century, and offers a problematic inheritance for someone like Xi. But nor, as we shall see later, can the Party jettison its past and say everything has changed. As in so many other areas, it wants to have its cake and eat it.

The CCP in the present day locates its legitimacy in three core areas. These are the pillars of its right to have power. They are set out in the first official comprehensive history of the Party, issued in 2011. The first pillar is its being part of the United Front to win victory over the Japanese in World War II. The second is its having unified the country after the Civil War of 1946–9. These first two are historic sources of legitimacy. The final one is its having started the 'reform and opening-up' process, which has been going on since 1978.[3] Each of the first two pillars has problems. As historian Rana Mitter and others have shown, the CCP played a largely subsidiary role in the victory against Japan.[4] It was mostly Nationalist armies that took the lead in that conflict. The Civil War is a less ambiguous victory, but it too is still unresolved, with the Republic of China, its opponent, continuing to exist on Taiwan seven decades after the war itself.

But with the third, economic reform, there can be less dissent and argument. Chinese officials throughout the last four decades have sounded most convincing and most confident when shooting out, staccato style, long lists of impressive economic statistics. They are too widely known to repeat here. Suffice to say that, since 1978, China has frequently attracted the description 'miracle'. Its economic rise has been a globally important, and in many ways unprecedented story – at least in terms of scale and speed. Only the most churlish would, or could, deny this. And the CCP is keen to take as much of the credit as possible. The third is, after all, the strongest of all its pillars of legitimacy, and the CCP's core claim to continuing in power in the way it wishes.

For all this play around where the Party locates the sources of its right to be where it is today, the simple fact is that the CCP exists for power. Without power – over the direction of Chinese society, and the economy – it would risk returning to the enfeebled, bandit-like existence it rose from. It looks keenly at the lessons to be learned from the fall of the Communist Party of the USSR and tries to avoid, in every way possible, what happened there. In this way, despite all the differences, the CCP continues to remain the child of Mao: desire for power is in its blood, despite the fact that it has to exercise it differently now. Even in a China where there is more diversity, and more complexity than ever before, whether in the cultural, legal or economic realm, almost always it is to the doors of the Party that one needs to come to find out who is calling the shots, who is holding power, who decides what happens. It is this organization that Xi leads, and it is in this evolving tradition that he sits. To understand him without understanding the Party would be like trying to comprehend music while being tone-deaf. Xi and the Party are inextricable. Its power is his power, and his power is solely derived from it. This has been an issue surprisingly little understood by many outside observers.

THE NEW MACHIAVELLI

It is audacious for Xi's Party, with its roots in terror, illegality and revolution, to present itself as the bastion of stability and justice six decades after coming to power by force of arms, insurrection and war. One wonders what the Party might try to do to counter a force like itself if one were to arise in the twenty-first century. Knowing the enemy has been one of the Party's abilities – knowing how to pre-empt and collude with them until the moment when the truth comes, usually too late to save the opponent. Flexibility, pragmatism and an ability to remake itself have been the CCP's great strengths. But this complicated hinterland is something that leaders to this day spend many hours trying to explain away. Xi himself has talked many times about there being no real division between pre- and post-1978 history. They form a seamless whole, with Maoism and Dengism only two different parts of the same story. He has addressed this issue often enough to raise the possibility that he suspects that his exhaustive explanation is not truly adequate. Xi's life, like that of so many of his generation, testifies to the contradictions and conflicts experienced by those born in the era of Mao who survived into the very different era of Deng. They were two very different worlds, and the link between them is a difficult one to explain.

If there is one source of power for the CCP that it cannot jettison, however, it is this control of the historical narrative: the justificatory story of its rise to power, the inevitability of that rise and the moral reasons behind it. As we shall see later, these issues weave in and out of Xi's own public pronouncements and speeches. Beyond the three pillars of legitimacy mentioned above, this is the meta-narrative, the basis on which even they rest and the reason why elite leaders now invest so much time and capital in them. The Party is in power, and has a right to that power, leaders like Xi say, because it restored dignity to the Chinese people after a century of humiliation at the hands of foreigners. The Party and the Party alone, in the words of the current Chinese constitution, allowed Chinese people to take 'state power into their own hands and became masters of the country', putting them in charge of their own destiny after a period in which that had been robbed from them.[5] It restored the unity of their divided, weakened land and returned them to their rightful place, at the centre of the world. This is the territory that no one else can challenge, or be allowed to challenge, in the Party's current line.[6] Those arguing for a more complex historical story over the last century and a half are in danger of being accused of lacking patriotism and being the lackeys of foreign forces and the enemies within who opposed this process and want to see China reduced to a weak, poor and divided place again. For many Chinese, whether they like or loathe the Party as an entity, this is a narrative that is difficult to resist openly because it is a difficult one to deny. The Party has indeed been in charge while China reunited most of the country and then restored its economy, which, since 1978, has become richer and stronger. Arguments that other governing forces and models, if given the chance in China, might have worked as well or better are easily dismissed by the simple, unassailable fact that it was the Party alone that presided while these things were achieved. All its misdemeanours and sins in the past, therefore, can easily be discounted with the riposte that things have now come good. The Party's tough medicine worked. And on the basis that it has, at least until now, been proved right, then its hold on power into the future remains justified.

The more analytically minded can easily see even in these arguments that the CCP has a proclivity to conflate its destiny and mission with those of the country as a whole. China's interests and the Party's interests are neatly married to each other so they appear as one. In this way, the Party has been able to recruit traditional culture to support its aims, something that would have been anathema in the Maoist era, when much of past Chinese thinking and creativity was disparaged as feudalistic and enslaving. The Party as China, of course, is a highly contentious idea. It is a perfectly valid proposition to say a Chinese person can be deeply proud of his or her country, its cultural and natural assets, and yet detest the governing Party. But for many, there is a pragmatic acceptance that as long as the reformist Party that has faced the world since 1978 is doing things that they broadly see as in the interests of the country they love and belong to, they will tolerate its grand claims, for today at least. The Party parasitically feeds off the prestige of and emotional attachments people have to their nation, trying to insert itself as the most viable, powerful and necessary defender of the country's ideals. This effort gives much of the Party's language about its role and nature a grand, all-encompassing purpose. Officials are keen to stress that it is simply not like a political party in the West, which is a mere plaything of special interests and marginal concerns. It is larger and greater than they are, able to contain the full spectrum of opinions and ideas, from left to right. It figures in this context almost like a state within a state, with its own universality and comprehensiveness. It reaches beyond the confines of mere political action and executive function, to be an entity able to discourse on cultural, ethical and spiritual issues. This aspect gives it an eerie similarity to the Roman Catholic Church, with its own autonomy and completeness. This is a parallel that I will return to several times throughout this book.

As the institution whose history in recent times has been the history of the nation, whose visions and ideals have also been the visions and ideals of the nation, the CCP is therefore able to locate much of its power in simply controlling the destiny of the country – taking up what it calls in official statements its 'leadership' function. This gives the Party the right to figure in all areas of broad decision-making, with the premise that what is good for it is good for the country, and what is good for the country is good for it. The Party is able to control this idea of the country's destiny, of its historic development and of its role. This, therefore, lies at the heart of its right to power. The next question is where that power is located, the power that someone like Xi has been able to link to himself and derive benefit from.

THE PARTY'S LEADERSHIP ROLE: RULE OF ITSELF, AND THE POWER OF FEAR

By 2013, Xi, as general secretary and leader of the CCP, stood at the head of an organization that had more than 80 million members. If it were a country, it would rank among the world's most populous. And, as noted already, in many ways, with its internal traditions, regulations and rules, it has often seemed like a country within another one, its terrain marked out by walls, mysterious but powerful-looking offices, and secret doorways and trackways leading to its chief offices. Its members have a Masonic sense of brotherhood, of joining rituals and rites of passage. The CCP marks the year with its own festivals, from the National Day on 1 October, which commemorates the founding of the PRC, to the session of the Chinese parliament, the National People's Congress (NPC) in the spring, and, finally, the most important event of all – the plenums and National Congresses, which act as temporal markers, pulsating through the years as the Party has grown older and grander.

No one would seriously claim that being a member of this organization per se makes someone powerful. For many, it seems the most their membership provides is slight access to sporadically useful networks, and preferential treatment for jobs in local or national government. Like the religious faithful, the most that might mark their being CCP adherents is very infrequent attendance at internal events, or the occasional communication from their local branch. Only as one travels inwards through the concentric circles of the membership does one start to come across people who might have real influence. Far away from the 80 million, there are the 3,000 attendees at the NPC, who have come to be significant in the modern Chinese power calculation. But they too have limits to their influence, and more often than not are simply legitimizing fodder for voting in the real players – the 200 full and 150 'alternate' members of the Central Committee (the latter being those who only attend some of the main meetings).

Even on this platform, however, there are questions about just how much clout someone has. Central Committees after Mao (when they were simply bodies bussed into Beijing from time to time to worship him and then disperse) have become increasingly tightly intertwined collections of separate networks, driven by different vested interests and ideas, collations of coalitions, as it were, where cohesion is illusive. Provincial leaders rub shoulders with military ones, alongside the

occasional academic and intellectual movers and shakers. Central-
ministry leaders take their place, as well as the directors of the vastest
state-owned enterprises (SOEs). Every so often, token non-state
personages have a role – the chair of home-appliances and electronics
company Haier in the early 2000s being among the best known. But
on the whole, the Central Committee at best opens the door to real
power. It does not guarantee it.

The Central Committee acts more like a room in the heart of the
Party that contains many doors. Penetrate these, and suddenly the
conversations being held become more significant and compelling,
and have rich, intricate links with the wider world around. In these
small committees, leading groups and advisory bodies the real matter of
where and how resources are to be deployed is discussed, and decisions
with binding force made. The central propaganda messages and key
ideology lines are decided at some, foreign-policy priorities are determined at others, and the framework for overall reform is established
at the most central. Xi, as will be shown later, has managed to fill the
chairmanship positions of most of these committees with either himself
or his closest followers. These are the people who truly run China.

There is one rung above them, which in the broadest terms sets
out the great political programme within which they operate. At
these heady heights is the Politburo, consisting of 25 members, which
itself is led by the seven-member Politburo Standing Committee – it
is here that the Olympians sit. Operating more like a philosophical
discussion group, having monthly retreats and awaydays, the Politburo
has been one of the best known, and least understood, of modern
political bodies. More important than a cabinet in the Western
system of government, yet ostensibly separate from day-to-day decision making, the Politburo owns the crucial function of dispensing
ideological, spiritual and political leadership. This description means
it covers nothing and everything. It has the broadest framework
within which to operate, which means it can wander into every area
of administrative and governmental life in the country. But like the
ideal city described in Plato's *Republic*, in a strange way China is really
run on the model of philosopher kings. The few reports we get of the

cogitations of the Politburo show mostly middle-aged men (with very few women) pondering the merits of market versus state, GDP versus human-development indicators, and happiness based on material goods versus happiness based on more intangible things. This group invites academics to speak to it, who attend, wait in thickly carpeted hallways, before being ushered with great apprehension into a boardroom in which the current immortals running China sit. Strictly instructed to give their presentations (keeping to time) and then, unless they are asked to stay, simply to stand up and leave, they go through the slightly surreal experience of standing before people who are immensely well known, but have no human engagement with them. Interaction is minimal to non-existent. The more cynical might wonder whether the whole exercise is in fact peopled by lookalikes and actors in order to dupe the outside world into believing that China is run by people with normal human lives doing normal things.

When we open the door to this final room, and disturb the seven members in their weighty deliberations, we also catch a glimpse of the place where Xi is most tangibly powerful, the place he had to take control of so that he could extend his influence elsewhere. It is primacy in this tiny community that matters most. Who rules over these men, rules everywhere else. Being ranked first in this group is the jewel in the crown, because from this group flows overall control of the key power entity in modern Chinese political life: ideological and strategic governance of the CCP.

The Party is a self-governing empire, and sets its own standards and objectives. In the West, those hunting for sources of power look at parliaments, courts, cabinets, armies and businesses. But there is nothing quite like the autonomy of the Party, which is in ultimate control of all these entities. It is the supreme one-stop shop. And that means that as one ascends the hierarchy of the organization, one gets increasingly giddy with the sort of authority an individual can have. The simple fact is that Politburo members can do as little or as much as they want. They have no terms of reference, no set objectives to achieve and no other bodies to be accountable to. The membership of the Politburo are meant to have oversight and final say over all policy areas. Security, economic targets, social stability and international affairs – all of these are performed to a mandate set by this body. But they work in a world without their own to-do lists and deadlines. Their job is to pass that work on to others.

If the Party is about occupying the prime directorial role in society, then its own governance is dependent on a small, tight-knit group of individuals who sit atop all of this. True to its Leninist roots, the role of this elite political vanguard, this small core of leaders, remains crucial. The Party's institutions and guiding ideology – just as they did nine decades ago in the CCP's infancy, despite all the immense changes over that period – remain faithful to this structure. Leninism may have been discreetly removed from the constitution of the Party and country since the 1990s, after the embarrassment of the fall of the USSR, but in spirit the Leninist inheritance persists. Dictatorship of the proletariat might be a thing of the past, softened with the ideas of the 'Three Represents' in the late 1990s, where all productive forces in society were embraced by the Party and became part of its leadership mission, but the notion that power might be dispersed widely and fractured such that an entity other than the Party might challenge and hold it to account remains anathema. Party members silently swear a vow of obedience when they join, and this represents an acceptance that the wisdom, righteousness and authority of the Party remain best expressed by its top leadership. These top-level political figures hold, therefore, a curious position as concurrent political, ideological and moral leaders. Again, the model of the Catholic Church becomes useful. If Party members are like religious believers, and the Central Committee is like the convocation of cardinals, the topmost Party leaders are like the Secretariat of the Vatican, and the general secretary, armed with doctrinal infallibility, like the Pope, is a rule-giver, spiritual nurturer and voice of doctrinal purity and correctness.

Power over discipline is crucial. And in the twenty-first century, the enforcer of this is the Central Discipline and Inspection Commission (CDIC), perhaps the most feared entity in modern China. Visiting the CDIC is an unsettling experience – its building stands anonymously in the western government region of Beijing and bears no markings, nor the slightest external sign of its importance. Even once inside its front courtyard it maintains its secrecy, having the same architectural paraphernalia as other official buildings: a modest marble lobby, meeting rooms and, in the back, smaller buildings, which serve as the nerve centre, the engine house of graft-busting. Visitors (and there are precious few of them) get glimpses of this inner bureaucratic world before being ushered into the main lecture theatre. It is here that the CDIC talks about undertaking innovative inspection tours, and conducting anti-corruption campaigns. The stress on greater utilization of the internet, and even having a public side, is new. This new public face includes attempts to convey to the outside world some of the work the organization performs. But its modesty is in fact a sign of how truly powerful it has become, an entity with the ability to demand discipline from Party members for the Party.

THE POWER OF THE COMMITTEES

One of the features of a ruler is their ability to turn existing structures to their own advantage, allowing their progamme to flow through channels that may not have been fully utilized before. The Party, after all, is not a monolith. Some parts of it, as has already been made clear, have more influence than others. Allowing too many voices can be distracting and dilute executive willpower and focus. In the 1980s, Deng Xiaoping had few formal roles after 1982, but maintained immense influence through a body called the Central Leadership Advisory Group, which was ostensibly constituted of retired leaders but, during the Tiananmen Crisis of 1989, had almost all major issues referred to it. This, in tandem with chairmanship of the Central Military Commission (CMC), gave Deng all the power he needed.

Xi's style partially seems to fit the 'leading-group' structure. Leading groups have been around for a long time. It was a leading group that served as the main instrument for the extremists during the Cultural Revolution, chaired by Jiang Qing. For the 40 years of the reform process, leading groups have played a key role. Part of their attraction for elite leaders derives from the fact that they are Party entities convened above the level of ministries, working across policy areas. Their function is also beautifully abstract and vague. They are there to formulate high-level guidance on policy, which is then handed to others to implement. They have the most valuable of attributes, therefore: great power, and no responsibility. Nor do they need to operate transparently.

Xi Jinping has been nicknamed 'the Chairman of Everything'. Of the eight best-known and most influential leading groups, he is chair of four. Not surprisingly, these four are the most wide-ranging in jurisdiction. He sits, for instance, as chair of the Leading Group of Overall Reform. He is also inaugural head of the newly established National Security Commission. In addition to this he chairs the groups for Foreign Affairs and Taiwan Affairs. This means that for the broadest menu of social, political, security and diplomatic issues, he has the most central role.[7] After him, four of his colleagues have chairmanship of one leading group each – Li Keqiang of the economics group, Zhang Dejiang of the group for Hong Kong and Macau Affairs, Liu Yunshan of the Party-Building group, and Meng Jianzhu (from the full Politburo, rather than the Standing Committee) of the group for Law and Political Affairs. Leading groups are covered by the constitution of the CCP rather than by that of China. As informal forums for decision making, therefore, their size, their freedom in terms of action and remit, and their ability to link different members of the elite and legitimize decisions are enormously useful. It is not surprising that Xi is so keen to use them.

THE POWER OF IDEAS

If this is the institutional structure of power in modern China, existing like the bones and veins of a physical body, how to describe the blood that runs through it and gives it life and force? Power is not just about ordering and doing. It is about thinking and influencing, reaching beyond people's bodies and into their minds and souls. Mao's power was never solely in his use of coercion. People could, and in Chinese history often have, rebelled against such tyranny. No, the Chairman's most powerful asset from the day he came to lead the PRC was an extraordinary emotional and intellectual appeal to a vast constituency of Chinese people. This gave rise to his threat in the Cultural Revolution that he could retire from Party posts and retreat back to the countryside to found a new party, start another revolution and reclaim power again. He almost certainly would, and could have.

The Party's history testifies to the fact that in the equations of power, it is not just physical force that matters, but also intellectual and ideational forces. Indeed, since the Party acquired power, the latter have become increasingly prominent. In the twenty-first century, in its seventh decade of leading China, the CCP has a hunger for ideas that almost equals the country's hunger for resources and energy to power its economy.

Ideology is often pooh-poohed by foreign observers. Many state that China is now an ideology-free zone, where capitalism rules the roost. This is flattering to the Western consensus, where history has ended and liberal polities preside over a future with unchallenged hegemony. In reality, things are more complicated. It is true that ideology is not important for the average Chinese, any more than pondering the philosophical basis of free-market capitalism is to a European or American. But for the elite, ideology matters deeply. It is often the difference between political life and death. Those who come down on the wrong side of ideological divides suffer. Power struggles are often framed as those between personalities and networks. But there are ideas behind these, ideas about the role of the market, of free enterprise, of social management and of the state and its final function. The Party might express these in off-putting and dense language in its internal documents, which the vast majority of people might never look at. But for the decision makers, these are crucial things. As I will write later, ideology is never far from Xi Jinping's thinking, and has become a major source of his claim to power.

Ideology, after all, underpins and underlines the fundamental claims of the Party. Trying to bridge the divide pre- and post-1978, between Maoist radical ideology and the embracing of Chinese-style capitalism afterwards, has taken immense thought and ingenuity. Perhaps it is impossible. But the Party ideologues, some of the most powerful people on the planet, have spent immense amounts of time and effort to square this circle. Their argument, expressed through Xi and his leadership peers, is simply that however unpleasant the social and human impacts of class struggle and mass campaigns during the Maoist era, the price was worth paying for the second phase of building 'socialism with Chinese characteristics' – the era from 1978 onwards when China was unified enough, stable enough and industrialized enough to open itself to foreign capital, free enterprise and a guided domestic market system. Throughout this period, policy changes have been accompanied by ideological justifications. The need to embrace foreign capital necessitated the ideological change expressed by 'socialism with Chinese characteristics' in the 1980s and 1980s. Under Jiang Zemin, the non-state sector, which had blossomed and become an increasingly important source of growth, was finally given recognition by the Party through the 'Three Represents' theory. China's need to wean itself off pure GDP growth and the immense imbalances and inequalities this had given rise to found ideological expression in Hu Jintao's 'harmonious society' and 'scientific development'. In Xi, the 'China Dream' expresses aspirations for a country with greater confidence and hopes – the affirmation of a bourgeois China with all the paradoxes that that entails. But every single one of these moves has been conveyed as being part of a coherent, consistent framework supplied by Marx, dialectical materialism, and the imperative to create a modern socialist state. In this context, ideology is the language of power, and those wishing to hold power in China have to become fluent in it, even if it is a language barely understood by most Chinese people outside the Party structure.

If there are important ideas the Party seeks to promote, control and articulate, then there is also a related language of that power – a discourse of leadership, whereby people in certain positions have the right to say things that have to be listened to, acted on and respected. There is a clear 'vocabulary' of leadership for the elite in modern

China, which makes political statements sound very different from the language of everyday people. Hu Jintao was probably the most extreme example of this, someone whose register was almost always impersonal, and whose messages were conveyed through slogans and in sterile-sounding speeches, whose most memorable quality was their total lack of memorability.

Xi Jinping's style is more direct. And there have been efforts by leaders from his generation around him to be a little freer in how they speak publicly. Party documents, though, resolutely remain in the register of the Communist functionary, with heavy internal references to 'Mao Zedong Thought', 'Deng Xiaoping Theory', the 'Three Represents' and the 'Theory of Scientific Development'. The use of this language in China is one of the most important indicators that an official may be intimately located in this nexus of influence and authority. Such power language is rarely about communicating, but more about asserting. Even other officials listen to it with their minds wandering, or half asleep. But it occurs as part of a performance, a display of a member of the Party elite's right to use certain privileged terms and vocabulary. The Party, therefore, has not only its own organizations, and its own narratives and customs, but also its own dialect.

CONTROLLING THE MESSAGE AND THE MESSENGER

If ideas matter profoundly in modern China to holders of power, then controlling the dissemination of information is also critical. Those who direct propaganda and undertake 'thought-direction' work are crucial members of the Party elite, and have a voice in the innermost sanctums of decision making. Getting the message right has always mattered to the CCP, from its earliest days. Mao's ability to craft this message was one of his core skills, whether through his writings or through the propaganda messages he supported. Slogans, campaigns, model workers, and narratives of liberation and empowerment that placed the Party leadership at the centre were all components of this. Materially, control of newspapers, films and cultural entities also played their role. The *People's Daily* newspaper, China Central Television, the Xinhua news agency and a raft of other information-centric entities were the institutional and material means that put the Party in charge of the message. And they were always directed by important Party figures.

Xi himself, in a speech to Party workers in 2013, admitted that the information work had never been more important, and never more complex. Media control in the era of Mao was straightforward. The country was sealed off. Ideas largely came from one source. The Party apparatus could turn on and switch off overnight news and with it the flow of ideas. People's indoctrination was exhaustive, and complete. Maoist ideas in the Cultural Revolution were written across the landscape on big posters daubed with large Chinese characters, enforced in meetings and mass campaigns, and illustrated with the 'Eight Revolutionary Operas', which were then the only cultural fare available. Those who even thought of trying to escape this onslaught did so at great personal danger. The only other option was nothing.

In twenty-first-century China, the internet has spread like wildfire. The Party has adopted strategic means to maintain control over some of its wilder impacts. A 'Great Firewall' keeps out contaminating ideas. Websites are policed by voluntary and employed armies of enforcers who take down instances of incorrect thinking. From time to time there are mistakes and missteps. But on the whole, rosy predictions at the dawn of the internet era that it would challenge the Chinese propaganda effort and enforce benign change have so far proved wide of the mark. If anything, as Evgeny Morozov has shown, the internet has been as much a blessing as a curse in China, telling leaders more about public opinion, but also letting them infiltrate and influence the ideosphere in subtle and insidious ways.[8] They are in good company. As the renegade CIA operative Edward Snowden showed in 2013, gleaming democracies like the United States and the United Kingdom had been up to similar tricks. The internet has been an opportunity too good for governments of any shade to ignore – they can snoop not just on people outside, but on those within.

For the Chinese power system, the internet still carries risks. Party members can be distracted by other intellectual or political ideas, and its tide of scandal and tittle-tattle sometimes carries flotsam about Party leaders and their unruly family and personal networks. Savvy netizens have created well-encrypted private languages through which subversive messages challenging official Party ones have been expressed. The many puns and synonyms in the Chinese language have been allies to their mission, causing probably the largest cat-and-mouse game in history – in which metaphors are searched for online and 'bad' messages eradicated, leaving that deemed wholesome intact. The continuous revolution to ensure the Party keeps up with this means the propaganda bureaus have to be on the move all the time.

In one area, however, the Party will forever have the upper hand. On information about one thing that interests almost everyone, it is the sole authoritative gateway – and that is news about itself. An industry of Party-watchers based in China, Hong Kong and Taiwan, as well as across the world, tries to read signals and track down inside information. From time to time events like the fall of Bo Xilai open up small cracks in the great wall that surrounds the Party's inner workings. But most observers suspect that the outside world knows very little about what really happens in the Politburo meetings, or when one major leader in China meets another. Occasionally, as with governments everywhere, there might be tactical leaking of news by one group attempting to damage another. Li Keqiang has seemingly been a victim of this in the last few years, with hints about his health circulating unofficially in late 2014, and, in mid-2015, about the possibility of his only serving one term as premier. But these tips are paltry fare to a famished outside world. The Party has been remarkable at keeping its business within itself. This information source is one it will not give up willingly.

Still, ideas are conveyed through language, and the way in which language acts as a key promoter of power agendas is a fascinating area. Once again, Mao was the exemplar of this, someone whose work was so distinctive that it gave rise to a new moniker – Maospeak. Academic Li Tuo, the inventor of this phrase, stated that Mao's language stood alone, on a promontory of its own, set apart from other kinds of speech acts and discourse.[9] The fact that this language, with its associated myths and ideological basis, was produced by a group of advisors that included, at some stage or another, individuals such as *People's Daily* editor Hu Qiaomu, ideologue Chen Boda and writer and radical Yao Wenyuan only shows how much effort was invested in it. Its ability through symbolism and the emotional resources of language itself to capture the emotions and allegiance of Chinese people was immense. Language has an intrinsic link to power. It is its external garments.[10]

In the period of Hu Jintao language grew sterile and formulaic from the elite leaders, and particularly from the more prominent of them. Hu never referred to any personal narrative, and kept his language as empty as possible of anything approaching a personal register.[11] His language was prescriptive and dominated by slogans. It is no wonder therefore that Liu Yunshan, while directing China's propaganda efforts, referred to this in 2005 in a speech to the Central Party School, the institution where Party officials are trained, in which he observed that officials' language was off-putting and rarely attended to by other cadres.[12] Chinese language itself is rich in symbolic and literary devices, and offers a huge resource for any leader, as long as he or she is willing to use it.[13]

Xi's language differs from Hu's precisely in this willingness to use a more personal register, and to refer to his past. There are many examples from 2012 onwards of him speaking in a very direct manner, either about his own life before becoming leader or about things he likes or has an interest in. He even refers directly to himself as a leader and to the challenges it brings: 'It is not easy to govern such a country,' he stated in an interview with Russian television in February 2014, 'so I must ascend a height to enjoy a distant view while planting my feet on solid ground.' As he continues, he pulls in his own experience: 'I worked in different regions of China for a long time, so I am fully aware that the differences are great between the country's east and west.'[14] He is also willing to use allusions from classical Chinese literature. In a single speech on innovation made in October 2013, he referred to Fan Zhongyan, a scholar from the Song dynasty, the ancient Book of

Changes, written by Sun Jing and Kuang Heng of the Han dynasty around the time of Christ, and Che Yin of the Eastern Jin dynasty, along with the modern Chinese nuclear physicist Qian Xuesen.[15] Such referencing is not unique to this speech, and has occurred several times since 2012. More importantly, his style is much less dominated by articulations of abstract ideology. So while he is willing to continue speaking about concepts as heady as spiritual values, inner worlds and moral visions, he tries to give specific examples of what these mean and how they relate to daily life. Some habits die hard, however. Despite condemning the use of slogans and 'empty talk' in 2012, Xi was to rely on an unappetizing list of slogans to 'distil' his outlook in 2015, when the 'Four Comprehensives' were released: to 'comprehensively build a moderately prosperous society, comprehensively deepen reform, comprehensively govern the nation according to law, and comprehensively strictly govern the Party'.[16] The search continues for a language of power that combines authoritativeness with humanity, and strikes the balance between emotional and rational registers in China.[17]

THE BOOK OF BLANK CHEQUES

There is one big difference between the China of Mao, and the China of the leaders who have followed: money. For Maoist China, poverty was a daily reality. The economy did grow during his period in power, a fact often forgotten today – but from the most pitiful of foundations, and often through blood, sweat and tears. Events like the Great Leap Forward and the Cultural Revolution impeded wealth creation. Mao was interested in many things as a source of authority and power, but money was not one of them. Business people were persecuted, and the private sector closed down from the 1950s. Even those who tried to sell a few eggs from a chicken they owned, or some grain from a patch of land on something resembling a free market, were playing with fire.

The ideological impediment to entrepreneurial behaviour was lifted from the late 1970s. From this point onwards, the phenomenon of wealthy Chinese involved in business returned. Very quickly, a small but growing group became rich, and could enjoy the fruits of their labours. By the 2000s this subset had become larger, and more important – important enough to gain membership of the Party. Money and material wealth are a source of power in almost every political culture. But the relationship between wealth and political influence is a complex one. Oligarchs may, for a period, have called the shots in Russia before Putin reined them in. But China has ensured that such a thing has never happened in its own territory. What has proved more challenging is the corrosive effect of money on officials and their family and other networks. This will be a major issue when we look in more detail at Xi Jinping, because in many ways his power is increasingly looking as though it is based on money rather than on moral, ideological and more intangible sources.

Money does matter to the CCP and its power in one key respect – the Party controls one of the prime sources of wealth creation in China, the SOEs, which still occupy much of the commanding heights of the national economy. It maintains a hold over budgets, through taxation and fiscal revenue. This is a crucial way of keeping provinces in line. Because the central government controls the purse strings, if provinces oppose it, it simply starves them of funding and lets that concentrate their minds.

And on money and its own budget, the Party is deeply secretive. It issues no accounts, and submits itself to no audits. The NPC, constitutionally the 'highest organ of state power', might be allowed to look each spring at the full government budget. But there are precious few lines in that covering the expenses of the Party, and what it, as an entity in its own right, might cost each year to run.

THE GUN

Mario Puzo's popular 1969 novel *The Godfather*, on which the series of blockbuster films was based, described part of the protagonist's logic as this: he would always try to reason and argue with people, but at a certain point, if they refused to give way, then he would get a gun out and shoot them. The seamless dichotomy of intellectual and brutal similarly served the Party well in its wild infancy. The hint that any refusal to comply might lead to beatings, torture and, in the most extreme cases, execution has been a powerful incentivizing force. The Party has not been squeamish about this use of force. Mao himself sneeringly described the attitudes of some to revolution as being akin to a pleasant 'dinner party' – and corrected them. Revolution was 'an act of violence'. And where necessary, violence had a place.

The Party now hankers for respectability, but the simple fact that it has total political and administrative control over legal force – the army and internal security services – shows that it still not only seeks to maintain a monopoly on political power, but also links this to having complete control over the powers of physical enforcement. For Mao and Deng, this gave them the trump card. In the Cultural Revolution, it could be argued that the People's Liberation Army (PLA) offered the last resort when the Party was rebellious and threatening to jettison the Chairman. Soldiers were sent in to run what had been civil organizations, and military leaders, represented by Lin Biao, were placed in positions of supreme political power. Deng too was able to rely on the crack troops of two regiments in the PLA to quell protestors in 1989 at Tiananmen Square.

For all its efforts to professionalize and become a modern fighting force, the PLA remains the military wing of the Party, and its mandate comes from a CMC chaired by a civilian – the general secretary of the CCP. Its core instruction in reformist China has been to assist the Party in strengthening the economy, to ensure that access to resources is unimpeded, and that the country internally and externally exists in a stable environment. This 'lips and teeth' arrangement means that there is no question about divided loyalties, and so far there has been little history of military leaders ever threatening the Party with coups – this is unnecessary as they are, in essence, one and the same entity, and they sink or swim accordingly in the same destiny.

Rumours that the Chinese army holds immense subterranean powers and is able to control more political territory than it might at first appear to stem from the idea that nationalist rhetoric is there to support the role of the PLA, and make it clear it is the final defender of China's interests. In recent years, PLA officials, such as the generals Liu Yuan and Xiong Guangkai, have made bellicose statements, sounding like they are setting policy parameters that the Party leadership has to follow. But these are probably overcooked claims. The PLA has historically been a faithful servant of the leadership, even if that leadership in the early generations of elite rule was mostly trained by and rose through the army's own stable. The Red Army, the former name for the PLA, was the child of the CCP, founded in 1927, six years after the first congress. Its narratives, political strategies and grand directives emanate from the Party, and its core leadership is, to all intents and purposes, appointed by the Party. For this reason, the PLA remains a guarantor of Party rule and power. And it operates as such with little real threat to its final master. The anti-corruption purges of 2013 onwards have lapped at the walls of the PLA, taking some significant figures down, usually in serendipitous symmetry with the purges within the CCP. This shows how permeable the boundaries are between them, and how profoundly, intimately linked they are.

Control of security services has also always mattered to the Party. Surveillance of people through neighbourhood committees in the Maoist period was extensive, and employed many millions of people, both paid and unpaid.[18] The Party's route to power had left it with a justifiable paranoia, and its leaders were perfectly aware that keeping tabs on people and what they were doing was crucial. A complex taxonomy of different classes and ranks of reliability and loyalty was created. Kang Sheng was the godfather of all this, one of the most unpleasant and reviled of modern leaders, but someone who maintained the trust of Mao until his final days. The security services in the twenty-first century remain the underbelly of power, something that by their nature cannot be explicitly talked about. And yet while they do not hunt down vast numbers of counter-revolutionaries as they did in the past, the Ministry of State Security (MSS), the Public Security Bureaus and the People's Armed Police (PAP), at national and local level, all undertake operations against those deemed separatists, subversives and common criminals.

Since the 2000s, the government, spooked by a series of unforeseen and highly disruptive protests that turned violent in Tibet, Xinjiang and Inner Mongolia, and dealing with sharply rising numbers of protests among citizens over matters ranging from pension payments to land rights, has supported a 'stability-maintenance' policy. This has broadly manifested itself in the ringleaders of specific kinds of protests being imprisoned, victimized and generally made an example of. Security services have been granted generous budgets, much as they have across the rest of the world in the post-9/11 era. Counter-terrorism efforts have increased. Much of this is legitimate. But the security services sit beside the PLA as a tool of supreme political usefulness to the Party, one over which it holds total control. Under Zhou Yongkang, Politburo Standing Committee member from 2007 to 2012, the enriched, empowered security services became akin to a private fiefdom, populated by agents able to swoop down on those it deemed antagonistic, and unleash a whole suite of extra-judicial powers, including extra-legal detention, threatened or actual physical violence, intimidation and bribery. The security services, surrounded by secrecy and enigma, are the agents best equipped to do the Party's dirty work. Empires of unaccountability, simply from the nature of their work, they have been remarkable bastions of privilege, something that may lie behind the removal of their vice minister Ma Jian on claims of corruption in early 2015. This is a sign that in an era of falling GDP growth and tightening belts, even the mighty MSS has to buck the trend and start delivering efficiencies.

BANDS OF BROTHERS, AND SISTERS

Alongside the institutional or corporate forms of access to power in modern China, there are also more amorphous factors: privileged and influential clans and their interrelationships. China under Communism may have buried feudalism and set its back against imperial orders; landlords may have been brutally dislodged in the campaigns of the 1950s. But in a society so vast there will always be the need for networks, whether provincial, familial or institutional. Belonging to these networks does matter, and the blood links among families who were investors in the capital of the Party in its early generations now often allow those families to draw rich dividends from this investment.

There may be 200 key power families in China, but perhaps no more than 20 or 30 really have meaningful clout. The most prominent of these are linked to the Dengs, and, more recently, Jiang Zemin's family. Mao's family, too, still plays a maverick role, though not perhaps as prominent a one as observers might expect. Mao's grandson has appeared at meetings of the Chinese People's Political Consultative Conference (CPPCC) in recent years, though more as someone gently mocked by the international press for his mostly irrelevant comments and lightweight style and noticeable only because of his ancestry than someone with anything serious to say. Clan links work through generations. The role of clans is always slightly uneasy and contentious because it enflames claims of unfair privilege and elitism, though with Xi Jinping, himself someone deeply embedded in this system through his father, they seem to have made a spectacular comeback. The simple fact is that the Party of the proletariat and peasant revolution has, nine decades after its foundation, become increasingly like something with an imperial inheritance line – a discreet royalty.

Clan links and connections have a number of benefits for those seeking power: access to other decision makers in the Party elite and the leadership, straightforward knowledge of why certain people can be trusted and have a vested interest in working in specific roles, and something akin to a 'brand value', which can be useful at least for name recognition, much as being a Bush or a Clinton has value in US politics. The description of Xi's path to the top given later will show that because of his family background he has been able to carry army, Party and other important elite constituencies, which have supported him as he has risen through the ranks. While never as crude as people giving allegiance through votes or other tangible displays of support, having a broad network of family facilitators is, of course, immensely useful.

Carefully defined clans can also express their power through control over key state assets and sectors of the state-owned economy. The family of former premier of China Li Peng, one of the leaders most associated with the Tiananmen Square crackdown, has in recent years been influential in the immense, strategically important energy sector. Former president Jiang Zemin's family has deep involvement with telecommunications, another vastly profitable enterprise. And the interests of the greatly respected premier under Jiang, Zhu Rongji, are related to finance. The link between clans and big-ticket business is, of course, a double-edged sword, giving access to almost limitless material and monetary benefits but also acting like a lightning rod for criticism and anger. The ways in which individual families with long, historic Party pedigrees have been able to turn their connections into something akin to business enterprises hijacked for their own narrow entrepreneurial purposes cause huge public anger and resentment. This phenomenon has become an increasing target for anti-corruption moves under Xi. Even so, prising apart leaders' families, in particular, and their desire to use Party links and privileges to become wealthy, has so far proved extremely difficult. Distributing political capital alongside financial capital has happened almost with inevitability for the Party as the country it governs has grown richer. But these clans and family links are also perhaps the most vulnerable source of Party power, and the one that may well radically change – ironically, under a man like Xi, who could himself be described as coming from this background.

THE PARTY OF RIGHTEOUSNESS

The majority of sources of different types of power described above may be said to be institutional, or tangible. They are things that exist, and through which influence and the power to control, dictate and direct events flows. But the blood flowing through this system belongs to two other sources of meta-power – ethical and emotional. These are the areas least written about or understood and yet perhaps the most crucial.

The ethical basis of the Party, because of its proclivity for violence right up to recent years, is problematic. The language of force,
coercion and raw power is one the Party speaks well. But when it
comes to justifying courses of action or things it has done, is doing
or intends to do on the basis that they are inherently right, things
become much more complicated. Marxism, in the end, did not gift
any system, whether in the former USSR or anywhere else, with a
particularly coherent body of ethical thinking. And while, since the
time of Mao, leaders have been happy to talk about qualities like
patriotism, sacrifice for the good of the country, Party mission and
even justice (rectifying the evils of the past and China's humiliation,
for instance), on the whole there has been no attempt to relate these
to being objectively right.

Part of this might be attributed to the way in which the Party
established itself from its foundation as atheistic, and asserted its own
values based on a strongly materialistic philosophy. To this day, Party
leaders like Xi have little problem stating that unless people are fed
and materially well off then they can have no meaningful cultural life
nor participate in the world of spiritual satisfaction. But the result
of this focus on the material is that China since Mao has become a
battleground of granular interests, where people and networks slog it
out against each other. Nobel laureate Liu Xiaobo offers perhaps the
most accessible and forensic critique of the Party system's moral challenges as it has transformed itself into a governing party and tried to
shed its revolutionary roots. He describes a world in which powerful,
largely unaccountable Party officials justify almost everything they do
on the principle that might is right, and in which they can get away
with murder, sometimes literally.[19] Egotistical, self-serving behaviour
creeps into most areas of life, with cadres above a certain level freely
helping themselves to public goods, looking after their own networks
and setting up a parallel world where they can enjoy material, sensual
and monetary benefits just because they are Party members. The
thinking that has been dominant in the last 30 years as China has
become wealthier is that members of the Party elite can do what they
want, simply because no one can hold them to account. Talking about

performing to ethical standards, when the main objective has been delivering GDP growth as a basis for promotion, has been regarded as an abstract indulgence.

The Party cannot ignore ethical issues, however, partly because of the immense resentment that cadre malfeasance gives rise to, and partly because, as the key entity in society, with a position of leadership over all the main areas of life, having no programme to try to explain systematically the philosophical basis of its rule looks incongruous and threatens to eat away at its legitimacy. It states constantly that it represents much more than its own parochial vested interest. But how can it truly do this without having access to a body of ideas, principles and values that extends beyond itself and applies across the whole of society?

Having moral authority is a core source of potential power for the Party, and one that it historically has alluded to in placing itself on the side of delivering justice and fighting against oppression for Chinese people in the 'liberation' period. In power, however, its moral authority has been undermined by the Maoist excesses and then the period of material enrichment, when so much of this early justice narrative was forgotten. One of the interesting moves by Xi Jinping has been to attempt to reclaim this moral high ground, partly through restoring the ethical fitness of key cadres by disciplining them and cleaning up their corruption, and partly through describing the Party as being on the side of justice, healthy and clean living, and selfless virtues. In February 2014, for instance, speaking at a study session of the Politburo, Xi stated that 'we' (presumably the Party) must 'respect and follow moral standards, to pursue lofty ideals and to reinforce ideological and moral foundations of socialism with Chinese characteristics'. The Party, he went on to say, had to help people 'upgrade their moral outlook, for the fostering of civic virtues in society'.[20] Ironically, some of the resources of ancient philosophical systems like Confucianism and its 'inverted golden rule' ('do not treat others as you would not treat yourself') have been recruited into this effort, with Hu Jintao referring to the need for the Party to have people-centred policies and to take people as the key, and Xi himself saying that 'to cultivate the core socialist values we must take traditional Chinese culture as the base'.[21]

Corruption has been a particular theme of Xi's period in power and will figure later in this book. It is also one of the most illuminating when looking at ethical issues. Does the CCP consider corruption something that is intrinsically wrong, asserting self-interest against consideration of others? There is plenty of evidence that, in fact, the discourse of anti-corruption in contemporary China differs from that of, for instance, the definition given by the Organization for Economic Cooperation and Development (OECD), which speaks of officials using their public positions for private gain, something that is regarded as wrong in any circumstances.[22] In China, as some officials have admitted, it is almost impossible not to use public positions for your network's gain. Some of these networks, in fact, can barely be controlled and trade off assumed links with an elite leader even if there is in fact no substantive, active connection. Corruption has become, as scholars like Andrew Wedeman have pointed out, something that is almost tolerated as part of the sludge accruing from rapid development, and campaigns against it (at least until Xi's) have been tactical, highly politicized and more tools of Party empowerment than exercises undertaken to ingrain better behaviour in governmental and Party officials in China.[23] For the Xi campaign since 2012, the political dimension of such a fight – undertaking a series of probes and purges against internal enemies in the Party, clearing away potential opponents such as Zhou Yongkang and Bo Xilai, and attacking inefficient behaviour in the state sector that threatens stable Party rule in an era of slowing growth – trumps the ethical dimension, however blurred the lines between these two realms appear. The anti-corruption clampdown illustrates well just how hard it has been, even under Xi, for the Party to assert that its behaviour is truly based on objective ethical values rather than Party self-interest. Whatever the true foundation of its actions, however, to state it is prosecuting this campaign because the Party is on the side of objective justice, virtue and moral values is a major source of authority and power. For this very reason, the Party's discourse on these issues is always slightly ambiguous, and sometimes incoherent.

EMOTIONS

Many studies make the CCP sound like a machine, one that has various inputs and an internal rationalizing process on which it operates, and that then issues carefully calculated outputs.[24] But the Party appeals for emotional support all the time, and one could argue that under the leadership of Mao it always let emotion win out over rational calculation. Notions of national honour, pride, dignity and status have played a crucial role in its major messages, in the historical narratives its chief ideologues have crafted for it to stay in power, and its mass campaigns and propaganda. The Chinese constitution of 1982 refers to the role that the Party played in making Chinese people the 'masters of their own house'. Stirring sentiments are inspired through Party-sponsored art, music and language.

It has become difficult to remember just how much during its past the Party appealed to the power of emotion for support. Leaders like Deng Xiaoping avoided high-blown rhetoric and stuck to policy pragmatism and a language appropriate to convey this. Jiang Zemin was little better, although he often allowed his own emotions to boil over in public – from being reduced to floods of theatrical tears at Deng's funeral in 1997 to exploding with rage at Hong Kong journalists who compared him to a latter-day emperor in 2000. But the emotionless era of Party rule reached its apogee in Hu Jintao, whose speeches, as noted earlier, contained no personal register, and who spoke in a long litany of slogans and theoretical memes that left even the most devout slumbering during his appearances at the Party congresses. Hu's robotic style of speaking, while it sometimes strayed into forced flowery language, was unlikely to enthuse and motivate a wide audience of listeners. Even worse, it seemed to represent the mismatch between the power elite and their dialect and the rest of the human race.

Xi Jinping's use of the phrase 'China Dream' from late 2013 has attracted widespread commentary. There have been passionate debates inside and outside China on what precisely this dream might be. What is not in doubt is that it appeals once more to the emotions of the

Chinese people, and links the Party to their ideals and hopes, things which the Hu era's fierce commitment to material development at the cost of everything else never attempted to do. Emotional force is something that a Chinese leader appeals to with some trepidation. Mao was the greatest master of it, and his utopian, idealistic messages during the Cultural Revolution decade of mass movements sanctioned widespread upheaval, careering violence and profound divisions in society. Mao's genuine ability to capture the feelings of many Chinese people inspired blind devotion and worship. One long-term Beijing resident from Europe once described this era to me as 'the closest China has ever come to a religious movement'. But for generations after Mao, seeing just how terrifying an emotionally mobilized and aroused population in China could be was a sobering experience. Bo Xilai, in his vaunted campaign to resurrect some aspects of Maoist emotional mobilization while in Chongqing from 2007, is the most salient illustration of this. His 'red song' campaigns and reuse of Maoist-style slogans and messaging made central leaders like Wen Jiabao profoundly uneasy.

Not appealing to people's emotions, however, even in China, is impossible. As Martha Nussbaum has written in her book on Western-style political systems, emotions offer some of the most important ways to reach out to the public for support:

> Public emotions, frequently intense, have large-scale conse-
> quences for the nation's progress toward its goals. They can give
> the pursuit of those goals new vigor and depth, but they can
> also derail that pursuit, introducing or reinforcing divisions,
> hierarchies, and forms of neglect or obtuseness.[25]

Intellectual arguments about policy or philosophy of governance, or debate about rational courses for future action, are well and good. But they reach a limited constituency, and often have far less compelling force than messages, even if underpinned by sound intellectual credentials, that aim for emotional support. For the Party, most of this emotional power is located in its increasing appeals to nationalism, and to sentiments of a rejuvenated China restored to its correct honour and status as a leading nation and major global player. Often, this drifts into targeted campaigns against 'old enemies' like the Japanese, or even the Vietnamese. Chinese politics is only likely to get increasingly 'emotional' in the years ahead. This is inevitable because emotional appeal is one of the most important, and forceful, forms of 'intangible' political power.

THE GEOGRAPHY OF POWER IN THE MODERN PRC

When some observers blandly state that the CCP only cares about staying in power and maintains an iron focus on this objective, it is worth pondering the various institutional, organizational and less tangible forms of power promotion and manifestations of authority. Power, as the philosopher Michel Foucault famously showed, is a dynamic, complex, organic thing. It cannot be easily labelled.[26] It drifts across hard and soft sources, sometimes using force, sometimes using inducements, often seductive and frightening at the same time. The CCP has shown in its elite leadership an instinctive understanding of where power lies, and how best to get it.

The question that comes back after all this careful delineation of the topography and typology of power in China is a fundamental one. What, in the end, is this power for? Power for power's sake is not, finally, a satisfactory answer. At some point, this collapses into self-interest, emotional and ethical bankruptcy, and popular opposition. That, surely, is self-defeating. The CCP claims it holds power for specific reasons – because it alone has the true path, the true ideas, to deliver a great, strong, powerful country. And China will be a great, strong, powerful country under its rule, its leaders state, because of the Party's intellectual, cultural and spiritual vision for that country. Unlike leaders in democracies, therefore, the CCP makes surprisingly grand claims about its vision. It does not just promise to deliver a good living standard, a world where the environment will be better and where people can live more peaceably, but something beyond this – a society where the delivery of people's material, cultural and spiritual needs will be perfected. Today, even in the second decade of the twenty-first century, the CCP remains close to its idealistic, utopian roots. It believes, in ways that most Western leaders of recent years do not, in scientific development, and in procedures, rules and a body of truths that will lead to a better world, one slowly approaching perfection. From Marxism, the Party maintains its convictions about historical progress: through thesis and antithesis to synthesis.

The Party vision is a crucial element of its rule, and one of the main sources of its legitimacy. As an organization, the Party, and the Party alone, has this holistic vision, and, most crucially, the means to deliver it through its monopoly on power. Multiparty parliamentary democracies might muddle along from election to election, mapping out abstract ideas of a better future but on the whole just trying to improve things slightly, and deliver pragmatic, measurable outcomes, but the CCP, free of elections, can drive towards the first 'centennial goal' in 2021, and the even grander one in 2049, setting itself landmarks far into the distance as it aspires to make its visions a reality.[27] Many of those who engage with the Party practically, be they business people, diplomats or foreign government officials, might be astonished to know that the Party has this idealistic, dreamy underbelly. They would see it as a hard-nosed, narrow, ruthless machine. But that would be to ignore the very sophisticated ways in which it has been able to monopolize emotionally appealing, stirring narratives from the past into the future, which elide the Party's and the country's aspirations from the time of Mao onwards. And Xi Jinping is the man in charge of China at a time when this task has hit a crucial crossroads. It is to his story that we now turn.

2
XI THE MAN

Man has three ways of acting wisely. First, on meditation; that is the noblest. Secondly, on imitation; that is the easiest. Thirdly, on experience; that is the bitterest.

—Attributed to Confucius

Such has been Xi Jinping's success at dominating domestic and international political agendas in China since 2012 that it is hard to resist the idea that there was some inevitability about his rise, and that he was predestined to occupy his current position. It is useful to be reminded that he was almost unknown as recently as the mid-2000s, and even then appeared only as a likely contender in a list of names – and not even the first-ranked. Chinese politics is often talked about, inside and outside the country, as being a highly deliberative, structured process in which the great collective intelligence of the Party manipulates and guides things to their best conclusion. This ignores the plentiful evidence that, in fact, it is often a scrappy, chaotic process, and outcomes are more often than not chanced upon rather than carefully planned.

Anyone predicting Xi's becoming CCP leader in the 1990s would have been regarded as crazy. In 1997, as a sign of his unpopularity, he famously missed out on election to the Central Committee of the Party, and direct entry into the central elite, by one position. Only machinations managed to get him a slot. In the early 2000s, commentators like Cheng Li of the US Brookings Institution referred to Li Keqiang as a more likely heir apparent to the newly installed Hu

Jintao.[1] Xi's great asset of his relationship to his father, a major military leader under Mao during the era of the Sino-Japanese War and the Civil War, and a member of the core group of national elite leaders for the opening decade of the PRC's existence, was, for much of his life, also his greatest liability. In his youth, it was the cause of ostracization and victimhood. In his middle age, it became a convenient target for opponents to attack, showing that he belonged to a self-serving faction of offspring of former elite leaders who were riding on the coat-tails of the older generation rather than relying on their own particular skills.

The hagiographic account of Xi issued by the official state news agency, Xinhua, in 2012 during his visit to Guangzhou points to a leader who has all-round experience at different levels of government, someone authenticated by his time as a sent-down youth during the Cultural Revolution, and a person who only went to university as a mature student and therefore enjoys a legitimate link with the common people of China. 'He arrived at the village [in Shaanxi Province] as a slightly lost teenager and left as a 22-year-old man determined to do something for the people.' 'The needs of the people weighed heavily on Xi's heart,' it continues later. It claims that Xi once said: 'Officials should love the people in the way they love their parents, work for their benefit, and lead them to prosperity.'[2]

Beyond its profoundly paternalistic tone, this presentation of Xi as someone with authentic grass-roots networks, someone who has a specific story to tell justifying his position, is striking. Xi differs from Hu Jintao, his predecessor, in a number of ways. But perhaps the most notable is his willingness to use his own life story, his personal narrative, to give himself political validation. This story says he has earned the right to be general secretary through his varied experience, his lifelong commitment to serving the rural constituencies of China and being able to speak to them, and his fundamental belief in the mission of the Party. This elision of Xi's interests and the Party's is a complex one, and will be looked at later. But in terms of the use of his biography to promote himself as the best leader the Party could have, there can be little argument. More than either Deng or Jiang, and far more than the faceless Hu, Xi has tried to tell a story about himself and his journey towards exercising power. And many parts of that story relate precisely to the sources of power covered in Chapter 1 – his links to the military, to elite Party leaderships, to the Party itself and its various narratives. What Xi has also displayed, as is becoming clearer, is an instinctive understanding of how to fit these various locations of power together, and how to mobilize them and use them to his advantage.

CHILDHOOD

Xi Jinping was born on 1 June 1953 in Beijing, the son of Xi Zhongxun and Qi Xin. The fact that he was born in northern China is the reason his name has the 'ping' character, from 'Beiping' (northern peace), the old title for Beijing.[3] He was the third of four children, with two older sisters (Qi Qiaoqiao, born in 1949, and Qi Anan, born in 1951) and a younger brother (Xi Yuanping, born in 1955). His father had enjoyed a distinguished military career during the wars with the Japanese and then the Nationalists, and was working in the 1950s in the propaganda ministry. His mother was also a cadre, working during the years of his birth and infancy in the Marxism–Leninism Institute, a place she had to attend from Monday to Friday, often being away from home. This meant that in his earliest years, Xi was largely looked after by his father.

Over this period, Xi enjoyed a typical elite youth. He went to Beihai Kindergarten in central Beijing, along with many other children of the newly installed top elite, among them the country's then president Liu Shaoqi, the influential economist Chen Yun and, most significantly, Bo Yibo. Many of these, after growing up, figured in Xi's subsequent career either as allies or, in the case of Bo Xilai (the son of Bo Yibo), opponents.

The 1950s figure in national memory now as halcyon days, a time when China, after its hard-won liberation, enjoyed a golden era of good governance and idealism. Mao in this early period of rule lacked the megalomaniacal instincts that were to figure so calamitously in the 1960s and 1970s. Rule was largely consensus-driven, with a presiding sense of urgency about building and reconstructing China for a bright, wonderful future. Clouds only started to appear on the horizon with the Hundred Flowers Campaign in 1956, and the subsequent anti-rightist campaigns, which were used to silence some of the dissent that had begun to appear. But by all accounts Xi's earliest years were simple, pleasant ones. He went to the 1 August Primary School after leaving kindergarten, another favourite for high-level leaders' children of the time.

This relative level of calm was to be irrevocably shattered in the summer of 1962. Beijing politics had become increasingly tense; fractures had started to appear in the leadership after the failure of the ambitious but wholly impractical Great Leap Forward. Far from improving China's economic position and making it a rival of developed nations, it drove the country into what is now largely seen as a man-made famine. For three years from 1959, millions suffered. As many as 50 million died. The fallout from this included fierce arguments from 1959 onwards between the topmost leaders, the most famous of which was a confrontation between Mao and one of his chief allies, Peng Dehuai, the minister of defence. Peng had attacked the situation in the countryside, where he said the economy had fundamentally collapsed. Mao took this as an attempt to seize his own power, and while he seemingly stepped back from the frontline for a while, he merely bided his time.

Xi Zhongxun, Jinping's father, was popular with Mao as a result of his previous military career in the north of China. But for others around the Chairman this only made him a better target. His most dangerous enemy was the founder of China's secret police, and one of the most fundamentally unpleasant of a Party core that contained a number of people verging on the psychotic. Kang Sheng, trained in the USSR, went under a multitude of aliases and seemed to rejoice in occupying shadowy places. He became Mao's intelligence tsar during the Yan'an years when the Party was in internal exile and fighting for survival. This meant that he had acquired considerable political capital, much of it through prosecuting vicious purges against perceived opponents of Mao, such as Gao Gang. Xi Zhongxun's vulnerability was his portfolio: propaganda, where he had deputy-ministerial rank. Part of his remit was to oversee the vetting of cultural products to ensure that they carried no covert or unhealthy messages. In 1956, Zhongxun gave permission for the publication of a novel about Liu Zhidong, a revolutionary martyr from the early era of CCP history, by a writer from the Workers' Publishing Company. This was only after extensive consultation and revision. The problem with the novel when it appeared was that it mentioned Gao Gang, a figure who was basically considered *persona non grata* after his exposure as an enemy of Mao, and banned from all explicit public reference. Gao himself committed suicide after his fall in 1954. Kang Sheng had found Xi Zhongxun's moment of weakness.

Kang Sheng had no doubt not read the book; nor for that matter did he care greatly about its contents, beyond the fact that in mentioning such a taboo figure it gave him the perfect chance to attack Xi Zhongxun.[4] As with the Cultural Revolution three years later, obscure arguments about literary works and themes did have real political consequences. Zhongxun was accused of supporting a work agitating for the posthumous rehabilitation of Gao Gang. This took place at a time when Mao and those closest to him saw conspiracies and attempts to remove him from power everywhere. The main impact for Zhongxun was that he was dismissed from office almost immediately. Kang demanded he be expelled from the Party, something akin to a death sentence, but Mao himself overruled this in a rare act of clemency. Zhongxun simply became a house husband, looking after his children, with no employment and no future in the Party.

The worst, however, was yet to come. With the start of the Cultural Revolution in 1966, Zhongxun's case was once more examined, but this time the accusations against him were expanded. He was accused of being a key leader in the 'north-east anti-Party clique'. The purge of the clique itself was to end in more than 60,000 suffering and more than 1,000 dying. Xi's father was effectively expelled from Beijing in early 1966, in order to undertake 'thought reform' through hard labour. Once again he was lucky, even though it didn't look that way at the time. Outside the hothouse of Beijing, he ceased to be of any interest to Kang, who seemed to have forgotten him – he was busy at the time promoting a huge number of other campaigns against bigger fish, the most important of whom were President Liu Shaoqi and his close associate Deng Xiaoping. This meant that Xi's father was largely spared the violent 'struggle meetings' at which crowds vehemently denounced those selected as class enemies and mass criticisms were unleashed on figures like Peng Dehuai, who was dragged back to Beijing, kept in a male lavatory and made the target of more than 100 large-scale public denunciation sessions, several of which resulted in him being wounded.

XI'S SENT-DOWN YOUTH

Unlike Hu Jintao, or most other elite leaders in China, Xi Jinping's life during the Cultural Revolution is widely known. This is probably because he was on the right side. His father's disgrace meant that Xi was unable to join the Red Guard groups established at the time, and therefore had no connection with their acts of violence. Nor did he become involved in any other radical movements. His greatest suffering was simply to be removed from his closest family when barely an adolescent, and sent in 1969 to the countryside.

He was not alone in this. One of the defining features of growing up during the Cultural Revolution was the experience of *xiaxiang*, being 'sent down' from cities to rural areas in order to experience first-hand life on the land. 'Between 1968 and 1980, some 17 million young urban Chinese were forcibly rusticated after completing secondary school,' French scholar of the phenomenon Michel Bonnin has explained:

This massive organized migration was undertaken as part of one of the most radical political movements ever to emerge in the People's Republic of China, because in principle these urban youths were to become peasants till the end of their days [...] This experience deeply marked an entire urban generation. It overturned the lives of the millions of young people

involved (more or less half their generation) and the lives of
their parents, brothers and sisters, and impacted urban society
as well as a broad swathe of rural society, which was obliged to
accommodate these burdensome guests.[5]

Bonnin's study looks in some detail at the ways in which this experience
created its own narratives and culture. It inculcated in a whole generation a sense of belonging to a very particular period, a generation
that saw disruption, family break-up and alienation by being sent away
to places where they were strangers. The closest experience to this in the
West was the evacuation of urban children to the countryside during
World War II in the United Kingdom. In many ways, the Cultural
Revolution was framed as a war – a war, as Jiang Qing, Mao's wife and
one of its chief protagonists, stated, that was waged in words rather
than actions, 'to touch people's souls'. The sent-down youths were
partly soldiers in this war, and partly its victims. This ambiguity for
those who experienced this period remains to this day.

Xi is not alone in his experience of being a sent-down youth in
the seven-strong Standing Committee of the Politburo that he sat at
the head of from 2012. Li Keqiang, Wang Qishan and Liu Yunshan
were all sent from urban areas to be rusticated and educated in this
way. Another member of the committee, Yu Zhengsheng, suffered a
more specific, more traumatic fate, his sister possibly dying, either
at her own hands or others', as a result of vicious retributive attacks
because his father had been Jiang Qing's lover before her marriage to
Mao. Xi, at least, while he suffered long separations from his mother
and father, was able to belong to a rural community and to try to
create a new life there.

For all its discomfort and bitterness, being a sent-down youth
has paid political dividends for Xi. Biographies produced about
him in the official Chinese press refer to this period as giving him
an intimate understanding of rural life in China, and enabling him
to understand the challenges of farmers, who still made up almost
half of China's population in 2010, according to the national census
undertaken that year. It has given him the status of someone akin to

a peasant emperor (a term sometimes used to describe Mao), and the era is presented as one in which it was Xi's good fortune rather than a disaster for him to learn first-hand what conditions were like in the vast Chinese countryside. All of this ignores testimony that shows just how harsh conditions were in this period. Country people were often unwelcoming to those who had few skills to contribute and were more often than not a burden on their food and other resources. There are plenty of examples of youths being beaten, bullied or sometimes even killed over this period. The majority experienced poverty and loneliness.[6]

Xi Jinping was sent to Shaanxi in 1969, another fortunate choice as it has been the key revolutionary base for the Party since 1935 when the Long March led it there, and was elevated subsequently to one of the most sacred spaces in modern China. It was also where Xi's father had been based for a number of years before 1949. Xi was based in a small village, Liangjiahe, from the late 1960s to the early 1970s, and worked a number of jobs – from barefoot doctor (a phenomenon of the time in which wholly unqualified people were able to undertake medical roles in backward areas), to manual labourer and a mechanic for agricultural vehicles. In 1972, around the time of China's rapprochement with the United States and an easing up of the intensity of the Cultural Revolution, after appealing to the then premier Zhou Enlai, he was able to visit his father, still in detention, the first time he had seen him since the start of the movement over five years before. Two years later, despite his father's ongoing problems, Xi was finally able to enter the CCP after more than ten attempts to join. Most accounts that have surfaced in the years since show him to have been a popular, down-to-earth person when he was a worker in rural China, and someone who maintained links with the villages where he had worked even in his later life. He was known as someone who liked reading, but who was also practical and able to do hard manual work. He was tall for his age, and regarded as without Beijing airs and graces.

Xi's rustication ended as abruptly as it had started. He returned to Beijing to undertake studies as a 'Workers' Brigade Scholar', a special category for those whose education had effectively ended a decade before and who had been deprived of the chance to attend university or college. He has spoken of his time in rural China with fondness in the years since. It was a time when he was able to think things through on his own, learn from experience rather than through books and study, and cultivate a certain toughness and resilience. He himself has reportedly said that the rustication period of seven years taught him two things:

> One was to let me understand what is realistic, what is the meaning of seeking truth from facts, and what the people actually are [...] The other was to strengthen my self-confidence. As the saying goes, a sword grows sharp when rubbed against a stone, and men grow stronger through hardship.[7]

The accounts that exist from those who knew Xi during his time being sent down indicate that he was popular and fitted into the small place he was sent to. His elite background was neither a hindrance, nor a help. He was independent and stood on his own two feet. The abandonment and separation from both his parents and his siblings, however, must have been wrenching. It is interesting therefore that he has adopted such an admiring posture towards the man in many ways responsible for his fate and that of the many millions in a similar situation: Mao. Xi's attitude to Mao will be looked at in detail later, but it is worth simply noting here that on only a personal level Xi has every reason to resent Mao and his period in power, and the suffering they visited on his father and himself. But he has never once articulated anything that could be remotely interpreted as reflecting resentment of Mao.

EARLY CAREER

Xi's return to Beijing was to coincide with changes that were to prove dramatic and epochal. In the mid-1970s, the capital had the air of somewhere witnessing the final act of a Wagnerian opera, a twilight of the gods with Chinese characteristics. At the centre of it all sat the aged, deeply ill and feeble Mao surrounded by contesting courtiers and cliques trying to manoeuvre themselves into place, awaiting his death. Intrigues occurred almost constantly, with Deng Xiaoping summoned back from countryside labour in 1974 only to be felled again in 1976, his great patron Zhou Enlai too ill with throat cancer to protect him, finally succumbing to the disease in January. This time has come to be characterized, at least in internal histories, as one in which the radical Gang of Four, led by Mao's wife, aimed to monopolize power, abusing and misleading the incapacitated dictator. It is almost certainly far more complex than that. Beijing politics in this era was chaotic and exhausted, the Maoist utopian programme discredited, and the country ripe for change. But nothing could happen until Mao himself died, in September 1976. Within a few weeks, the Gang of Four and their main networks were gone, swept away by arrest and detention.

For those who survived the previous decade, there was a feeling akin to the ending of a war. People were able to return to their homes, or at least what was left of them, and families could be reunited. Xi's own father was finally able to come back to the capital in 1978. His son by that time was near the end of his chemical-engineering course at the elite Qinghua University. But whatever courses he took were incomplete, such had been the decimation and destruction of education under Mao. The main benefit of attending university was to link him with Chen Xi, who assisted him in his study for a PhD when he was a rising official in the late 1990s, and who was subsequently to be a mentor and one of Xi's closest confidantes.

Qinghua University had been one of the hotbeds of radical student protest in the earlier part of the Cultural Revolution, less than a decade before. But by the time Xi attended the Beijing-based university, while it was still convulsed by criticisms of its president, Liu Bing, for being anti-Maoist, there was nothing approaching the violence that Xi's predecessor as national leader, Hu Jintao, may have seen when he was a student graduating there in 1966.[8] Xi was to enjoy a reversal of fortune for his family in the Qinghua years. Supported by one of the great elite leaders, Wang Li, in 1976, Xi Zhongxun was fully rehabilitated in 1978, and then almost immediately appointed second secretary to Guangdong Province in southern China in May of that year. This was a place that was about to figure as the frontline of one of the greatest reconfigurations of modern history. A state that had set its face against any form of market activity and foreign capital, and that had gone out of its way to bury entrepreneurialism, was dramatically to embrace all three. And Guangdong was to be the key location for this process, with Xi's father playing a prominent role.

REFORM OR PERISH

It is one of the great mysteries of twentieth-century politics that a septuagenarian who had been a faithful servant of the CCP since the age of 16, who had promulgated and implemented some of the most ruthless purges in the anti-rightist campaigns in the 1950s, and then been brutally felled himself in the 1960s and 1970s (not once, but twice), should have risen back to prominence and sanctioned changes that saw China make an almost 180-degree turn.

Deng Xiaoping has been described as the most famous pragmatist of modern times, someone who carried a skin-deep commitment to Communism alongside a profound desire to see his country succeed and become strong and powerful again. Part of his own journey of transformation can be located in the dark years from the end of the 1960s into the 1970s when he was as politically ostracized and isolated as it is possible to imagine. Like Xi Zhongxun, he was never expelled from the Party, but was removed from almost all effective positions of influence, confined to a tractor factory and working in menial jobs in Jiangxi. It was there, several years after the event, that he heard of the crippling of his own son Pufang during violent denunciation sessions in Beijing in 1967. Accompanying this was his daily experience of the grinding poverty and lack of development in rural areas, which he finally could see first-hand. Like the famous dissident Wei Jingsheng, ironically his great nemesis in the late 1970s, he was haunted by the question of how such poverty could still exist in a country that had been promoting socialism for more than two decades. Around 1973 and into 1974, before he was summoned back to Beijing, he evidently underwent a dark night of the soul, in which his lifelong faith in one form of Communism was changed into something different. This was nothing as crude as a repudiation of his former beliefs, but instead a desire to marry socialism to the mission to raise China and Chinese people's lives to a wealthier, better level.[9]

After Mao's death in 1976, his gradual rehabilitation saw him use his massive prestige to reacquire authority and to fill Party and ministerial slots with his own people, by which he meant people sympathetic to a less dogmatic creed than Maoism, with its commitment to class struggle and violence as a tool to enforce change in society. China, Deng felt, had had quite enough of this. Now it was a case of treading a different path, one that took economic growth as its key mission. It was a simple idea, but one that went against the grain of many others in the leadership who were still married to the Mao charisma despite all the suffering they had seen.

The changes Deng and the leadership around him (of which Xi Zhongxun was a key member) were to implement have been commented on exhaustively. This attention is appropriate. They were radically to change the face of their country, and the world, and played a large role in securing the status that China enjoys today. In many ways Deng saved the Party when it was most in peril of simply imploding in nasty factional battles, with different groups trying to enter the vacuum that Mao's death had left. Like all true political egomaniacs, Mao left no satisfactory successor, having destroyed all those who looked remotely like being capable of replacing him during his life. But Deng was the great survivor, and someone who had a military tactician's genius for picking his moment and his territory. There was no overnight commitment across the country to the suite of policies which would be described as 'reform and opening up' in the years afterwards. Instead, there were incremental changes, the most significant of which was to allow a small cluster of places on the Chinese mainland, from Shenzhen to Zhuhai, to exploit their geographical proximity to developed external markets like Macau, Hong Kong and Taiwan to establish manufacturing zones. These zones exploited the one thing that China had in abundance – cheap labour. Factories sprung up across these Special Economic Zones (SEZs) that the Deng leadership sanctioned, creating goods that were then exported for foreign capital. It was to prove a simple but immensely effective plan. Shenzhen was to transform from a small sleepy town largely dependent on fishing into a city with 40 to 45 per cent growth rates in the mid-1980s, a place where skyscrapers were thrown up with such abandon and speed that an eighth of them simply collapsed within the first year of being built.[10]

Deng's reforms were not universally accepted, and while it is less commented on today, there were plenty in the leadership who were either apprehensive about what he was doing or directly opposed to it. For them, the Maoist dream lived on. The most pernicious were purged along with the Gang of Four for their reputed crimes in the decade previously. But many served in the Party, complaining or opposing reform as a betrayal of Communism. To them, manufacturing for foreign capitalist systems and taking foreign money went against their most fundamental beliefs. Leftists were to remain powerful critics of the main Party line, and still, to this day, poke their heads above the parapets to wave the flag of Maoist fundamentalism. But it was because of people like Xi Zhongxun, promoted to first secretary of the Guangdong Party Committee in 1980, that the reforms were pushed through.

He may have made an even more direct contribution. Many impute to Xi Zhongxun the idea of the SEZs in the first place. The story, perhaps apocryphal (it does not appear in any of the official material put out by the Party about his career), is that while on an inspection tour of Guangdong he saw the suppressed entrepreneurial instincts of the people, and thought this should be harnessed. With the dismantling of communes in 1978, and the ideological invitation issued that year to 'seek truth from facts' and liberate thinking, Xi the elder may have wondered why certain carefully marked-off areas could not become incubators. If they failed, then there would be limited fallout. After all, these were only a handful of cities in a vast, continent-sized country. But if they succeeded, they would serve as real ripostes to critics, and as models for others to follow. Hu Yaobang, the newly installed general secretary working with Deng in Beijing, came to Guangdong in 1980 and was convinced of the idea. The rest is history.

This direct link with one of the most successful and popular policy changes the Party has achieved since coming to power is an immense political asset for Xi Jinping. He could not, in this sense, have a better paternal legacy to lay claim to. Untainted by any trace of extreme leftism (Zhongxun was already sidelined well before the Cultural Revolution in 1966), his father was on the side of the angels right at the start of reform. Other figures from the pre-1978 period all carry baggage with them. They are either contentious in the Party, or people with other political liabilities. Bo Yibo, another of the 'Eight Immortals' from the founding generation of leadership, did allow one of his sons, Xilai, to go into politics. But Yibo was always linked to the attacks on other figures, particularly Hu Yaobang, whose removal from Party leadership in 1987 he supported. For Zhongxun, there is no such air of contamination. His brief period in Guangdong was the best time to be there. And this gives his son a powerful authenticity when he speaks of 'reform and opening up'. His father was utterly central to it, at a time when it was risky to be so.

MILITARY CAREER

For Xi Jinping himself, the late 1970s and early 1980s were years spent in Beijing. Unlike Li Keqiang, then studying law at Peking University, he had no link with the 'Democracy Wall' protests over the winter of 1978–9 – a short-lived movement in which citizens in the city were able to post grievances and demands for political change on a public wall in the Xidan district in Beijing. He finished his degree and was, probably through his father's intercession, given a position working for a member of the Politburo and one of the key leaders of the CMC, the body consisting of both Party and army people that had control over the PLA. The ultimate vehicle of Party 'rule of the gun', the CMC was to be Deng's key political asset, and the body on which he served as chair right up to 1989, long after he relinquished other formal posts. It set the overall strategic direction for the country's massive military forces. In 1979, when Xi started working for Geng Biao, the PLA was undergoing a fundamental reappraisal. It had experienced combat in Vietnam in 1979, which had proved deeply unsuccessful. Sucked into the neighbouring country on its south-western border, the army had suffered huge losses. Its equipment and personnel were shown to be out of date and inefficient. As part of the whole modernization process, it had to turn itself from a peasant guerrilla force, as it had been established by Mao, into one capable of fighting in modern war conditions. That required technological, cultural and political change.

Geng Biao was from a traditional military background, a highly respected soldier already in his sixties when he got to know the young Xi, and someone who looked like the veteran of multiple military and political battles. Xi helped Geng prepare for his visit to the United States, where he was one of the leaders mandated to go outside China to look at models and ideas for various aspects of its technological and economic reform. Once back in China, however, Geng started to experience troubles over the issue of Hong Kong and what to do with the stationing of military personnel and troops there upon its reversion to Chinese sovereignty in 1997. Deng had curtly rejected the original proposal from British diplomats that the arrangements for Hong Kong's New Territories – the areas of Hong Kong on the mainland, which, unlike Hong Kong Island, had only been ceded to the British on leases rather than in perpetuity – might be extended beyond their 99 years. But within his rubric of 'one country, two systems' there were many details that still needed working out, one of which was the role of national defence and how Hong Kong and the PRC might work together coherently. Geng and Deng had unspecified differences on this, and it was for this reason that Geng reportedly told Xi in 1981 or 1982 that he should look for a more promising career elsewhere. Being too closely associated with him might quickly prove a liability. However intended, it was to prove good advice. Xi left Beijing in 1983, and his career in the military, in order to work in provincial China. He was not to return to central politics again for another 25 years. While it is tempting to interpret this as a very early sign of ambition and destiny, in fact it was probably more of a pragmatic move. Military careers offered less scope; society was becoming increasingly civilian, and the simple fact is that influence for anyone who was ambitious lay in many other areas than simply the military.

THE PROVINCIAL YEARS

The 1980s are now looked back on as a golden age of reform, an era in which China was at its most liberal and adventurous. Hu Yaobang, the general secretary presiding over most of this era, is one of the most highly regarded of modern Chinese central leaders, a man with an extraordinary career, in which he survived being put before a Japanese firing squad in the Sino-Japanese War, and was then sidelined in the Cultural Revolution. A British government official who met Hu during his visit to London in the 1980s referred to his energy and charisma, which came across despite language barriers.[11]

Hu undertook the promotion of radical reform in the agricultural sector, removing state control over much of the rural economy by implementing a system in which farmers were able to sell their surplus crops back to the state for a profit. Embracing controlled market economics in this way was to improve productivity almost overnight.[12] A country that had known tragic famines barely two decades before now experienced grain surpluses. The countryside had suffered badly in the Cultural Revolution, often becoming lawless and brutally violent. But in the 1980s it became a place of transformation and change, with Town and Village Enterprises (TVEs) spearheading entrepreneurialism, and small unofficial banks lending money to China's emerging class of private business people.

Xi Jinping entered this world by first working in Zhengding, a village in Hebei, the province around Beijing. In going to the lowest possible level of government in the country to be an official he might have been following his father's advice to seek broad and wide experience, and start from the bottom and work his way upwards. Village committees had no formal status even in the new 1982 constitution. They existed under townships, with little if any fiscal powers, as what was loosely termed 'semi-autonomous entities'. But they were significant enough to be granted a suite of direct election reforms from 1987. Villages were still where almost 85 per cent of the country's population lived at this time. And, most importantly, they had to implement some of the least popular central-government policies – collection of taxes and the one-child policy being perhaps the two most egregious. In many ways, local officials at this level stood on the frontline, and were the face of the state as experienced by the vast majority of people. They were often unpopular, regarded as brutal, corrupt and venal. In surveys even into the 2000s, they were shown to be the least liked kind of official, the ones who were most blamed for poor policies and misuse of power. A report by two journalists in the early 2000s from Anhui Province painted a picture of people who had godlike powers, and were unafraid to use high levels of violence against those who crossed their path. Being a grass-roots leader, therefore, was a harsh and unglamorous political training.[13]

Perhaps it was made even harder by two factors. The first was that, while in Beijing, Xi had married the daughter of a diplomat intimately involved with Hong Kong issues who was then posted to the United Kingdom to work at the embassy there, taking her with him and leaving Xi back in China. The semi-official explanation given now is that the marriage failed simply because the couple were unable to live in the same place. Xi also rejected the idea of either living abroad, or availing himself of an opportunity that was beginning to open up for his generation: studying outside China. The two divorced around 1983. Xi's ex-wife reportedly lived in the United Kingdom for a number of years and then moved to Hong Kong. Very ironically, therefore, China, a country with a reputation of being traditional in family matters, has, in the last seven decades, been led by five key figures, three of whom (Mao, Deng and Xi) have been divorcees. The

United States and United Kingdom, bastions of liberalism, have only been led over this period by a sum total of two – Anthony Eden and Ronald Reagan.

The second factor was more ominous. While testimony to this day shows that Xi was regarded as a hardworking, competent and popular village official who used his background from Shaanxi in the Cultural Revolution to good effect, his overall boss, the Party secretary of Hebei Province Gao Yang, evidently felt little affection for him. Gao regarded Xi as someone from an elite background who was imposed on the province through family connections, not personal ability. Gao reportedly suspected that Xi had enjoyed something akin to imperial nepotistic favour, and had little time either for Xi's leadership style or for him as a person. There might be some truth in this. In Beijing during this era, the central leaders were discussing succession issues. The generation of the 'Eight Immortals' – the people instrumental in bringing the Party to power over the 1930s and into the 1940s, and then running it, through thick and thin, from 1949 – were now largely in their seventies and eighties. Some were in poor health. But there was a real problem, and one that Deng saw clearly, in stuffing elite positions with the offspring of this generation. Blood lineage might have been the basis for claiming someone was a good revolutionary in the Cultural Revolution, with bad family background being one of the worst stigmas that a person could carry. But in this reforming China, the key priority was to have a new leadership of people promoted through ability and skill, not through background.

For this reason, an arrangement was informally reached whereby older leaders were able to denote one of their offspring as a potential successor, allowed to play a political role in the future. Bo Yibo famously settled on one of his sons, Xilai. Xi Zhongxun, who had two sons, proposed the elder. For the other Bo and Xi siblings, their futures were largely to involve business. This too has resulted in complications that will be discussed later, because the simple structural issue is that access and proximity to their powerful political relatives has been of clear, and often highly contentious, commercial use. As China has grown richer, this issue of making vast sums out of blood links has developed into an open sore, and one that Xi has had to address directly.

There were plenty of other reasons that Gao Yang might have resented Xi. He was barely 30, and had been parachuted into the position. And his ambition might have grated. For all its manifold benefits, an elite background has been a double-edged sword for most of the period the CCP has been in power. Elite families attacked each other during the Cultural Revolution, and links to people like Deng over this period, as seen in the case of his badly disabled son, were not good things to have. Later, even when things stabilized, being the son or daughter of a high-level leader was a blessing in some ways and a curse in others. In the 1990s it was particularly unpopular, with more and more people feeling that the Party was a self-serving business that looked after its own. This clannishness was only diluted a little by having outsiders like Hu Jintao, with no family links to the Party's current or former elites, as Party secretary. And despite the fact that Xi mentioned little or nothing about his father's prominence, and has remained largely tight-lipped about it to this day, this must be one of the reasons why he did not get the right number of votes when he stood for Central Committee membership in 1997. In many ways, in the early part of his career at least, Xi succeeded in spite of his elitist links. But the claim that these have given him unfair advantage has never quite dissipated.

THE FUJIAN YEARS

Fujian Province, a vast coastal area directly opposite the island of Taiwan, has historically been one of the great trading zones of China, with merchants from earlier dynasties setting out from its shores to trade as far as Indonesia and deep into the South and East China Seas. One of its main cities, Xiamen, was designated an SEZ in 1980. For a northerner like Xi, arriving in 1985 to township-level work in this province would have been as much a cultural wrench as being sent to work in Italy would be for a British person. Even the local dialect was utterly different to the standard Beijing one. Food was less meat-based, with more fish and vegetables. And the climate was warm, semi-tropical, the summers hot and humid and the winters mild.

To this day, Fujianese constitute a disproportionate number of overseas Chinese. The long coasts of the province offer a natural outlet and inlet to the wider world. It is a place that has a reputation for openness. And it was also, when Xi went there, embracing the reforms started a few years before with abandon, particularly because it was able to attract huge amounts of investment and trade from the developed economy of Taiwan facing it – though it was separated by 100 miles of water and was a million miles away in political terms. When in Fujian Xi had the good fortune to work with a veteran leader, Xiang Nan. As one commentator stated, if Deng was the great architect of 'reform and opening up' nationally, then Xiang Nan was the master of reform for Fujian, a person who was to perform the same service for his province as Xi's father had for Guangdong.[14]

Xi's three years in Xiamen left a deep personal impression. This was probably because they gave him the first real experience of what 'reform and opening up' meant in practice. Rural Hebei in the north was a long way from the action. But in Xiamen, Xi had come to the frontline of 1980s reform. Factories were established in the city region, capitalizing on the Taiwanese, Japanese and South Korean companies putting some of their manufacturing capacity there. It would be here that he would see some of the wealth creation that reform inspired – but also some of its problematic side effects.

Xiamen was to figure more than just professionally in Xi's life path. It was while based here that he romanced, and then married, in September 1987, his second wife, Peng Liyuan. Peng, who was to be one of the most famous singers of traditional songs in China, was, like Mao's wife Jiang Qing, a native of Shandong Province. But she had spent most of her adolescence and early career in Beijing, training at the national music academy. Reports of her first meeting with Xi indicate she was underwhelmed. But their marriage endured the long separations in the years afterwards, when Xi stayed in the provinces and she was in Beijing. Up until the late 2000s, Peng was far better known than her husband. The dynamics of their relationship and alliance will be dealt with in more detail in the following chapter.

NINGDE: BACK TO BASICS

Xiamen provided urban buzz. But CCP leaders are put through a number of assessments and career-progression processes conducted by the local and national Organization Department, the Party's human-resources arm. The key here is to extend the experiences of leaders and test them out in new situations with a view to seeing if they can be promoted. Xi left relatively developed Xiamen, therefore, and was sent to Ningde, a township in one of the poorest parts of the province. This meant returning to hardship again, even though it was geographically a larger area. But it was a form of promotion. Now he was the district Party secretary, presiding over a complex place at about the time the shine started to come off China's early post-Mao reformist zeal, with a host of new pressures and responsibilities. Inflation, student dissatisfaction with corruption, and elite conflict led to the sidelining of former Party leader Hu Yaobang in April 1987. But it also meant the end of the influence of many of his allies, among them Xi Zhongxun. Once more he was under a political cloud. Ironically, it was fellow Party elite leader and elder Bo Yibo who maximized his family gains from Hu's fall, energetically criticizing his right-leaning, overly liberal tendencies and taking part in some of the vehement denunciations of him.

If Xi Jinping was affected by this, it didn't show in his public utterances during this time. He has since, in fact, made grand claims for the things he learned while in Ningde. It was here that he 'learned to liberate his thinking, inculcate good cadres, deal with poverty and promote openness from top to bottom'.[15] And it was in Ningde that he gained first-hand experience of one of the problems of reform: the rising levels of official corruption. Fujian, after all, like many other areas of provincial China, had gone from being poor to experiencing new ways of making money and new levels of wealth. Nice houses were being built. Officials were suddenly in the position to exploit their work to make good money, taking backhanders and illegal inducements. Many of them considered this no more than a just reward for their suffering in the previous decades under Mao. One of the key sources for local-government corruption was requisition of land for sale to property developers to become commercial premises. This was to prove one of the most contentious and hated phenomena of the next quarter of a century, and still figures today, although to a lesser extent simply because so much land has already been sold that there is little left to make money from. Giving farmers poor compensation for their land and then smothering it with factories or high-rise residential accommodation was a rich source of revenue for cash-poor local governments. Ningde was no more immune than the rest of Fujian, with Xi complaining in November 1988, during a clampdown on official malfeasance in this area, that thousands of government workers were taking money from land sales that they had no right to. It was here that, for the first time, he began to address the theme of how Party and government officials should not go into politics in order to enrich themselves.

It got no better on his move to the city of Fuzhou to be Party secretary there in May 1990. Fuzhou was the largest urban centre in Fujian, and had become a gleaming, modern-looking place on the money that had been invested in it over only a few years, with a new airport and new roads and infrastructure. But 1990 was not an easy time for reform. A year before, in June 1989, the Tiananmen Square uprising had convulsed the capital, spreading across most of the rest of urban China (its impact on the countryside was negligible). Even in Xiamen there had been demonstrations. The issues of corruption and the consequent discontent that had figured two years before, when Hu Yaobang had been sidelined, had not disappeared. Inflation exacerbated the problem. Initial lack of consensus in the leadership led to indecisiveness, so that by late May the students were perma- nently camped out in the central city area in Beijing, even managing to disrupt a visit by Mikhail Gorbachev, the leader of the USSR. Deng and the elderly leaders proved that they still carried the most influence by authorizing a military intervention, which led to perhaps more than 1,000 casualties (precise figures have never been issued by the authorities).

The impact for Xi's father was clear. He reportedly took a position of opposing military intervention, and maintained his loyalty to Hu, who had died in April from a heart attack. Too elderly and important a figure to purge, he was allowed to go to Shenzhen, far away in the south, where he was to live for the next decade until his death. For his son, the 1989 events figured not so much as a problem of social and political stability but for the questions they posed about how any local government could maintain the momentum for economic development and opening up when there was so much uncertainty in Beijing. Deng had ominously warned, when thanking crack troops who took the lead in quelling the revolt in mid-June, that part of the blame for what had happened lay in the complicated international situation outside China's borders.[16] Within a few months, the Berlin Wall fell, and a host of Communist-backed regimes across Eastern Europe collapsed. Communism itself seemed under permanent attack, its validity as a system on which a government could base itself highly questionable.

Fears that China might steer itself away from the whole reform strategy were strong throughout late 1989 and into 1990. Foreign investors withdrew. China became more ostracized, with a series of arms embargoes placed on it by the United States and the EU in particular. The CCP settled on a new leadership, headed by Jiang Zemin, formerly the Party boss in Shanghai, who was regarded (erroneously, as it turned out) as a lightweight and Deng's puppet. Leftists in the Party such as the redoubtable Deng Liqun returned with a vengeance, implying that June 1989 had been inevitable the moment the country strayed from Maoist orthodoxy. Growth fell to its lowest level in a decade.

In fact, it was early in 1992, during a tour of the SEZs, including Xiamen, that the ageing Deng recommitted China to the path of reform. His celebrated 'Southern Tour' would have been witnessed first-hand by Xi, one of the local officials Deng was seeking to empower and support as he proceeded around the zones declaring that China had to continue to reform and open up, and deal with problems like

June 1989 as they arose. It meant that places like Fuzhou were given a second lease of life. And that meant that Xi's career could progress. He was finally elevated to provincial-level leadership as a deputy governor in 1996.

Being a provincial-level official allowed Xi to stand for the Central Committee of the Party at national level during the 1997 National Congress. Controversy over this continues, because it saw Xi humiliatingly come 151st in the list of candidates for alternate membership of this all-important body, which at that time only numbered 150. It was a place where he could experience real power if he succeeded in joining. In order to sort this mess out, the simple solution of extending the number to 151 was deployed, violating the neat pattern and raising the suspicion that this had been mandated by Jiang Zemin, the Party leader, precisely so Xi could join. In 2000, Xi was elevated once more from deputy governor to full governor of the province. But only two years later he was moved to Zhejiang, a coastal province to the north, this time to be Party secretary. And as is widely known in China, it is in this position, rather than governorship, where the real power lies. In effect, Xi had been given his own province to run.

ZHEJIANG: THE FAT YEARS

Unlike Fujian, Zhejiang might not have been a location for one of the earliest designated SEZs, but it certainly compensated for this by inventive entrepreneurialism that became world-renowned through what is called the Wenzhou model. Wenzhou, one of the least developed districts in the area, had a population that had long learned to rely as little as possible on officials and government, and to get up and make its own way in the world. Poorly served for infrastructure into the 1990s, and with limited educational and financial assets, it was the amazing ability of Wenzhounese to travel through China and then into the wider world and set up networks which supported their largely family-run export businesses that most attracted attention.[17] Wenzhou entrepreneurs figured in manufacturing, textiles and ceramics. Some went to Beijing, where they set up businesses, working with their contacts back home and selling goods nationally; some went to Europe, proving so successful that they were blamed for effectively shutting down much of the native Italian textile business because of their competition. The ancient city of Prato in the north of Italy became inundated with Chinese people, many hailing from the Wenzhou area. Others went to New York or Sydney, and in later years Africa and Central Asia.

Zhejiang as a province had traditionally been purely agricultural. But its proximity to Shanghai meant that when that city gained SEZ status in 1990, this was de facto extended to Zhejiang. By the late 1990s, even the fact that the province's Party secretary, Zhang Dejiang, had studied economics in North Korea, and written in a journal article that he regarded the non-state sector as problematic and politically disloyal, did not prevent more than 70 per cent of its GDP growth coming from private companies.[18] Exploiting its location between the coast and the vast central and western areas of inland China, Zhejiang indirectly gained two big fillips just before Xi arrived to take up the post. The first was China's entry into the World Trade Organization (WTO) in 2001, which saw a new energy committed to internationalization and reform in the economy. The second was the lifting of prohibitions against business people being members of the Party. By 2002, Jiang Zemin had stated that non-state-sector business people were still one of the forces making up the vanguard of progressive development in society, and as such were allies of the Party and eligible to join it. This gave them a new legitimacy, and in a place like Zhejiang, where they already had a huge informal influence and importance, this was immensely significant.[19]

Xi served as Party head in Zhejiang at the zenith of the time when provincial careers were all about delivery of good levels of growth. All other considerations, from environmental to social, were secondary to this. And over these years growth came flowing like water from an open tap. One of Xi's first priorities was to support local enterprise – companies such as the internet start-up Alibaba,

created by Jack Ma (Ma Yun), a native of the province who had
briefly been an English teacher before going into business. Xi was
also hugely supportive of Geely, another major emerging employer
similarly owned by a private-sector businessman, which made cars
for the domestic market. Within a decade, both of these companies
were to make a mark outside China, among the first to do so, with
Alibaba making its founder Asia's richest man by late 2014. For all
its chaotic dynamism, however, the Zhejiang that Xi came to suffered
from underperforming exports and low inward-investment levels. He
was to address this, attracting McDonald's, Motorola and Citibank
to set up branches there. In his four years in Zhejiang, exports rose
an extraordinary 33 per cent year on year, ranking fourth nationally.
He also encouraged almost 2,000 enterprises to invest outwards into
116 countries.[20] In order to raise Zhejiang's profile internationally,
during interviews he held with American author Robert Lawrence
Kuhn for a book on Chinese leadership Kuhn was writing in 2005,
Xi sought the author's support to set up a Zhejiang week in the
United States.[21]

While his son was serving in Zhejiang, Xi's father died. Still based
in Shenzhen, Xi Zhongxun had experienced a minor rehabilitation
during the 1999 celebrations of the 50th anniversary of the foundation of the PRC, when he had been invited to attend the National
Day event in Beijing on 1 October. Xi Jinping has been described
as a loyal son and someone who wants to live up to his father's
expectations. But they had a relationship that was often interrupted
by forces from outside, and this must have caused complications.
For Xi, there are problems with referring explicitly to his father
simply because of the lingering accusations of nepotism. There are
also issues about just how close the two were, as they were effectively
separated for so many years, from the early 1960s right up to 1978.
Did Xi ever resent this and feel any sense of abandonment? Or is he
trying to fulfil some inner mission of retribution over the way his
father was treated? Around the fall of Bo Xilai, rumours circulated
that there had been some deep-seated antagonism between the two,
that their families had clashed in the Cultural Revolution, and then

again during the fall of Hu Yaobang, when Xi Zhongxun clearly took the side of Hu, and Bo Yibo, Xilai's father, actively worked against him. This sits oddly with Xi's extremely positive words during Bo's pomp when the former visited Chongqing in 2010 and lauded to the sky the things Bo was doing there. We can only speculate on the nature of the relationship between Xi and his father. It is almost impossible that Xi will ever enlighten us on the true nature of such a personal matter.

LEADERSHIP SPECULATION: SHANGHAI AND THE TWO LIS

Around 2005, in the build-up to the next National Congress two years later, attention started to focus on who might replace Hu Jintao when his term as general secretary came to an end in 2012. Hu's own succession had been plagued by rumours that he had not been allowed the scope and freedom to exercise power fully because of the constant interference of the 'retired' ex-president Jiang Zemin. Jiang maintained a formal role in the CMC, always the main trump card of Chinese politics, right up to 2004–5. There was speculation that he had surrounded Hu in his first Politburo with figures who owed allegiance to him and in some ways belonged to him. The most obvious of these was Zeng Qinghong, the Svengali of Chinese politics at that time, a man legendary for his Machiavellian modus operandi and serpentine skills, who had secured not only a Politburo Standing Committee seat but also a role as vice president.

The 'clash' between Hu and Jiang was based on speculation and rumours rather than hard evidence. But succession was seen as important, simply because whoever emerged in 2007 was almost certain to be elevated five years later. The main issue was that person's rank in the pecking order when it was announced. In the years just before 2007, three names appeared regularly in speculation: Li Keqiang, Li Yuanchao and Xi Jinping. And the two Lis were, for a long time, preferred over Xi.

This was for a number of reasons. The first was simply that Li Keqiang was viewed as close to Hu Jintao, and therefore able to enjoy the support of an incumbent in his bid to be Party boss. He was a highly regarded provincial administrator like Xi, someone who had managed provinces as diverse as Liaoning in the north-east and Henan in central China. Both had thrown up huge challenges: Liaoning had had a nasty fire disaster in a nightclub that had been mishandled by local officials, for which Li took ultimate blame as the most senior provincial leader. But the problem in Henan was worse, with long-term mismanagement of a scandal in which blood donated by locals for money had become contaminated with HIV and led to a precipitous rise in AIDS levels across some areas of the province. Li came to the province after this affair had blown up, but he was unable to resolve its aftermath well. For this reason, he was viewed either as someone who had bad luck, or, even worse, as a poor crisis manager.

Li Yuanchao had a less complex background. His main adminis-trative job before 2007 was to lead the wealthy province of Jiangsu, neighbouring Zhejiang to the north. Here he had piloted a number of reforms concerning elections at township level, which won plaudits from liberals. He was seen as someone who was more open-minded and international in his outlook than his peers, partly because he had briefly attended courses at the John F. Kennedy School of Government at Harvard in the 1990s.

Neither Li followed the pattern of the largely technocratic super-elite leadership dominant at this time. Around Hu sat people who overwhelmingly had degrees in engineering. Li Keqiang, however, had studied law, and Li Yuanchao history. What they did share with Xi, albeit to a lesser extent, was that they were both from Party-aristocracy backgrounds, with Yuanchao's father being a former senior leader in Shanghai and Keqiang's father-in-law having been important in the China Youth League, an organization Keqiang joined and in which he was influential in the 1980s. Indeed, it was in the Youth League in the 1980s that he was to meet his supposed patron, Hu Jintao, who then had a leadership position there.

As 2007 drew closer, clues were gathered from the appearances and prominence of the candidates. The Xi–Li–Li troika remained constant, but other names, from Wang Yang to Bo Xilai, also regularly appeared. Bo Xilai in particular seemed to be an increasingly high-profile figure, first in the provinces in the north-east and then as a trade minister, in which role he could be seen sticking up for China in trade wars being waged across the world.

One of the strange aspects of Xi's career is just how often, at critical junctures, the ill fortune of others, usually with little or nothing to do with his intervention, has served his own purposes. In 2006 rumours started to circulate that the Party secretary of Shanghai, Chen Liangyu, was in trouble. Some recounted how he had had shouting matches in a couple of Politburo meetings with the then premier Wen Jiabao, mostly over the powers that allowed a provincial-level entity like Shanghai to run its own affairs. What was more widely known was that the city had been using some innovative measures to address a problem across the rest of China – pension-provision shortfalls. The one-child policy, along with rising living standards, had created an immense retirement-age funding problem, with large amounts from government budgets being spent on looking after the elderly. Many of these people had been – through government service, work in large SOEs or army careers – wholly dependent on their state pensions, with an expectation that they would always be looked after. But with reformulation of the ways in which local governments could raise funds through direct and indirect taxation, and of what they needed to give to the centre (which increased from the early 2000s), as well as increased responsibilities for social welfare and other forms of public spending, local governments were starting to find servicing large pension commitments increasingly difficult.[22]

Innovation at the provincial level has always been a tricky issue in a system as sporadically, and often capriciously, centralized as China's. This will be a subject that recurs later in this book. Many of the reform-era policy changes originated with local governments – something that is best exemplified by the 'Household Responsibility System', which was illegally used in Fengyang, Anhui Province, after the death of Mao, but only sanctioned nationally several years later. The same could be said of village elections, which were tried out in the remote areas of Guangxi and Sichuan before they finally received wider permission, and were then extended to the whole of the rest of the country more than a decade later. Innovation from the bottom up has become something of a tried and tested means in China – but for all the examples of new methods that were tried out, judged successful and then embraced by upper levels of government, there are many more that proved unsuccessful and often resulted in castigation or the sidelining of official careers. The Chinese system has proved to be one in which risks can be taken, but the punishment for those ending in failure is prohibitively high.

An attempt to set up a national pension fund had already been made by Zhu Rongji during his time as premier, but the plan was regarded as too complicated. This meant, a decade later, that local governments still had no systematic way of making sure they had enough funds to deal with the claims made on them by the retired.[23] Shanghai under Chen Liangyu had attempted to establish a number of more commercial investment vehicles, the profits of which would be used to fund pensions. The result, according to central-government claims, was extensive illicit use of funds for personal purposes and full-blown corruption. The first warning that the Beijing leadership was about to do something was when a local businessman associated with the scheme and its investments in Shanghai property was taken in for questioning. By late 2006, rumours of Chen's political demise were so prevalent that it seemed he had already been removed. His formal detention for investigation in early 2007 was therefore not a surprise. What people were more interested in was who would be appointed to replace him, in view of how Shanghai had been seen in recent years as a major launch pad for political careers (when not serving, as in Chen's case, as a graveyard for them as well).

Only a few months from the National Congress later in the year, the announcement that Xi, still not even a member of the full Politburo, was to be the replacement was taken as a sign that he had finally poked his nose just slightly ahead of the two Lis. For this reason, as explained in the Introduction, Xi went out of his way to keep a low profile, giving no ammunition to any potential rivals and enemies and doing the most risk-free, soporific things (such as meeting delegations, including people like me!). His tactic worked. In October 2007, he was appointed directly to the Standing Committee. More crucial than this, he came out of the door of the Great Hall of the People a few steps ahead of Li Keqiang, and ranked one place above him. He had won the race. He was the heir apparent.

There is a small postscript here. With an eerie symmetry, around the same time that the leadership changeover was due to occur in 2012, one of the most aggressively ambitious and effective of the crop of contenders to new positions, Bo Xilai, was also removed from contention because of his wife's involvement in the murder of a British businessman and the resulting fallout. It has been little remarked on, but both Chen's and Bo's falls happened at the best possible moment for Xi, and made him their main beneficiary. There are two ways to interpret this. The first, with surprisingly high currency in China, would be to impute it to a profound, deliberate scheme among some Xi-supporting leaders. Others, with whom I agree, would simply put it down to extraordinary luck on Xi's part. And Fortuna, as Michael Ignatieff made clear in his excellent book on politics in Canada, is incalculably precious in politics, more so than in perhaps any other field of human endeavour.[24] The question, then, is how well someone uses it.

BEING A PROVINCIAL LEADER IN CHINA

A simple answer to the question 'Who runs modern China?' would be: the Central Committee of the CCP, and in particular its 200 or so full members. These are the people who might be said to be the elite. They run the Party; they constitute the Politburo, and they have direct strategic input into all major policy decisions through entities like the leading groups. There are plenty of caveats to this answer, of course. But in essence, the Central Committee is the single body with the greatest clout.[25]

Membership in recent years has comprised a mixture of provincial leaders, central-ministry leaders, army generals, key SOE presidents, academics and think-tank directors, and, very occasionally, a non-state representative. The only thing they seem to have in common is that they are all Party members. Of these different clusters, the largest is that consisting of provincial leaders. They have the biggest voting bloc.

Provincial leadership is immensely important for the modern Party. Jiang Zemin, Hu Jintao and Xi Jinping all came from careers directing the Party at the most senior level in provinces. Hu and Xi in particular spent the majority of their careers outside Beijing. This at least is a characteristic that these very different people share with each other. It is an understandable one too: China's provinces have populations that can easily outnumber most other nation states in the world – Henan and Sichuan contain more than 100 million people each. These 'states' have GDPs that make them equivalents of major European or Asian countries.[26] Shanghai's is the same size as the Finnish economy, and Guangdong's the same size as Indonesia's. Being the Party leader of a Chinese province therefore is a huge job. Final accountability to the central government for stability and prosperity of a province lies with this figure. Failure means instant recrimination. This is something the well-ensconced Wang Lequan experienced in 2010 in Xinjiang, when his inability to foresee and then deal with the aftermath of the riots in July 2009 led to his removal and sidelining into a lower-profile job in Beijing.

The life of a provincial leader is a tough one, not only because of the pressure to deliver targets, but also because they are almost always outsiders, parachuted into areas where they are not native, but surrounded by people who are locally born and bred. This is a deliberate structural attempt to try to erode the clannish nature of provincial politics in China. A local leader would be regarded as having too many vested interests and narrow parochial concerns to be trustworthy and to be able to keep out of the clutches of invasive, pushy networks. An outsider is harder to 'own'. One of the issues around Chen Liangyu was that he had spent most of his career in Shanghai. He had become too comfortable there, and too protective of a place he almost regarded as his own personal fiefdom. Overmighty provinces that start to think they can take on Beijing are a major headache. This tactic is one means to avoid that happening.

But it does cause problems. Provincial leadership is a lonely business. In his years in Fujian, and then Zhejiang, Xi had little if any family life. Peng Liyuan was enjoying her stellar career in Beijing. His daughter, Xi Mingze, born in 1993, was largely away from him (just as he had been away from his mother during much of his own early youth). Added to this was the fact that Xi made big efforts to ensure that family members did not try to move into areas where he had authority and use his official position to undertake business. In Shanghai, he reportedly ordered his younger brother to get out of the city while he was there. Many other provincial leaders, however, were unable to resist this temptation – one of the claims used in the final attack on Wang Lequan in Xinjiang was that he had let his Shandong cronies come to enrich themselves in his 'kingdom'.

Even without all these problems, provincial Party bosses have to live in a world where they are, if things go well, simply passing through. They have little interest in undertaking risky moves that might upset their career progression. They also have to be careful not to alienate or take on local networks, which might ignore, or simply sabotage, their policy-implementation orders. Their deputies, many of their governors and their whole bureaucratic support structure are locals, people who are more likely than not to stay in place once they have moved on, and therefore have even less incentive to take part in changes that might make them unpopular, exposed or vulnerable.

The prize for succeeding in the baptism by fire that is provincial leadership in contemporary China is a high one because of all these challenges. Those who are seen as doing a good job are elevated. Many provincial Party bosses are already sitting on the Politburo. It is only a step away from the core of power, the Standing Committee. And of the Standing Committee that was appointed in 2012, six of the seven forged their careers in provincial leadership, with five (Xi, Li Keqiang, Yu Zhengsheng, Zhang Gaoli and Zhang Dejiang) having spent the vast majority of their lives outside Beijing. Xi was therefore right when he said that one should not go into politics in order to make money in China. For access to real power, rather than financial or commercial forms of it, the hard road of isolated – and isolating – provincial politics has in recent years been the most reliable way to Beijing. It is little wonder therefore that so few are keen to travel along it, and that so many who do experience calamity and hardship along the way.

HEIR APPARENT: THE TIGHTROPE ACT

If there is one position more difficult to be in than that of a provincial leader, it's that of the heir apparent. The record of those poised to take the top job in the PRC has been a lamentable one. Few professions have a higher failure rate. Of Mao Zedong's long string of potential successors, one was left to die of untreated cancer on a cell floor after being felled (Liu Shaoqi), one died mysteriously in a plane crash while fleeing the country after an alleged coup (Lin Biao), and only the final one, Hua Guofeng, survived, only to be slowly outmanoeuvred and sidelined by Deng. Deng did no better, even though his choice of successors were treated a little more gently. Hu Yaobang has already been spoken of. Zhao Ziyang's perceived failure to respond correctly to the 1989 upheaval brought him 16 years under house arrest. Jiang Zemin was an unlikely third choice, and only worked because other possibilities were too divisive and he was the least objectionable to the widest group of Party leaders. Hu Jintao's 'succession' under Jiang was imputed to his being an official in his early career who was favoured by Deng, and imperially mandated as a replacement. This explanation seems elegantly simple. The fact that even when the succession happened in 2002 it was scrappy and left Jiang lingering for so long slightly undermines it. Power in China, like anywhere, is a hard drug to kick the habit of.

The precedent of 2002, however, was regarded as putting in place what should happen in 2012. In sinological terminology, it 'institutionalized' the process, and was one of the most important ways of showing that the Party was no longer the plaything of an all-powerful leader, but something with rules, regulations and internal processes that had to be observed. Even so, following the changes ushered in in 2007, there was a great deal that remained unclear right up to the moment Xi stepped out in mid-November 2012. There was nothing preordained or automatic about his final success.

One of the first tasks Xi was given was to chair the coordinating committee for the Beijing Olympics, to take place a year later, in August 2008. This was a job fraught with challenges. The government had spent a reported US$ 42 billion on preparing for the event. China's capital had been remodelled, with a large number of disgruntled residents made to move from homes where some had lived all their lives to newly constructed suburban buildings on the outskirts of the city. Battles over compensation increased. And already there were problems with where some of this vast tranche of money had gone, with rumours circulating that it had disappeared into the pockets of greedy officials and their cronies. Moreover, there was the even more serious issue of deteriorating air quality, something the city had suffered from for many years and that now threatened to hinder the performance of Olympic athletes.

Things were made even worse by a series of events throughout 2008 in the lead-up to the games. At the end of April, what initially appeared to be skirmishes in Lhasa, the provincial capital of the Tibet Autonomous Region, developed into full-blown riots resembling those that had rocked the area in 1987 and 1989. Tibet has always been a complex place for the central Chinese state to govern, ever since its full assimilation into the PRC in 1959. But these riots, under the glare of international attention, were particularly problematic because they disrupted the developmental logic of the ruling elite from Beijing, who were convinced that, with trickle-down economic growth, Tibet and its inhabitants would lay aside some of their cultural and political reservations about the current situation and see that sticking with Beijing was their best bet for a prosperous, powerful future. Enough people disagreed with this to leave a number of buildings in the city centre in smouldering ruins. Security personnel flooded the area. The few foreign journalists around were tracked down and evicted, with a news blackout imposed. Barely four months before the Olympic Games were due to open, this was the least welcome news for Hu Jintao and his government.

Perversely, a huge tragedy some weeks later created a great deal of sympathy for the Chinese government internationally, when more than 80,000 people were killed during an earthquake in south-west China in the Wenchuan area of Sichuan Province. This time premier Wen Jiabao initially led the charge, quickly going to the affected area and declaring that the central government would spare no expense or effort. Thousands of volunteers, among them reportedly Xi Jinping's wife Peng Liyuan and his very young daughter, Mingze, either helped raise funds for the relief effort or directly participated in disaster relief. This was, in many ways, one of the best volunteering efforts in a society for which the concept, until recently, had been a completely alien one. International partners were also welcomed, from Japanese to British. The only issue was the later handling of dissatisfied residents and activists who pointed out that many of the collapsed buildings were schools and public places, while government buildings had evidently been constructed to higher standards and remained standing despite the terrible tremors. Activists like Tan Zuoren raised questions about this disparity, for which he was rewarded by being put on trial in 2009 for subversion. The artist Ai Weiwei, attending his trial in Chengdu in order to speak in his defence, was beaten by local security agents.

All of this was accompanied by two other issues, both related to the outside world. One was international criticism of the actions of state-owned companies in Africa, where China was accused of being amoral in its behaviour, supportive of regimes such as that of Sudan, which were being criticized for their human-rights records, and generally driven by greed and lack of principle. The phrase 'genocidal Olympics' was coined, and director Steven Spielberg withdrew from a role as artistic advisor for the opening ceremony. The second issue, connected to this international criticism and the domestic concerns outlined above, was the huge controversy dogging the Olympic-torch procession as it made its way across the world en route to Beijing. Somewhat naively, the route planners had felt that this offered the opportunity for a global celebration of China and its new prominence. What transpired was more daily proof of just how ambivalent people were on this issue, particularly in the United States and Europe. The worst manifestation of this was in Paris, where a disabled Chinese sportswoman was jostled and manhandled by protestors, gaining terrible publicity back in China. French companies were targeted and right-wing nationalistic bloggers like Wang Xiaodong, one of the authors of the rabble-rousing *Zhongguo bu gaoxing* [China is not happy], published a year later, had a field day. For them, this was a perfect illustration of the fact that there were many in the outside world who were hostile to the very idea of an Asian nation like China being ascendant again. Visceral anger at perceived slights bubbled over so that the torch procession, far from being a masterclass in soft power, became a PR catastrophe for almost everyone involved.[27]

In hindsight, the whole Beijing Olympics saga was a vast learning process for everyone. The outside world discovered even deeper reservations about this newly resurgent global power. China saw unequivocal proof of just how much more work it needed to do to build a better and more understanding coalition of support beyond its borders. Bussing in loyal crowds of mostly Chinese students studying overseas to cheer themselves hoarse at events connected to the Chinese government only went so far in this soft-power war. Each side clearly had big issues with the other. Not that we can conclude from this that Western constituencies were unified in what they felt and thought. Apologists in the United Kingdom came out with sonorous screeds of praise for everything China had ever done, while their opponents spat blood with rage at how a place that was an evil dictatorship in their eyes was being granted legitimacy by the outside world. There were no easy answers to such disagreements. But this was probably a good thing. The 2008 Olympics, whatever else they did, bid farewell to black-and-white notions of China, about which easy judgements could be made. It was the end of a period of innocence, in which China was easy to praise or condemn depending on what your political stance was towards it.

For Xi, though, all of this was academic. His one priority was to ensure that the event was perceived among his peers as a success. If it went badly, then his pole position was in jeopardy. Perversely, he was in a race not dissimilar to the ones the athletes took part in, only for him the stakes were far, far higher. One terrorist attack, particularly during the opening or closing ceremony, one Tibetan demonstration while any significant leaders were around (or any incident that involved them in any way) or, perhaps worst of all, Chinese sporting failure in the games themselves could have destroyed his ambitions. As it was, the three weeks of the tournament were a success. China came top of the medal tables for the first time ever. There were no serious security incidents. Squadrons of pesky foreign journalists there to cover the games went away without any killer stories. Even the Beijing weather behaved. The person who most gained in August 2008 was not on the field or in the pool, but sitting in the VVIP-registered seating as a member of the Politburo.

STABILITY

Physically, the games left monumental, and largely unused, facilities scattered across the capital and other locations in China. But it did mark a profound change in the leadership's philosophy of governance. The uprising in Tibet, followed by the July 2009 disturbances in the massive north-west region of Xinjiang, spooked the leadership of Hu Jintao and Wen Jiabao. It made them jumpy, and even more resistant to relaxing their grip on the core levels of control. And it made them even more wary of the outside world and its agenda. Events like the 'colour revolutions' of the mid-2000s in Eastern European and Central Asian nations, which had once been satellite states of the USSR, prompted a renewed bout of soul-searching by thinkers and the leaders they advised in Beijing. The pernicious role of the outside world in these events, particularly a power as zealous as the United States, was fingered as a major source of unrest. The United States and its allies simply held to a view of the role of government and of the actions that government should undertake which was different to that of Beijing. This created a narrative of the United States' hidden purposes and agendas that many Chinese officials and policy makers signed up to. From Tibet to Xinjiang, Taiwan, Hong Kong and even other parts of China, this notion of enemies supported by disruptive outside forces who were working to undermine the Beijing regime took deeper hold.

From 2008, therefore, two new characteristics of rule started to appear in China. The first was a steep increase in funding for the security services, and an increased mandate for them. Under Politburo member Zhou Yongkang, they became increasingly well resourced. With direct access to the elite leadership, they were supported by a philosophy of 'stability maintenance' (*wei wen*) in which ringleaders and those seen as disruptive or troublemakers were removed, and made an example of. Classic cases of this include the removal and then prosecution of veteran dissident Liu Xiaobo, whose driving role in writing and then disseminating the Charter 08 documents asking for more political reform was regarded as seditious by the Hu leadership. In fact, little that Charter 08 contained violated Party thinking, or at least its rhetoric. But the very fact that the Party was not consulted or included in this political event meant it was almost duty-bound to respond fiercely. The crime of Liu, and of Charter 08, was to violate the unwritten rule that the CCP alone had the right to articulate the language of political debate in China. Others could not occupy this territory without threatening the Party. Despite Liu never once proposing violent opposition to the CCP, and saying that he sought constructive debate, he was deemed a threat to national security. In fact, it would have been more accurate to say that he was a threat to Party security, a crime that was in many ways deemed worse.

The second characteristic was a rising level of ideological opposition to foreign modes of governance, of civil society and of political reform. The commitment to reform itself was not questioned. China still needed to reform, as leaders from Hu downwards testified. But it had to do so on its own terms, not on a template supplied by the ill-meaning West. Parliamentary democracy, overmighty and interventionist law courts, or disruptive civil-society actors were all enemies to China's peaceful development and its rise to being a great, strong country. The Party alone was its strongest guarantee of being able to undertake this journey without suffering the same fate as the USSR or its other, lesser acolytes. Figures therefore like Wu Bangguo, number two in the Politburo next to Hu and chair of the NPC, went to great lengths to remind listeners that China did not desire any of these things, and wanted to find its own path.

Since coming to power in 2012, Xi Jinping has been accused of driving China towards a more nationalistic and assertively exceptionalist direction. But these memes were already well in place by the time he took up position, and the forces driving them were deepened by two other major external events – the Global Financial Crisis, and the 'Jasmine Revolutions' in the Middle East, beginning in Tunisia. Both events complicated the image of liberal, multiparty democratic systems among the Chinese elite, and among the general population. The ways in which the United States and the EU started to experience issues around their own governance played into the hands of more conservative Chinese thinking. It proved that simply copying these external models on the assumption that they would lead to the best economic and political outcomes was naive. In many ways, it also eroded the idea that the CCP could ever be complacent about the help it might get from the outside world. It could not rely on such major partners as the EU or the United States to refrain from causing problems for China, even in the economic realm. More liberal Chinese started to have a difficult time pointing at models such as the European and American ones and claiming that they were the best in terms of stability and efficiency: these countries were undergoing real crises, and there were profound questions about how they too needed to reform.

For the Chinese leadership, the Jasmine Revolutions, from Tunisia to Egypt and Libya, and finally Syria, simply underlined the messages that had come from the 'colour revolutions' of a few years earlier. They showed that the United States and its allies were forever interfering, foisting their ideology on partners who then suffered as a result. This distrustful mindset only increased among many influential Chinese. The more extreme among them became convinced there was a concerted campaign directed from Washington to destabilize and undermine China. For them, stressing the uniqueness of what China was trying to do, and relying as much as possible on its own abilities, were key. Xi has remained within this rubric. He has simply continued to articulate scepticism about using foreign ideas without adapting them to unique Chinese circumstances. On the precise nature of these unique attributes, however, there is rarely much detail. The mantra remains that China has to find its own way and do things on its own terms.

2009 was a year of anniversaries. The 60th of the founding of the PRC was one of the happier ones. However, as though to highlight just how complex the messages the CCP needs to promote in the most recent era have become, even something as benign as the 90th anniversary of the 4 May student uprising in 1919 was not straight-forward. The students of this period had been responding to the unfair treatment their country received at the Versailles Peace Conference held at the end of World War I, where, despite being neutral, they had seen the north-east of China carved up, with parts handed to the Japanese. This continued the humiliation of the colonial adventures in China from 1839 and the First Opium War (1839–42). Even Germany was granted concessions. The students had demanded science and democracy, one of the great rallying calls of modern Chinese politics, and something that remained a demand down the years, even to the time when the Communists came to power three decades later, promising they would deliver. 'It is impossible,' historian of this period Rana Mitter states,

> to understand how thoroughly [Chinese] society of over a billion people was changed in the course of a hundred short years without returning to examine the experience and possibilities of that short period of promise in the early twentieth century.[28]

In terms of science, perhaps the Party had kept to its word. With the Deng reformist period and its 'Four Modernizations', science had been carefully married to ideas of power and progress. Education and industry supported the production of a new generation of Chinese scientists, building up indigenous capacity in order for the country to claim back its historic role as a great innovator, which has been outlined in the epic series of books *Science and Civilisation in China*, begun and edited by the British sinologist Joseph Needham. But for democracy, things were far more complex, and the 4 May celebrations of 2009 needed to be marked in a context where political change with Chinese characteristics was the key demand. By far the most controversial of the 2009 anniversaries, however, was that marking the half-century since the 'annexation' or 'peaceful liberation' of Tibet (depending on your point of view). With the 2008 disturbances still weighing on the Beijing leaders' minds, this was a tough landmark to handle. Low-key 'celebrations' were held in Lhasa and other areas in the autonomous region, and a high-level meeting was convened in Beijing, with some of the Dalai Lama's representatives, to discuss what might be done in the region. Nevertheless, there was nervousness throughout 2009, culminating in major meetings in the capital, at which new guidelines on how to handle the management of Tibet were issued. The Party's main objectives remained stability, economic progress and ethnic unity.

SUCCESSION: STEPPING OUT OF THE SHADOWS

When 2012 came and the political succession was in sight, Xi's assets were simple. He stood as the highest-ranking official in the hierarchy who would not need to retire when the National Congress occurred. His propagandists had been assiduous in ensuring that his varied and deep networks in a number of areas were known. Around 2008, a journalist who worked for one of the state papers based in London passed me one of the biographies that had recently been issued about Xi in Hong Kong. He had a knowing look on his face, and said portentously that this man was worth watching. Sometime later another contact told me that a number of other individuals posing as journalists were suspected of working directly for the MSS. They were, in effect, spies. That meant they were probably far better informed than journalists.

Receiving messages in this way was interesting. But there were questions over why Xi was getting this support. He had taken final responsibility, quite late in the day, for the Beijing Olympics. But he had not been at the forefront of the response to the looming financial crisis lapping at China's door from the outside world during the meltdown that year. Nor had he been connected with tricky social issues, unlike his peer, Li Keqiang, whose portfolio as vice premier included welfare and macroeconomic development. He was most famous outside China for loud comments he made while on a visit to Mexico in 2010, in which he had complained about foreigners with full stomachs and nothing better to do than attack China. Even during the felling of Bo Xilai, he had been largely out of sight – almost literally so when he simply disappeared for almost a fortnight in September 2012, cancelling appointments to see figures as godlike as Hillary Clinton, then US Secretary of State (something that, according to a member of her team who spoke to me afterwards, caused particular rage among the Americans, who felt initially that the snub was deliberate). Why was Xi in such a powerful position when the National Congress arrived in November that year? What did he have that his competitors didn't?

A large part of the problem with trying to answer this question is simply that despite the many hundreds of millions of words written during and after the 2012 succession, there is one glaring, underlying fact: this was a process in which rules were being made up as it went along. The talk of precedent held a little water – but only up to a point. The simple truth is that there was no manual or neat set of regulations held in the central Party compound setting out the process and the ways in which a clear winner might be legitimized and then appointed. There were some processes that had been used before – the idea of time limits, for instance, for Party appointments to specific positions. There were abstract promises to consult with Party members at all levels, and to then canvass votes and ideas on who should be appointed after all of this was reflected on and distilled. But rather than clear internal rules setting out processes whereby quantifiable outcomes might be produced (like numbers of Party-member votes), the Party gave the impression throughout 2012 that it was more like an organization undergoing complex, largely invisible chemical reactions within itself. Somehow, through these opaque processes, a sort of answer was emerging, but it was never as crude as putting two, three or more names on a board, placing votes beside them and declaring the one with the most to be the winner. It was rather an attempt slowly to manipulate, move and develop a consensus, during which any dissension was rapidly swiped away, and a final outcome magically appeared, giving everyone involved the sense that they had taken part and contributed, even though they could not describe how they had done this, or see any overt evidence of the ways in which their ideas about who might succeed had made an impact. The leadership succession therefore was an extraordinary, almost organic process in which the Party was partly convincing its membership, and partly being convinced. It belonged more to the realm of magic than political science.

After all, this process had one overarching justification, and that drove everything else. This, ironically, came back to the all-important issue of stability. Just as the 'stability-maintenance' regulations were being enforced in society, sometimes with considerable violence, so too was the Party inflicting on itself strictures that ensured there were no schisms, internecine fights or divisions that threatened to get out of control. These became most worrying around the time that Bo Xilai fell, when there were real reasons to believe that elite division in particular could set one portion of the Party against the other. The Party is in many ways a coalition, trying to sit under one roof. There were any number of scenarios by which this outwardly harmonious show might have been scuppered. Bo did have popular public support, at least in the places he had served, delivering on populist programmes like affordable housing and better working conditions, and he projected the sense that he was accessible and listening to people. But the elite, even those contemplating sticking their necks out to support him, had second thoughts, weighing the risk of collective Party implosion at such a vulnerable time against parochial gain. Rumours that Zhou Yongkang alone showed dissatisfaction with Bo's treatment were the only sign that there might be internal dissent.[29] On the whole, the Party elite membership, through fear of stirring up instability, kept rank.

WHERE DOES XI'S POWER COME FROM?

If we revisit the list of sources of power in contemporary China given in Chapter 1, we can try to marry Xi to each of these and see the ways in which he could count on their support and harvest political and power capital from them. There were broadly two sources of power: the institutional, tangible and material (the Party, central ministries and their executive authority, and the PLA) and the abstract, intangible and ideological (control of narratives, new ideas, ways of speaking and emotional appeal).

China might have more than 1.3 billion people, but the real contenders for Party leadership narrowed down to the tiniest demographic. First they had to be Party members. That reduced 1.3 billion to 82 million. Then they had to be above a certain age (anyone under 50 was extremely unlikely to be considered suitable, through lack of experience in a system in which administrative training and track record are evidently important). They couldn't be military personnel. Nor was it likely they would be outside the Central Committee – 82 million comes down this way to 200. In fact, it was difficult to consider anyone outside the full Politburo – 200 becomes 24. And of these 24, in 2012 more than half were retiring, and in any case they had to be part of the Standing Committee. That brought it down to two – Xi Jinping and Li Keqiang. In this way, what looks like a hugely crowded field rapidly becomes a pretty empty one.

What did Xi have, therefore, that Li didn't? This is not just a simple question of patronage. Xi might be talked of as 'Jiang's man' and Li as 'Hu's'. Some came out with suggestions that as Deng got the chance to designate Hu a future successor, so Jiang could designate the one after that. This has an appealing simplicity and elegance, but seems too straightforward by half. Patronage there may be, but it is made up of a number of different ingredients and elements.

Looking at Chapter 1's list of power sources, tangible and intangible, symbolic and real, the interesting aspect of Xi is that he seems to marry many of these together. He did inherit through his father a dense support network within the Party elite, with links to those on the more liberal side around Hu Yaobang, and to the traditional heartland of the Party establishment – the Dengs, and even back to Mao. This at least meant he was a known quantity, and someone who gained access to people through established links with them. But there is also the issue of narrative. Plenty of others also had such links: Bo, for instance, or Yu Zhengsheng or Wang Qishan (through marriage). Many offspring of former leaders go into politics in China, after all. It is not rare. Why, of all of them, has Xi been the victor? Is it something to do with the fact that his father seems to have made few enemies, and to have garnered a lot of broad support, taking part in no nasty intra-Party cleansing campaigns and occupying jobs where he did positive, reformist things, rather than getting involved in some of the murkier business of Party rule? An elitist background is not a straightforward asset. It can be problematic. There were plenty of unpleasant things that former leaders had to do, and this could resurface and be used against their families when they were hoping to secure political futures. Xi's father ranks as relatively unproblematic. Even the claim that his son was only successful because of his father's support is a complicated thing to prove. If that were true, Xi might have played safe and just stayed in the military in the early 1980s, enjoying an illustrious career there. That he made the move to civil government shows at least some of his own instinctive political ambition. He knew real power in China in the end didn't lie with the military, and he did take a risk in going down to a local-government entity. Few others did this.

Having a narrative for himself was important not so much for the people, or even for the broad Party membership, but for the inner elite of leaders. With his father's story, he supplied this. It brought with it one massively important source of institutional support. The Party in 2007 put him in pole position to become leader, and supported him throughout the following five years, because it was by then in its collective interest for him to succeed smoothly. If there had been problems, then of course there was no reason why Xi couldn't have been sidelined or removed. Outsiders have to remember that this is a process in which there are no real cast-iron rules.

In addition to this, Xi also had ideological appeal. The most important characteristic here was simply to have no bold, grand new ideas, but to stick relentlessly to the primacy of the Party, the parameters of Dengist reform, and to the stress on respect to be given for the CCP's Maoist roots. The one issue that Xi did speak about in the years 2007 to 2012 was that the Party needed to serve the people, that the people were the prime responsibility and, in the words of his Xinhua profile in late 2012, that the people should be regarded as 'parents'.[30] This was compatible with Hu's talk of taking people as the key, but it also burnished Xi's populist credentials: although not original in itself, it at least seemed to be a theme he could express for himself in a different way and for which he could take ownership.

There was also the extensive political use of his provincial record, which Xi exploited to claim not to be a pampered product of central ministries – an insider contaminated by their elitism and bad habits – but someone who had real experience of China's rural areas through being sent there to work as a youth, someone who could present himself as an underdog, despite his elitist background, and who could demonstrate to other Party figures the ability to deliver efficient if unspectacular rule. Ticking off not only parts of his CV that garnered more popular appeal, but also elements that proved to hard-nosed Party operatives that he was someone who could be entrusted to work for what the Party most wanted and needed – to stay in power – was a double gift. These were not things Li could demonstrate so easily. He might have been from a humble background, but that meant his links into the Party's patronage networks were a little less developed than the 'peasant emperor' Xi, who could enjoy the best of both worlds. And finally, whereas Xi, as head of the Central Party School from 2007, had some excuse to wander into ideological areas, Li spoke narrowly, albeit impressively, on his core area – economics. He followed the agenda. He did not have an easy way of setting himself apart.

So if the question was asked directly and frankly (and there is no evidence that it ever was) to either contender, or anyone else bothering to put their name forward, 'On what basis do you think you should be appointed Party leader?' the answer had to be the candidate's ability to demonstrate both the capacity to do what was expected of the job, and something far more difficult: that they had the right, morally as much as administratively, to be in this position. This is no more than an admission of what an odd job CCP leadership is. What, finally, is the general secretary's core function? It is not to gain power on the back of a specific manifesto. That, in a consensus-based organization, is already in place and functioning. It is not to direct the government, but to give it broad political and ideological leadership. In that sense, it comes closer to a spiritual position like that of the Pope, or the Archbishop of Canterbury. Its role is to supply a vision, to exemplify particular moral qualities and, finally (most important of all), to display a profound and convincing belief in the Party, and the Party mission. This is what makes it more accurate to say that the position chooses the person, rather than that the person runs for the position. Active agitation for the top slot never seems to work in China. Passive acceptance seems to be the trick, something that privileges intuition by a contender over raw ambition. And this means that, for candidates, it is more about displaying real, deep-down commitment to the Party, showing it is part of their lifeblood, something they absolutely belong to and will serve faithfully, without ego or personal gain. At a time when the Party has become the custodian of the world's most dynamic economy, when it is in the key position to enjoy the material fruits of this success, this is a particularly hard posture to adopt.

Xi Jinping became general secretary in November 2012 because in the end he was able to convince the core elite of the entity placing him in this position that, from his background, his life story and his administrative record, he believed profoundly and completely in the mission of the Party, and in its moral right to rule. He may be the sole person in China who fully believes in this mission, but he is the one person who has to. He is general secretary not because he is defending an organization: he is there because he is defending a faith. And in his years since the 1980s he has shown almost consistently that he was a true believer.

MAGICIAN OR WARLORD?

Anyone trying to come up with an easy model to make sense of China's political system today is immediately struck by how much of a hybrid it is. It has elements of the country's imperial past, the lingering warlord mentality of the CCP's roots (and its use of violence) and now the technocratic discourse of a post-modern, developmental market state. No wonder Chinese politicians confuse observers. They seem to operate in three realms of leadership, and draw on resources from all of them. How do individuals who find themselves in the middle of this behemoth make sense of their role? Max Weber, the great sociologist, stated in his lectures on the vocation of politics in the 1920s that in the past there were two dominant kinds of leader: the magicians and prophets on the one hand, and the warlords and gang leaders on the other.[31] But in the modern world, Weber said, these figures tended to appear as leaders of political parties, who had a vocation compelling them to do what they were doing. In this scheme, where does a leader like Xi Jinping sit? Is he a sorcerer and prophet, or a warlord and gang leader? Mao Zedong, someone Xi appealed to much more than expected after coming to power in 2012, could be described as both. Deng, Jiang and Hu, however, were more mundane in their articulations of power. What, then, is the nature of Xi's vocation, his inner calling?

Conviction is important in politics everywhere – the perennial question is what, in their hearts, politicians really believe in. Too much flexibility and they are vulnerable to the accusation of being flip-floppers, unprincipled or vacuous. But those who stick firmly to one set of principles can also be run down with claims of dogmatism. Pol Pot in Cambodia was consistent, and evidently had profoundly held and coherent beliefs. But no one would sensibly claim that this was a good thing in view of the terrible consequences it had. Deng was regarded as more pragmatic, and for his critics someone who turned his back on much of what he claimed to have believed in before coming to ultimate power in China. Yet his policies have so far been regarded as immensely successful.

It is common for observers of Chinese politics to say that for leaders in this system it is not about belief, that Communism as a creed is dead, that the country is run on a massive exercise of doublethink in which on the one hand capitalism in its most raw form rules the day, while on the other the Party is stuck with having (rhetorically, at least) to dress up its statements to give the impression that it does indeed believe in Marxism–Leninism. Chinese leaders are accused of caring only about power, of being hypocritical and of saying one thing while in their hearts believing another – or nothing at all. This is a remarkably patronizing way of viewing them. Anywhere else, especially in democracies, we would hunt for some real beliefs leaders might have. But Chinese leaders are not accorded this courtesy. They are straightforward. They believe nothing, cling to power no matter what and have no vision for what to do with that power beyond making their country richer. This at least seems the dominant assumption about them.

It is rarer to argue that in fact they do have convictions, and that they do believe in the things they say. They believe to such an extent that they do ruthless things in order to defend their beliefs. In this context, it is the Party as an institution that is the sorcerer, prophet, warlord or gang leader. Just as a Western company is, the CCP is like a person. It behaves like one, defends itself like one and has people who articulate its collective beliefs and passions. In this context, neither Deng, Jiang, Hu nor Xi can really be seen as being like emperors in an imperial system. The Party is the emperor, seeking a kind of immortality by using these transient figures. They are its spokespeople, its deliverers of infallible messages.

The CCP leadership provokes much cynicism. It is regarded as self-serving and hollow, and the language of its leaders as insincere and manipulative. But as historian Yuval Noah Harari has pointed out, when talking of political elites everywhere:

It is quite common to argue that the elite may do [what they do] out of cynical greed. Yet a cynic who believes in nothing is unlikely to be greedy. It does not take much to provide the objective biological needs of *Homo sapiens* […] That is why cynics don't build empires and why an imagined order can be maintained only if large segments of the population – and in particular large segments of the elite and security forces – truly believe in it.[32]

Having seen how Xi came to power, and what he has done while in power, what sort of model, therefore, can we use to understand him, to see into his political soul? The best, in fact the only, way to answer this question is to look at what Xi himself has said.

XI AND PARTY: FRIENDS OR ENEMIES?

Within his own discourse, Xi is a servant. He serves the Party. In a talk at the Central Party School in September 2012, two months before becoming president, he talked of people needing a sense of history, and of the role the Party has played in guiding China's modern history and articulating its national vision. The CCP has an almost sacerdotal role in this history, represented as something for which Chinese people sacrificed themselves in the past, something that always represented the good of the country, and in which people could put their trust and faith. The Party is 'the first under heaven', and for this reason has to be built up, defended and strengthened.[33] The way to do this is to ensure that Party officials represent and exemplify its moral qualities. And they can only do this if they believe in the Party, in the Party's historic role, in what the Party represents and in what its collective values are.

Xi returned to this concept of service to and by the Party when he addressed the world after emerging as leader in November 2012. In his comments to the press he explicitly stated that the Party had sometimes lost touch with the people, and that this was a contradiction that had to be dealt with, simply because for him the Party represented the common interests of the people, so there should be no gap or space between it and society. Soon after his elevation he visited Guangzhou, and continued along this line of thought. Standing on the sacred territory of reform, the place his father had been so instrumental in supporting in the early 1980s, Xi exploited the reformist narrative, recruiting the symbolism of Deng's great Southern Tour for his own purposes. Talking about the continuing mission of the Party to change, he also stated that this did not mean blind Westernization. The great temptation throughout the last 35 years had been to equate reform with an adherence to Western values and beliefs. For Xi,

> there are people who think that reform and opening up is the same as adopting Western universalist values, Western political systems, and if these things don't happen, then it's not reform. This is mistaken and distorts what we are doing. Of course we want to raise the banner of reform, but our reform is one that will continuously have Chinese characteristics.[34]

Once more, in Guangzhou he returned to the issue of the quality of cadres, their beliefs and their moral standing. The USSR, he stated, fell because of its sloppiness, its lack of ideals. 'To run the country well we must first run the Party well, and to run the Party well we must run it strictly,' he said on 17 November 2012, while addressing the National Congress.[35] Party-building in these circumstances is the key. The CCP must maintain close ties with the people. It must seek popular support. If its key representatives, its priestly caste of elite leaders, are mired in corruption, alienating the public, unable to 'restrain their own family and staff', then 'it will eventually lead to the destruction of a party and the fall of a government'.[36] Celebrating the 120th anniversary of Mao Zedong's birth, in 2013 Xi returned to the need for public support, and the means to achieve this: 'people are the creators of history'; 'before the people, we are always students.'[37] A year earlier, he had stated that 'everyone has an ideal, an ambition, and a dream': 'The Chinese Dream is, in the final analysis, the dream of the people.'[38] The role of the Party was to be the great intermediary for this, the midwife to the birth of national idealism.

UNBURYING MAO

One of the challenges for any leader in China since 1976 has been to take a position on Mao Zedong. He has been like an immense felled tree placed in the middle of a yard that people can choose to go over or around but which they cannot ignore. This is because there are two Maos. The first, the dictator, has not been dealt with kindly by history. Almost yearly, new evidence is produced, inside and outside China, of the colossal costs of his intolerant and self-centred rule. But there is also Mao the brand, the symbolic Mao whose image is sporadically available in the country, and whose propaganda value and continuing emotional appeal as the great national unifier and warrior hero has proved more enduring – but also more pernicious.

As the Hunan activists who splattered red paint across Mao's image during the 1989 disturbances discovered, those who choose to debunk or attack the Chairman are guilty of sacrilege. Mao transcends the person who lived into the 1970s and whose utopian revolution died alongside him in 1976. The Mao who survived after this was someone who appeared in narratives of national liberation and empowerment, and who really did found the China Dream that Xi so often refers to: the dream of becoming a strong, powerful nation. For Xi, therefore, taking a view on Mao has been one of the hardest tasks, one that makes him most vulnerable to attack from the many fervent supporters the Chairman still has in the country, as well as from the increasing number who regard him as a liability and a badge of shame.

The way in which Xi has addressed this issue is by stressing the absolute unity between China pre- and post-1978. For any observer, the PRC under Mao was a wholly different place from that which followed his death. The Party managed an almost 180-degree turn. Fundamentally, before 1978 the core task of the Party was to effect cleansing of the class ranks through mass campaigns and class struggle.

Its ethos and language of power were wholly different from those of the Party after 1978, which accepted that economic production and growth were the keys to success and national strength. Xi has focused on the common vision between these two eras – creating a strong country through a strong Party – rather than on the lack of unified means by which to do this. He has talked of the Party being almost like an epistemic community, a repository of knowledge and wisdom in which the Chinese have managed to invest their ideas, the wisdom that has come from their mistakes, in order to continue building towards their common aim.

Xi explicitly referred to the issue of the 'two 30 years' (that is, the three decades leading up to 1978, and the three decades after that date) in remarks he made in 2013. Pre- and post-1978, China was led by a Marxist party, he has stressed.[39] Superficially, however, the forms of Marxism in the two periods seem very different. The challenge, as he reportedly said at a Politburo meeting in July 2013 at Beidaihe, the seaside resort where annual top-level Party retreats are held, was 'how to find the common points between Mao Zedong Thought and Deng Xiaoping Theory', so that this difference could be bridged.[40] The Party needed to have unified thinking on this, to avoid the accusation of being self-contradictory and intellectually divided, and to exist as one entity in the Mao era and afterwards. Denying Mao and his contribution, particularly of his thought, was therefore not a good idea. Of course, Xi admitted, the Party over its history has made mistakes. But these could all be learned from:

> The Cultural Revolution taught us a moral lesson, and the Great Leap Forward was a distortion of the path of development. But we can also regard them as a kind of rich resource. What can we learn from them? That we need scientific measures, and democratic construction.[41]

So while there have been modifications and changes, repudiating the pre-1978 Maoist era wholesale is impermissible. Class struggle may no longer be necessary, as it was under Mao, but class still exists, and the Party needs to think about this. And while dictatorship belongs to the old world, Mao's notion of the people's democratic dictatorship is still crucially important.[42]

There are harder-nosed reasons why the Maoist legacy is something Xi would want, as a new leader, to appeal to. The dictator, who caused his own father so much suffering, and who had such an impact on his own early life, may not be a person Xi harbours fond memories of. But the propagandist, the master of Chinese symbolic politics, the person in modern China who could be said to have most truly understood where power was located, how to use it and how to keep it – his was an inheritance worth trying to tap into. And what a list of assets using Mao's name gives to Xi, or any other pretender for that matter: his impeccable nationalist credentials, for one, and his stress on Party cleansing and on holding to the mass line. More important than all of these, however, was to emulate the Maoist way of conducting politics. This was more elusive, but boiled down to a unique and powerful truth. Mao himself had a clear vision of the best means by which the CCP could wield its power. It was not by becoming some bureaucratic machine, but by holding on to ideals and emotionally mobilizing people. The Party had to reach into their hearts, through its messages and propaganda. Mao was not a cynic. His greatest danger was his exuberant idealism. This gave those who attacked him a difficult target to bring down. In attacking him, they soon found they were attacking the Chinese people's hopes and dreams, or at least the very successful Maoist articulation of these. Mao may have said that power came from the barrel of a gun. But that was only pointing to the instrument and means. The real source of power was in the thinking and ideas of the person holding that gun. And here, Mao was able to reach deeper and quicker than any other Chinese politician of modern times.

The consensus in the post-Mao years is that power no longer comes from gaining the belief and reaching into the ideals of the one carrying the gun, but from having enough money to pay that person off. With its success at material wealth creation since 1978, it seems that the CCP now has enough money to buy the loyalty of the Chinese people.

But just how sustainable and successful is that new strategy? Is this truly where power has relocated itself? Loyalty is an elusive quality, and people are fickle. Material wealth has created a dual allegiance, competing with and sometimes even usurping the demands of the Party. Tainted officials have wandered from the fold, using the Party to enrich themselves, assuming that the material wealth they have acquired will make their positions secure and forgetting the values they are meant to represent and act on. From these nodes, networks have sprung up, with competing loyalties, violating the wider social mission of the Party and threatening the kind of fragmentation that existed before 1949. This will be dealt with in more detail in Chapter 4. Xi, from his past and current behaviour, in this context has had one great intuitive insight that has given him the edge over his peers. Despite all of this focus on wealth, in the end money is not the source of power, or at least not in its purest and most durable form. Moral, symbolic and idealistic appeals really control allegiance. This has become the main territory that he has sought to secure. So while he is not Maoist in his ideology, he is very Maoist in his understanding of the need to locate durable power and gain traction on it.

This is consistent with his behaviour during his time as a provincial official. In Fujian, during its era of enrichment in the 1990s when endless amounts of money were flowing in from Taiwanese investment, and the infamous Lai Changxing Yuanhua scandal was unfolding, he was emboldened enough to say to a local journalist that one did not enter politics for personal enrichment. On 1 March 2012, while speaking at the Central Party School, just on the eve of taking the reins from Hu Jintao, he repeated this. Before more than 2,000 cadres, he stated that some joined the Party and embarked on political careers simply because they regarded it as a route to riches and wealth. Safeguarding the Party's moral role was difficult, he admitted. But it was the only sustainable future. Money and material goods were not the real source of political authority in the country. That was achieved through more intangible forms of leadership.[43]

These were brave things to say when it was clear that it was precisely to enrich their networks and make a good financial return for those who had supported them that people went into the Party in the first place. Xi's own family had been incriminated in this: a Bloomberg report appeared only shortly after Xi had spoken that highlighted the property and wealth of his own immediate family in Hong Kong.[44] But these were relatively small amounts compared to the billions linked to figures like Wen Jiabao, or the hundreds of millions claimed for Bo Xilai. While embarrassing, Xi's family's behaviour was the image of restraint compared to that of other elite leaders' families. Mao had waged war against the Party's becoming a bureaucratic, self-serving behemoth. Xi's new mission, it has increasingly become clear, is to wage war against its becoming the ultimate corporation, a money-making Midas machine that turns all it touches to wealth, at least for its top members. His tactics have therefore been to restore the Party to its idealistic roots, to cleanse its elite leaders in order that they can perform their function as leaders, rather than wealth dispensers, and to do this through a mixture of managed crisis and fear. This, in essence, is his political programme. And it is why Mao is still of immense importance for him.

3

XI, HIS ENEMIES AND HIS FRIENDS

> *Tzu-kung asked about friends. The Master said, inform them loyally and guide them discreetly. If that fails, then desist. Do not court humiliation.*
>
> —*Analects* 12.23

When China's international relations are examined later in this book (in Chapter 5), the world is described as one of concentric circles, with China in the middle, and other powers and countries arranged around it, in order of their importance to the needs of the centre. Similarly, Xi sits at the heart of a dense network of interlinked personal relationships that emanate away from him in circles. This is not a static network, ossified into factional allegiances that hardly change as the years proceed, but something highly dynamic. As with most courtly systems, people fall in and out of favour. There are no hard and fast rules dictating who is in and who is out. Those who seem to be successful today can disappear tomorrow as challenges and demands in the wider environment cause new faces and forces to appear. Conversely, those out of favour yesterday can be elevated today. It is an environment of almost ceaseless change.

From Xi, we can plot at least a number of different categories of relationship. The most settled of these are his kinship and intimate links – with his family, his wife and his daughter. The next category consists of political alliances – his closest allies on the Standing Committee of the Politburo and then in the Party more broadly. After these are friendships – people he has been close to in the past,

but where there are no clear institutional links. Next are the bureaucratic supporters, people with whom he works from day to day, and
who implement and fulfil the Party mission with him. There are
intellectual influences beyond these, from advisors, those who have
his ear and whose ideas have had some visible impact on him. These
people in particular don't necessarily have to be Chinese. Outside
all of these categories are those who matter to Xi because they are
threats, antagonists or, in some cases, outright enemies. If a list like
this implies an easy taxonomy, one point needs to be cleared up
immediately: if we were to try to visualize these relationships around
Xi and their depth and commitment, there would be many overlaps,
duplications and people who started in one class and then moved to
another. Some relationships were important in the past, and are less
so now. Some may become more significant in the future. But if we
were to look on power like a map, then these are the people who
populate the territory. They are the ones who need to be understood
in order to get closer to the nature of Xi's power and the ways that
he exercises it.[1]

FAMILY BUSINESS

As the great sociologist Fei Xiaotong made clear in his work on the
nature of Chinese social links, despite all the changes and transformations that Chinese society has gone through in the modern era, the
fundamental role of family bonds has remained relatively stable.[2]
Mao's brand of Communism tested it to its limits, pitting fathers
and mothers against sons and daughters in the Cultural Revolution.
Still, in rural China, the remarkable mobility of contemporary life in
the country has not eroded the sense of strong obligations between
blood relatives. A favourite task for anyone learning Chinese is to
try to master the vast array of terms used for family relations, and to
grasp that simple English terms like 'uncle' or 'aunt' can be divided
into maternal and paternal equivalents, and then refined even further.
Obligations to respect elder family members inherited from ancient

Confucian codes still linger, even though hierarchies of the past have been disrupted by social and cultural changes in the era of the one-child policy.

Market China has seen the monetizing of relationships. The relationships bearing most financial fruit are those with major political figures. The examples are legion. Former premier Li Peng's family has accumulated immense wealth in the coal and energy sectors; Jiang Zemin's has gone successfully into telecoms. Former premier Zhu Rongji's family is associated with finance. Wang Zhen, a lauded figure of past elites, apparently castigated his offspring for exploiting their links to him for crude money-making a few years before his death.[3] But he is part of the minority. There is a clear financial benefit to be gained from links with the political elite, and the closer these are to the Politburo, the more value can be gained. That means that brothers and sisters, sons and daughters of leaders stand in the frontline and have to make a conscious decision either to enjoy the benefits of their connections or to spend their lives turning down the hordes of people who come their way. For aunts, uncles, cousins and even more distant connections, the challenges of handling the opportunities still exist, even if they are reduced in intensity.

Not belonging to a direct bloodline does not put any limitation on this exploitation. Those marrying into families with elite links can also enjoy the benefits. Ironically, while the fifth-generation leadership in China is one in which men dominate the top levels, their offspring are mostly women. Xi Jinping and Li Keqiang both fall into this camp. The day in the future when their daughters decide to marry will see individuals with no prior links to their father-in-laws' networks become connected in such a way that they can then create a whole new group of people with close links to the Chinese elite of elites. In-laws, whether on the male or the female side, have become some of the most active utilizers of the benefits of being associated with the CCP elite. In many ways they have more latitude to work in areas like business. This even extends to foreigners. One of Xi's nieces, according to a report in the *Daily Telegraph* in late 2012, is married to British national Daniel Foa.[4] The article claims that he derived at least some benefits from the link. Few brakes are put on the flexibility of patronage in modern China.

Xi's carefulness about his closest family is well known. Reports of his asking his younger brother to stay out of business while he was Party secretary in Shanghai sit alongside tales of his mother summoning family meetings in recent years to tell everyone they had to be very careful about how they behaved and what sort of public perceptions there might be about their businesses and wealth.[5] The Bloomberg reports of 2012 about just what sort of property Xi's closest relatives were linked to in Hong Kong came at an unwelcome time, weeks before the National Congress expected to achieve Xi's final promotion.[6] But at least they did not involve Xi's daughter, for the simple reason that she is barely out of adolescence and has had little time to do more than attend Harvard as anonymously as possible and get her degree there. Maybe her chance to embarrass her father by becoming deeply linked to business interests, inside or outside China, will come soon. Hu Jintao's children's involvement with business, particularly in Africa, was the source of great discomfort for Xi's predecessor.

The most powerful family influence on Xi, however, is his wife, Peng Liyuan. The role of the first lady in Chinese politics has never been a straightforward one. Of the five elite leaders of the last six decades, only the wife of Mao Zedong became politically active. As indicated in Chapter 1, this proved disastrous. The profiles of the wives of Deng, Jiang and Hu ranged from low-key to non-existent. There seemed to be an unwritten law that they should be seen and never heard, existing as far as possible in the shadows. With Peng, however, Chinese politics has a new phenomenon: someone who was far more famous than her husband – even up to his appointment as a Politburo member in 2007.

Peng highlights a number of important issues. First, she unleashes the political capital that can be gained from having a glamorous celebrity wife. She is indisputably a political asset, someone well known among a wide domestic public, most of whom are indifferent to politics but might be reached through her. Second, she has her own authentic links to the military, a constituency that definitely matters to Xi. More important still, she contributes hugely to the narrative that is being built around him: a more human leader who is less remote than his predecessors. Through his association with Peng, Xi has a more suitable persona for the era of Chinese social media, where even figures previously hidden behind walls of authority have to work harder to gain a connection with the public that can be used for their own political purposes. Peng is a massive asset here. She breaks the rule that Chinese elite leaders don't have private lives that they can disclose or be comfortable about.

Peng Liyuan was born in 1962, during the final era of the famine caused by the Great Leap Forward, in Shandong Province, one of the worst-affected areas. She has a younger sister and brother. Her family, at least on her mother's side, was moderately prosperous before the 1949 revolution. Even after this they managed to maintain their cultural level; her parents worked in the artistic field, and were classified before the Cultural Revolution in the clunky terminology of the period as 'intellectual elements'. But after 1966, the social status that they had been given, and the fact they had distant relatives living in Taiwan, marked them out for rough treatment. Peng's maternal grandmother, who had been particularly involved in her upbringing, was labelled an 'old landlord element' and paraded through the streets. Her father was labelled one of the dreaded 'five black elements' – groups identified by Mao as enemies of the Cultural Revolution – expelled from the Party and put in what was called at the time the 'cowshed', a term covering various forms of incarceration and 'correction by the masses'. In 1971, the whole family was sent down to a rural area, where the nine-year-old Peng had to look after her sister and brother. Her experiences over this period therefore can be described as just as unpleasant as those of her future husband, if not more so as she was younger and would have been less prepared to cope. Apparently unspectacular as a student when she started primary school, her one great talent even this early on was music, at which she excelled.[7]

Peng has enjoyed a different sort of patronage to Xi. In many ways, her career typifies the sort available to an ambitious woman in a culture like China's, which often remains highly divided along gender lines.

While Xi had to keep officials above and around him happy during his career, Peng needed to cultivate teachers and influential directors. Her earliest teacher, a singing instructor called Gao Chengben, at least recognized her abilities. But her most influential patron when she began performing in Beijing in 1980, at the beginning of the reform era, was Li Bo, a veteran music teacher who had been at the revolutionary base in Yan'an in the 1930s. A performer, theorist and teacher, Li was nicknamed the 'father' of modern Chinese music, and was hugely influential by the time he came across Peng. When lessons at the Chinese Academy of Music restarted in 1980 after the long inter-ruption of the Cultural Revolution, he was appointed director. Closely linked to Deng Xiaoping, he had seen Peng perform that year during a concert in Guangzhou, where she had sung a typical song from her Shandong home. One account of their first meeting has Li asking her how old she was, and, when she replied '18', then telling her she had great raw talent but needed to have discipline. 'Where can I learn to do that?' she asked innocently. 'I know of a place,' Li answered. From 1980, therefore, she studied at the institution he directed in Beijing. This remained the key place for her work for the next 30 years.[8]

Peng was in the right place at the right time. The 1980s saw a momentary explosion of relatively liberated artistic expression. For the previous decade, during her childhood and adolescence, foreign music had been banned; performances were limited to the Eight Revolutionary Operas produced under the artistic and political direc-tion of Jiang Qing. They consisted of stirring tales of Chinese revolu-tionary liberation and class struggle performed in a hybrid style: part traditional Beijing opera, part Western ballet. What other productions there were fitted within the rigid ideological template of the time. It is one of the ironies of modern Chinese history that a movement bearing the name 'cultural' was in fact highly philistine and restricted. The real 'cultural revolution' came from 1980 onwards, when musical and literary ideas started coming in from the outside world once more, and people were freer to express themselves.

One of the great collective moments for Chinese over this period was the Chinese Central Television (CCTV) *New Year's Gala* programme, broadcast annually on the eve of Chinese New Year. Watched by more than half a billion people, it consisted of a gala performance of singing, comedy, drama and dance. Politburo members were often shown sitting in the front row of the studio audience, nodding approvingly at the wholesome family entertainment. The New Year performance is like the Super Bowl in the United States, offering a moment of collective national experience. People gathered around the newly bought TV sets that were starting to populate the country and saw acts ranging from new renditions of the ancient art of comedy double-talk to performers dressed up in military gear singing their souls out for the love of their motherland. It was through these performances that Peng became famous, dressed usually in her officer's clothing and hitting impossibly high notes as she praised the wonders of the new China. In a country dominated in the Maoist era by politicized model workers and grim-faced politicians, this was highly appetizing. Peng and figures like the singer Song Zuying were akin to new superstars, figures both palatable to the political elite and appealing to the people on the street.

For the newly divorced Xi, Peng, whom he married while still a provincial official in 1986, was a major catch. Her fame at the time far exceeded his. The marriage is even more interesting because for the next two decades the two had to pursue careers in different parts of the country. Peng continued her glamorous tours around the provinces and abroad, while Xi engaged in the slog of being a rising provincial official. This has led to stories of them frequently being estranged and even, at points, coming close to divorce. They carry shades of a Clinton-like accord, whereby two different, but complementary, political ambitions elide and override the various traumas and differences they have experienced together. The tabloid press of Hong Kong and Taiwan has produced stories of Xi being linked to news anchorwomen (this seems to be standard for top Chinese leaders – Zhou Yongkang was accused of something similar) and others during his life largely as a single person in the south. But the relationship has prevailed.

Peng is not without political baggage. Images of her serenading soldiers in congratulation after the 1989 Tiananmen Square massacre were taken down from websites when they started to resurface in the last few years. The fact that she is a World Health Organization (WHO) 'goodwill ambassador' for tuberculosis and HIV/AIDS, and an ambassador for the prevention of juvenile delinquency and tobacco control gives her role much more content and profile than those of any of her predecessors apart from Madame Mao. But her position as a ranking officer in the PLA also offers capital for her husband, and a tangible link to a crucially important constituency. It is hard to know if there was ever some moment in the past when a 'deal' was reached between them as Xi's rise to prominence accelerated. Certainly, her performances have decreased since 2007. Nonetheless, she has figured prominently in Xi's overseas visits, famously using her own iPhone to take shots when she was in Sunnylands, California, with Xi and President Obama in 2013 and making a speech in English at the UN in 2015.

As a soft-power asset, Peng is a great gift to Xi. But she may have a more fundamental function. The simple fact is that Chinese public and political life needs to be feminized. The CCP rose to power on the back of promises to support gender equality and fight against the repressive misogyny of traditional Chinese rural life. Yet while there have been women serving on the full Politburo, none has ever reached the Standing Committee, only 20 per cent of CCP membership is female, and since 1949 only two provincial governors have been women. This shows the Party has not lived up to some of its earlier, headier promises.

This problem has been exacerbated by the impact of the one-child policy. There have been cases of female infanticide and rural prejudice in favour of male over female children. China now has 50 million more men than women, with births split at 106 male to 100 females. The net effect of this has been to empower women. Urban women have become fussier about marriage partners, with many opting to remain single. The stigma of divorce has gone. Women figure in the entrepreneurial and business elites far more than in the political ones. Considering this, the Party ignores the support of women at its peril. Peng may well figure as a key part of this strategy to speak more to female Chinese. In contrast to the era of Hu, when there was almost complete silence on the leader's personal life and marriage, Xi's marriage has been used in his official biography as an essential part of his story, the narrative crafted to appeal to both the Chinese and non-Chinese public. 'In the eyes of Peng,' the Xinhua account issued in 2014 goes, 'Xi is a good husband and a good father. She always shows care and consideration for him.' For her, 'Xi is both unique and a very ordinary person.'[9] This solicitude extends to the widely observed sharp glares Madame Peng directed at a passive Xi during the opening gala of the Asia-Pacific Economic Cooperation (APEC) summit in November 2014, prompting him to respond quickly by raising his hand and waving it at the crowd, something that was noted even in a Western press largely indifferent to any information about China, other than its oft-predicted imminent collapse.[10] In the circle of relationships around Xi, therefore, the one with Peng is the most complex and the least easy to quantify, but in many ways the most important of all.

POLITICAL ALLIES: ONLY ONE TIGER ON THE MOUNTAIN

In mid-2012, shortly after the excitement of the fall of Bo Xilai and his wife Gu Kailai, and before the leadership succession itself, Wang Qishan, formerly a vice premier in charge of the crucially important 'Strategic and Economic Dialogue' (S&ED) with the United States, was appointed head of the Central Discipline and Inspection Commission (CDIC). This struck many at the time as poor use of Wang's highly regarded skills as an economist. Was he being sidelined to give more space to Li Keqiang, who was expected to take over the full responsibility for macroeconomic policy as premier in early 2013? According to a Chinese phrase, 'there can only be one tiger on the mountain.' Was this an attempt to ensure that conflicts between the two were avoided, and their portfolios carefully delineated?

   Neat explanations in politics anywhere usually hinder as much as they help. In Chinese politics, with its love of opacity and subterfuge, this is especially so. There was a chess-like neatness about Wang's being so elegantly sidelined to the CDIC. Even at the time, there were clues that this was a far more meaningful position than it at first appeared. In hindsight, the message was already becoming clear that corruption was to be a major political priority of the new leadership. And, beyond his economic prowess, Wang has another, less-noted but equally powerful quality: he is a formidable implementer.

Wang is a crucial figure for Xi, and the closest he has within the 2012 Politburo Standing Committee to a firm political ally. Li Keqiang and the other four have more amorphous links with the leader. But Wang has to succeed in his designated position as head of the anti-corruption body – and, as has been shown elsewhere in this book, the task of restoring moral credibility to the Party is seen by Xi as a battle he cannot afford to lose. Wang's failure, therefore, will also be Xi's. Their political fortunes are intimately tied to each other.

And their stories show that they have unexpected links. Wang is four years older than Xi; he was born in 1948, just before the revolution, probably in Shanxi Province, though some biographies say his actual birthplace was Shandong. His father was an engineer whose technical training made him consider moving to Taiwan when the PRC was established. He ultimately remained on the mainland, despite the fact that his intellectual background and foreign links caused him to be targeted during the anti-rightist campaigns in the late 1950s. In 1956, because of the construction opportunities for engineers, the Wang family moved to Beijing. About the same time as Xi, Wang was rusticated, and became a 'sent-down youth' in 1969, moving from high school in the capital to the Yan'an area of Shaanxi to work on a commune. It is hard to know if his time in Shaanxi overlapped with Xi's. Neither has referred to any link with the other at this time. In any case, the older Wang had different ideas, because the most important relationship he formed at this period was with a female colleague who, it transpired, was the daughter of Yao Yilin, a former national deputy minister of trade. Moved to the provincial capital of Xi'an to work at the Provincial History Museum (possibly with the support of his newly acquired top-level relationship), in 1973 Wang began studying history at the North-West University in the city, working in the museum until his move (after marriage and joining the CCP) to Beijing.[11]

Wang has been described as a maverick, someone whose leadership differs markedly from the technocratic style that prevailed under Hu. An historian by training, he worked in the Chinese Academy of Social Sciences in the 1980s, only starting his political career at the relatively late age of 38, when he became a government economic planner. Even more unusually, his main interest as an historian was the Qing and Republican periods, not post-1949. Even his status as a 'princeling' – a term applied to Party leaders who are related to former top-level figures, either as children or grandchildren – is indirect, and through his wife. It is not something he has thanked people for reminding him of. He was also reportedly deeply influenced by the Hu Yaobang era of Chinese-style liberalism in the 1980s.

His real skill, and the basis of his alliance with Xi, however, has nothing to do with links in the distant past, or connections with princeling patronage networks. The stand-out feature of Wang's career has been his ability to fix unpleasant crises with immense competence. Sent to Guangzhou in 1997, he cut his teeth by helping the Party secretary Li Changchun manage the fallout of the Asian financial crisis and the collapse of a local investment corporation, the first of its kind ever allowed to go bankrupt in China. Dealing with the huge number of bad loans, Wang Qishan took a major role, proving his abilities to the central leadership by avoiding provincial fiscal meltdown in an area that then represented 40 per cent of the nation's economy. After a brief period as the Party secretary of the island Hainan Province, his achievements qualified him for a return to Beijing as mayor in 2003 to deal with the fallout of a far graver crisis – that of severe acute respiratory syndrome (SARS). Mismanagement by the Beijing municipal authorities and the Ministry of Health during the initial phase of the disease's spread from Hong Kong in late 2002 into early 2003 had already led to the felling of two high-level officials. Wang was expected to restore at least some confidence and trust among the public in the government handling of the crisis. By April, better information management, control of people's movement and the public spaces of the city, and some sign of a strategy to deal with the disease before it began to get out of hand had resulted in domestic and international plaudits.

Wang was the mayor of the capital throughout its most intense phase of preparation for the 2008 Olympics. It was during this period that he showed his ability to handle corruption. In 2006 his vice mayor in charge of the vast construction projects commissioned for the Olympics, Liu Zhihua, was removed from office and accused of siphoning off tens of millions for his own networks. Several other high-level officials and business people fell in the same crackdown. Wang himself earned promotion, being elevated to vice premier in 2007.

Even if a factional structure holds good in Chinese contemporary politics, Wang Qishan fits into no easy category. A semi-princeling, he has no strong regional, SOE or institutional power base and served too short a time in provinces to have established a powerful network there. His main quality is an ability to push through hard policies and take on powerful vested interests. He does not show much fear of creating enemies, either. His first few days in the CDIC in 2012 were accompanied by reports that he had asked his staff to read the classic study of revolution in France by Alexis de Tocqueville from almost two centuries before.[12] The conclusion he had reportedly asked the 1,000 members of the CDIC to draw from this work was that the moment of danger for society from upheaval was not when it was impoverished, but when it was moderately well off and contending social and political forces had something worth fighting over. The work of the CDIC is infamously secretive. But under Wang there are clear signs of a highly tactical and strategic plan, whereby larger and larger targets have been slowly enclosed and then brought down, the most important of which so far being security chief Zhou Yongkang. The risk of this work creating extremely powerful enemies is high. Murmurs in 2014 of figures as lofty as Jiang Zemin and Hu Jintao becoming anxious remain unproven.[13] But for Xi, Wang has proved an effective and loyal ally, someone who is also unlikely to pose a threat through age, as a result of his not having children or a defined

power base among any of the usual institutional anchors in the Party
or government.

Less intense alliances also exist with three of Xi's other Politburo
colleagues in the Standing Committee. Li Keqiang is perhaps the most
complex: a man who has maintained a low profile, to the surprise of
many who predicted a much stronger role before his appointment as
premier in 2013. According to one journalist working at the *Southern
Daily*, an official CCP newspaper, Li's office at the State Council had
been lobbying newspapers in China to carry more stories about the
premier – such was the dominance of Xi over much of this period.[14] This
undermines the usual idea that the media in China is neatly state-directed
and subject to centralized edicts. Ironically, elite Party leaders have to
have their own media-relations strategy and work within an internal
market to sell stories about themselves to the domestic media. That Xi
Jinping placed his name so prominently on documents coming from the
Third Plenum – in particular his lengthy explanatory statement – was
telling, particularly when it was evidently mostly about economic reform,
firmly within Li's portfolio. Making a neat division between economic
and political issues is never easy anywhere, least of all in China. Given
that the government's core strategy is all about reform, Xi had in many
ways been handed a mandate to wander where he wished. Economics is
a valid area to take a prominent interest and role in as the main leader.

In 2014, unsubstantiated rumours circulated about how Li was even
considering retiring due to ill health. Maybe these arose from dissatisfaction expressed by him or his officials, or maybe they were started by
ill-intending bystanders supportive of Xi. The premier, though, still has
a big role in Chinese politics. In many ways, Li Keqiang has the ability
to derail the progress of the Party and government's reform package.
For someone who has been associated with problems implementing
policy in the past, it might not be so much about Xi manoeuvring to
get around Li, but about Li simply being exposed as less competent
than people thought he was. In 2015, rumours continued that Li might
retire in 2017 after one term.[15]

Liu Yunshan has a more abstract role. He is head of ideology and
Party-building. The sole member of the Standing Committee with no

substantial provincial leadership role on his CV, his elevation in 2012 caught many by surprise. He was regarded as stolidly left wing, and had been associated with problems over news management in the past. Liu, however, evidently has a closer link to Xi than was initially suspected. He took a leading role in drafting the Third Plenum statement, and has increasingly acted as an enforcer of orthodoxy among cadres, in particular through his role as president of the Central Party School. Loathed by many Party members as the voice of turgid control and ideological purity, Liu comes from a background in state journalism, and worked for the Propaganda Department of the Central Committee in the 1990s. He therefore has a long history of being a deviser of policies to control both the messenger and the message – a subject that Xi, as the next chapter will show, has devoted a considerable amount of attention to.

Finally, there is Yu Zhengsheng, Party elder, someone close to the Deng family, and a man with long provincial experience. Yu acts like the chief representative of the forces of conservatism, an elder states-man whose advice draws on his extensive career of ups and downs. He comes from the most heavily elitist background of the leaders, his links going back to the 1930s when his father Yu Qiwei (also known as Huang Jing) was briefly married to Jiang Qing, the lady who a few years later became Mao's fourth wife. Mayor of Tianjin in the 1950s, Yu's father died in 1958, but his family suffered persecution in the Cultural Revolution a decade later (his sister might have com-mitted suicide then as a result of her mother's incarceration over this period). Yu's background, however, is more complex than this. His great-uncle served as defence minister in the Nationalist government of Chiang Kai-shek in the 1940s. Yu himself studied and then worked in ballistic-missile technology during the 1960s and into the 1970s, regarded as a priority area that even continued when other technical subjects were stopped at the time. But the most difficult aspect of his background is his brother Yu Qiangsheng, who worked as a military spy before defecting to the United States and, in effect, disappearing in the mid-1980s. That Zhengsheng has been rehabilitated from this is a sign of his deep loyalty, most of all to the Deng clan, whom he came to know well when linked to Deng Xiaoping's disabled son Pufang in the 1980s through his involvement in the Chinese Welfare Fund for the Disabled. Yu Zhengsheng is the ultimate modern Chinese man without qualities, someone almost wholly lacking in any political persona, whose few speeches printed in the Party magazine *Qiushi* [Seeking truth] are devoid of a single distinctive idea or position. As such, he simply brings supportive constituencies for Xi, but offers zero ideological opposition. This, in contemporary Chinese politics, counts as a form of alliance.[16]

THE BUREAUCRATS

Members of the Politburo and Central Committee and heads of ministries have visibility. They are known, and their function is at least relatively clear. But there are more anonymous power holders in China, who inhabit the same shadowy world as unelected officials in Western bureaucratic systems. Supposedly servants of their political masters, they are often deeply influential through being gatekeepers, almost always close beside their patrons and bosses, able to whisper in their ears, arrange their diaries, and grant people access or keep them away. They are trusted in ways political colleagues are not, acting almost like eunuchs in the imperial system that prevailed until a century before, by neutering themselves and therefore gaining access to the most hallowed spaces – although the modern eunuchs are political, rather than sexual. There are three figures that occupy this space for Xi. The first is Ding Xuexiang, the second Zhong Shaojun, and the third Zhu Guofen.

From 2013, Ding Xuexiang's formal role has been as the unexciting deputy director of the General Office of the CCP Central Committee. In fact, his real function is to serve as Xi's private secretary. There can be few better placed in contemporary China in terms of access to Xi and knowledge of his day-to-day work. Ding, born in 1962, is the ultimate faceless insider, a bureaucrat from Jiangsu Province who first met his future master during Xi's brief tenure in Shanghai in 2007.

Ding had already worked in the Science and Technology Commission in the city under former city bosses Huang Ju and then the disgraced Chen Liangyu. Ding, according to Chinese media reports, attracted Xi's attention when he came to Shanghai because, despite his lengthy local career, he had been educated in the north and had some of the more direct manners and ways of speaking that Xi associated with that area.[17] Unable to take Ding with him to Beijing after he was promoted later in 2007, Xi managed to finally get him there in July 2013, when Ding was announced in the *Hebei Daily* local paper as accompanying Xi on a tour of the province.[18] Ding belongs to no specific networks, has no political links to anyone significant from his family, and has maintained the same low-key status as some of his predecessors. His main talent is an ability to write well, and to transfer his master's ideas into clearly written instructions. He also has a good link with Xi's Politburo colleague Yu Zhengsheng, who served as Party secretary of Shanghai from 2007 to 2012, and whose secretary Ding was. It is likely that Ding will replace Li Zhanshu, his current boss (on paper at least), who is due to retire in 2018, as director of the General Office.

Beside Ding is the even more low-key Zhong Shaojun, a man who was almost completely unknown inside or outside China until his appearance beside his boss in meetings with foreign dignitaries in early 2013. Xi took no personnel with him on departing from Fujian to assume position in Zhejiang in 2002, but it was while Xi was in Zhejiang that Zhong served as head of the local Organization Department in charge of personnel decisions, and then as Xi's personal secretary. They created a professional relationship that survives to this day. Zhong has carried his anonymity to heights unusual even in China, with minimal information about his career available in official sources. He is reportedly a graduate of Zhejiang University, where he completed a master's degree in analysis of cadre management, and he continued his studies with a part-time PhD at Qinghua after Xi's move to Beijing in 2007. His first appearance was in March 2008, when he accompanied Xi as vice president to the United States. He serves as the head of Xi's private office, and has been linked with the foreign-affairs portfolio in Xi's inner team, while also possibly covering Xi's chairmanship of the CMC.[19]

Still deeper in the shadows is Zhu Guofen. He figures in official literature only as 'President Xi's secretary'. Born in 1973, a native of Guangdong Province, Zhu studied in the Law faculty at Renmin University (also known as the People's University) in Beijing from 1995, before working briefly on a Party magazine issued by the Central Committee called *Secretary Work*. From 1998, he returned to Renmin University to complete a master's degree. He spent the next decade working in the Central Committee again, in various capacities, before coming to attention when listed as Xi's personal secretary at the 2013 Boao Forum for Asia conference. Zhu also accompanied Xi on his visit to California in mid-2013. If Zhong covers Xi's military portfolio, Guo sits on the Party and political side, dealing with Xi's position as CCP head.[20]

There are two other, better-known members of this inner bureaucratic group. The most significant is Li Zhanshu, mentioned above, who serves as director of the General Office but also as a member of the full Politburo. Born in Hebei in 1950, Li is a veteran insider bureaucrat with experience across several provinces in the last 30 years, culminating as governor of Heilongjiang Province from 2008. Linked with Xi as early as the 1980s when they were both serving in Hebei, Li has issued the same stern demands for discipline and moral rigour in the Party as his current boss – something that could be a result of his need to differentiate himself from Ling Jihua, an old colleague on the Politburo felled by anti-corruption investigations in 2015, whose former position Li now occupies.[21] The other member is He Yiting, based at the CCP Policy Research Office as a vice minister, where he is involved with anti-corruption and Party-building signature campaigns associated with Xi.

For all the attempts to link these members of the bureaucratic super-elite together, and claim that they are members of an informal think tank sitting at the heart of the government, the links between them are in fact very fluid, and only really cohere when it comes to their working closely for one man – Xi. They are not generators of ideas and intellectual stimulation – not overtly, anyway – but implementers and facilitators. The most influential figures on ideas for Xi, while linked to this close network, sit in a slightly different realm.

XI'S THINKERS

The sources of Xi's ideas, and the people who have most impact on his thinking, can be divided into those he has known a long time, and those he has inherited from previous leaders. Chinese leaders live in a vortex of protocol-driven meetings and highly scripted and choreographed encounters with the public and the outside world. Added to this is a barrage of paperwork. Some idea of what his daily routine might be like was issued in a Shanghai paper in October 2014. Up at dawn, and going to bed after midnight, Xi seems to be trying to emulate the infamously punishing work practices of China's nemesis in the early 1980s, British prime minister Margaret Thatcher, who got by on four hours of sleep a night. Even with a schedule as driven as this, there is the question of how fresh or new ideas get through, and how thinking ever gets done. Xi probably has a few minutes to take decisions on things ranging from the military to the Party, and from personnel to international issues. He can only survive by delegation, and that includes getting people he trusts to do his thinking for him while he struggles with the daily deluge of being a leader.[22]

Chief among these intellectual influences is Chen Xi, a classmate of Xi's in Qinghua in the 1970s, who pursued an academic career for most of his life before being made deputy director of the Organization Department in charge of personnel decisions under Xi.[23] Chen, a native of Fujian Province, studied initially at Fuzhou University Technology College before going to Beijing to attend Qinghua University in the chemical-engineering department at the same time as Xi. After returning briefly to Fuzhou, Chen went back to Qinghua and spent most of the next two decades there, becoming increasingly influential in the political and management areas of the elite university.

After a year's study leave at Stanford University in California in the early 1990s, Chen was appointed deputy Party secretary of Qinghua from 1993 and made full Party secretary in 2002. It was while Chen occupied the most senior position at Qinghua that his old friend and colleague Xi completed a doctorate there.[24] Serving as Party secretary of Qinghua until 2008, he was then made deputy minister of education from 2008 to 2010, and then, for only six months, served as deputy Party secretary of Liaoning Province before coming back to Beijing in late 2010 to replace the daughter of Deng Xiaoping, Deng Nan, as director of the Science and Technology Commission. Once Xi was elevated in 2012, Chen followed suit, being lifted into the immensely powerful Organization Department to be a vice minister there. Chen is seen as having created a very close bond with Xi while they studied together in the 1970s. If anything, it proves Xi's loyalty to his old friends, with stories of how graduates of the chemical-engineering department at Qinghua from the mid-1970s onwards would meet informally in Beijing at least once a year for a catch up from 2007, when Xi was back in the capital. There were also stories of how Xi, when unable to make the get-together, called old colleagues to find out how they were.[25]

Wang Huning is an inherited link, someone who has been influential in Chinese politics for over a decade, and proved himself the ultimate ideological survivor. Like Chen Xi, he is a refugee from the academic realm, having worked in the 1980s at Fudan University in his native Shanghai. His intellectual background is heterodox. He originally studied French but then moved into international relations, briefly studying in the United States as a postgraduate (something he has in common with all the key intellectual influences on Xi in this section). He was elevated during the era of Jiang Zemin in 1994 to be director of the anodyne-sounding CCP Policy Research Office, and stayed here for more than a decade. This position is immensely important because it serves as the 'think tank of think tanks', a kind of secular CCP equivalent of the Congregation for the Doctrine of the Faith of the Catholic Church, and provides great access to elite leaders and immensely powerful networks.

Wang comes across as the ultimate creature of the bureaucratic undergrowth, someone who has been imputed with being able to translate leaders' ideas into snazzy sound bites with Chinese characteristics. His fingerprints have been found, for instance, on the 'Three Represents' of Jiang, the 'Theory of Scientific Development' of Hu, and now Xi's 'China Dream'. This ability to 'feel out' the ideas of his political masters intuitively, and then give them some structure and definition, has meant that Wang has never become married to any particular viewpoint or ideological position. His reported lack of ambition and dislike of any sort of profile are also good qualities. He comes across as a twenty-first-century version of Henry VIII's Thomas Cromwell or France's Robespierre, someone who carries a night shadow around in broad daylight, and who simply appears beside Xi at key moments, in the best vantage point, to whisper and influence.[26] A member of the full Politburo since 2012, he is reportedly an insomniac. What can be gleaned from his work prior to his becoming a more invisible official and servant of the Party's ideological apparatus is that he locates China politically and intellectually almost always in distinction to the United States, a country that occupied the centre of his thinking as an academic. It almost certainly remains in this position in his years married to subterfuge and silence. Wang was bereft of any evidence of personal relations, apparently alienating his first wife with his bookish ways, though he reportedly remarried in 2015. Because of these traits, he is probably corruption-free, unlike Ling Jihua, a colleague who has suffered for the actions of his relatives (particularly his late son). Wang's isolation means he offers Xi the ultimate benefit – loyalty. Wang himself would probably see that as loyalty to the Party and the Party destiny under unified leadership. If anyone wishes to see the face of calculating, conspiring and unaccountable modern Party power, then they need look no further than the impassive, sallow features of Wang Huning.

The final influence is in the economic realm: Liu He, deputy of the National Development and Reform Commission since 2012, and, more importantly, director of the Leading Group for Financial and Economic Affairs. Mr Liu sat beside President Xi in early 2013, during a visit by the then US national security advisor Tom Donilon. According to people at the meeting, during the introductions Xi pointed to Liu and said: 'He is very important to me.' This statement is reminiscent of Mao's curt remark about his ultimate successor, Hua Guofeng: 'With you in charge I am at ease.' In this case, too, the mantle is a heavy one, and it is unlikely that Liu would have felt too relaxed or reassured on hearing the words.[27]

Liu He stands out academically and intellectually as a strong believer in markets. Educated partly at the John F. Kennedy School of Government at Harvard, where he attended a course in 1995, he has reputedly enjoyed a link with Xi since their time in middle school in Beijing in the 1960s.[28] It was Liu's input that was behind the acknowledgement of the role of the market at the Third Plenum in late 2013. As his assistant on the leading group, Liu appointed a Stanford-educated economist, Fang Xinghai, who had been working as deputy director of the Shanghai Stock Exchange for a number of years. Liu, however, is modest about his influence, having his office respond to a request for comment by saying that individuals in the system are limited in terms of their impact, and that the system is guided by collective decision making. Even so, it is interesting that ideas that Liu has been so closely connected to over the last few years have received such powerful expression in Party documents on the macroeconomy.

THE OUTSIDERS

Surrounded by walls of protocol and protection, how can Chinese leaders ever break out and hear new perspectives and ideas? Tales of Peter the Great dressing as a commoner and trying to mingle in the crowds of Moscow so he could take the pulse of public opinion come to mind. The story of Xi catching a taxi in 2013, which stunned the Chinese press, might be untrue, but it does capture something about how closeted elite Chinese leaders are, buried behind their walls of official protectors, security, advisors and minders. Often it seems like this human shield is there as much to protect the world from them as them from the world.

Xi has maintained links with some figures not belonging to the purely political or government world. Some of these have come to him through his own personal background. In the 1980s, his father showed great loyalty to Hu Yaobang, and at this time grew to know some of the latter's family, in particular his son, Deping. Hu Deping, born in 1942, comes from the generation before Xi's, who managed to complete their education (in Hu Deping's case at the department of literature at Peking University) before the Cultural Revolution. He returned in the 1970s to work in the History Museum in Beijing and has sustained his role as a liberal intellectual ever since, someone respected for his own scholarly interests as well as because of the positive image that his father maintained among those broadly sympathetic to liberal reform.

In July 2012, He Deping held a meeting with Xi, just as the final stage to the leadership change was getting under way. At this meeting, Xi stated that there needed to be all-out reform – but not reform that was disruptive. 'Economics must be stable but progress, politics must be stable but reform, and culture must be stable but change.'[29] An irrevocable part of this would be through maintaining Party discipline.[30] Xi's words to Hu refer to the challenges facing China as 'unprecedented'. They were worked up into a note circulated to senior leaders at the Central Party School, and gave one of the clearest signs that, once in power, Xi wanted to move more quickly and radically than the previous leadership.

One issue the meeting with Hu Deping raised was just how ambiguous views about the 1980s and the era of Hu Yaobang really were among the political and intellectual elite. When former premier Wen Jiabao wrote a *People's Daily* editorial praising his old mentor Hu, many felt that it showed he was out of step with the other leaders around him. Hu Yaobang had been blamed for precipitating the problems that had led to the Tiananmen Square massacre in 1989. Despite sporadic rumours of a revised judgement, there remained great sensitivity about this event. Xi showed no signs of going soft on this issue, marking the 25th anniversary of 4 June in 2014 with a harsh clampdown, taking in a number of activists and lawyers who had attended a seminar in May in Beijing asking for a reappraisal of Tiananmen. Despite this, Hu Yaobang was someone linked to almost every other member of the elite. He had been a patron of Hu Jintao (no relation) and linked to a whole swathe of younger officials who were now coming into positions of real influence through his roles in the China Youth League and then the Organization Department, which he led before becoming general secretary of the Party. He represented an authentic strand of reformist liberal politics, albeit with Chinese characteristics. While he was no democrat, he did believe in having liberty and looseness in the system for innovation, new ideas and entrepreneurialism. The fact that the Xis and Hus have a family link is also important. Only via this route was someone like Hu Deping able to get the sort of access he had in July 2012, just weeks before the succession itself in November that year.

ENEMIES

If we can learn a lot about someone from the friends they have and alliances they maintain, then we can probably learn as much, if not more, from knowing who their enemies are. The great literary critic Samuel Johnson commented that if someone really wants to understand himself, then listening to what his enemies say about him is a good place to start. Understanding Xi means understanding who opposes him. A book in Chinese trying to answer this question puts only two people in the enemy camp – the president of the United States and Liu Xiaobo, imprisoned winner of the Nobel Peace Prize.[31] This is a gross oversimplification. Xi's deadliest enemies are almost certainly those who sit closest to him, within the Party. They are the people who have the most immediate means to harm him.

Of these, the group broadly assigned the title 'leftists' is the best known, and the basis of its opposition to much of what has constituted reform in the last three decades has been exhaustively discussed. The

notion that in the second decade of the twenty-first century there might
be a cohort of diehard Maoists still banging the Great Helmsman's
drum in China, despite the daily avalanche of news showing that the
country now is almost like another planet compared to its pre-1978
existence, is an unsettling one. Maoists seem like stranded Japanese
in the South East Asian jungles, struggling out of the thick forests
decades after World War II ended to find that they have been battling
for all this time in vain and that their struggle is long over. But there
is a very serious side to why Mao remains so potent in contemporary
China, and why invoking him is so combustible politically, despite
the fact that his mandate remains as slippery and hard to capture after
his death as it did when he was alive. The crucial, incontrovertible
difference anyone can accept between the China of Mao and the China
of today is the spiralling inequality now. It is this that the most serious
supporters of Mao invoke in their attacks.

In 2012, the Development Research Centre of the State Council
(DRC) and the World Bank co-produced a report on the challenges
facing the country in the coming two decades. The report, *China 2030:
Building a Modern, Harmonious and Creative Society*, was a bible of
modern reform, proposing deeper marketization of the economy and
the factors of production, a much larger role for the non-state sector, a
wider reform of government and administrative functions, and a more
aggressively green agenda. If there was a coherent, lengthy statement
(the report came to more than 350 pages) of Western-style neoliberal
economic values imported lock, stock and barrel to the PRC, this was it.
'Direct government intervention may actually retard growth,' the report
stated. 'Instead, the policy emphasis needs to shift even more toward
private-sector development.'[32] Arguing for a scaling back and redef-
inition of the role of government and the state, the report continues:

> The expanding middle class is increasingly vocal in its demand
> to participate in the discussion of public policy [...] The gov-
> ernment should respond proactively to these needs and grant
> rights to individuals, households, enterprises, communities,
> academia, and other non-governmental organizations.[33]

This crisp statement encapsulated all the great red lines for the more socialist-supporting contingent in Chinese society, most of whom regarded 1978 not as 'Year Zero' for the renaissance of China but as a catastrophe from which the country looked likely never to recover. For them, these celebrations of the market, of an emerging middle class, of the non-state sector and of the surrender of the state were stages of capitulation to Western-inspired capitalism, which was being sneaked in by bribing and seducing Chinese people with slightly improved living standards while allowing a new elite to become obscenely rich.

On 15 July 2012, 1,644 prominent economists within China responded to the report with an open letter. Their political target was the premier Wen Jiabao, firstly because he was regarded as the most zealous liberal reformer on the Politburo Standing Committee, and secondly because he was viewed as the primary political patron of the report – despite its falling more under the immediate jurisdiction of the vice premier in charge of macroeconomic affairs at the time, Li Keqiang. Thirdly – and as further proof that, despite its often abstract public veneer, politics in China is almost always intensely personal – the premier was targeted because of the widely known fact that Wen Jiabao's family were among the most venal and rich of the political elite, with his wife Zhang Peili in particular and his two sons being associated with dizzying fortunes. This was to be very publicly documented in the *New York Times* only a few months later.[34] For Maoist and leftist complainants, therefore, there couldn't be a better combination than this sort of report, with this kind of content, produced by these partners and under the patronage of this specific individual. They launched their salvo.

The letter categorized *China 2030* as a direct challenge to the Chinese socialist system. It was, the authors said, 'an attempt by Wen Jiabao to introduce multiparty capitalist politics' into China, and to attack SOEs. The signatories of the letter stated that this had been the consistent trend of Wen-supported policy throughout his period as premier. In 2010, they said, only 27 per cent of the economy was in the hands of the state sector; the remaining 73 per cent was in the non-state sector. This statistic was a monument to the surrender of the economy into the hands of entrepreneurs and business people who had self-interest rather than care for the country at heart. The 1,644 economists argued passionately that to downgrade the SOEs in this way was fatuous. In the energy, chemicals, materials, telecoms and construction sectors, the state had to maintain its guiding role, because these were 'critical to preserving the independence of our economy' and could not be watered down by non-state agents. The advantages of SOEs had been ignored in the report, including the fact that they were the most competitive in taking on enterprises outside China, and, importantly, were the major source of revenue for the central state so that it could discharge its welfare duties. Of tax revenues to the central government, which made up 70 per cent of all government fiscal revenue in the PRC, more than half came from SOE contributions, with the rest being a mixture of individual tax, foreign-enterprise tax, consumption tax and, embarrassingly, tobacco tax. To downgrade the state system was politically and economically to bite the hand that fed. More importantly, as fellow Politburo member Wu Bangguo had stated during his powerful defence of SOEs at the NPC in 2012, the annual meeting of China's parliament, SOEs had been a source of stability for China during the Global Financial Crisis of 2008 onwards, when the export markets in Europe and North America had dried up. Without SOEs at this time, China would have been sucked into the same collapse as elsewhere in the developed world. Government control over SOEs was therefore considered a critical mechanism at times of crisis like this to ensure that external folly did not jeopardize China's economic stability.

But there was a far more virulent tone in some parts of the letter, one that drew from the rich tradition of nationalism in Maoist thought. The authors of the letter stated that the DRC and the World Bank were nothing more than stooges for Western-led (for which read American-led) capitalist infiltration into China. Their tactic was simple: they were covertly seeking to weaken and destabilize China in precisely the way they did with the fall of the USSR and its central planning system in 1991. When the USSR collapsed, consultants and representatives of the International Monetary Fund (IMF), the World Bank and other organizations trooped to Moscow and foisted on it disastrous policies that saw its strategic government assets carved up and handed over to oligarchs, its welfare system collapse, its life-expectancy rates collapse and its national prestige plummet. While the West celebrated this moment as the end of the Cold War and the moment when Russia liberated itself and returned to its senses after 74 years of Communist folly, for many in China it was an existential disaster, a capitulation by Russia to self-harming policies that led to precipitous decline, unleashing the anarchy of the Yeltsin years and showing that the West in the end was never a true friend of anyone except itself. The consensus of the many seminars, round tables and consultations in the PRC right up to 2013 on the collapse of the USSR was therefore overwhelmingly critical. The one agreed point was that the whole post-1992 story of Russia showed precisely what China should not do, not what it should emulate.[35]

This, in essence, is the Maoist critique of China in the twenty-first century: that it is a country led increasingly by revisionists who are surrendering to precisely the sort of Western influence that Mao resisted so heroically throughout his career; that it is a place where the state is turning its back on the common people, where precisely the sort of bureaucratic business elite that Mao had waged successive campaigns against, culminating in the Cultural Revolution, is reappearing. Mao himself had wearily admitted to the US journalist Edgar Snow towards the end of his life that he had failed to change much in China, and that future Cultural Revolutions would need to be waged to dig out the profound problems of elites and bureaucratic power holders left over from history. But in the China of Hu Jintao and Xi Jinping, the bureaucrats and their patronage networks linked deeply to business and money had come back with a vengeance. The families of the 'Eight Immortals', the leaders who had been active in the CCP from the earliest period of its founding up to the first decade of the twenty-first century (Bo Yibo was the last to die, in 2007, at the age of 99), were symptomatic of this, with most of them accruing wealth and property both inside and outside China, and monetizing their revolutionary family inheritance. The struggles during the foundation and rise to power of the Party, and then its stewardship of the country after 1949, were not meant to end up here. The nadir of this was the announcement in May 2013 that Kong Dongmei, granddaughter of the Chairman, came 242nd on the Forbes China Rich List that year, with a fortune in insurance made along with her husband Chen Dongsheng. Even more stomach-churning was the fact that despite this vast wealth, she had run a bookshop in Beijing promoting Communist culture and written four books about her grandfather. Major General Mao Xinyu, also a grandson of Mao, had stated in 2009 while he was part of the CPPCC that 'the Mao family heritage is honest and clean. None of the Mao family members have entered business. They all live on their modest salaries.'[36] Kong proved him wrong. If the direct family of the great man himself could not keep clean, then what hope for the rest of the country?

ONLINE CRITICS

The internet has entered the lifeblood of contemporary China, but only 20 years before 2013 the number of mobile-phone and internet users in the country was almost non-existent. Now China holds the world record for both. Unsurprisingly, those proclaiming to be faithful Maoists are speaking through various online portals, the most prominent of which is the Utopia website. Utopia was founded by Fan Jinggang and Han Deqiang in 2003. Fan has been the most prominent face of the website and the small Beijing bookshop it is associated with. He was born in Hunan, Mao's home province, in 1976, the year of the Chairman's death. According to an interview in 2012, the inequality that Fan witnessed on coming to Beijing as a student in the 1990s was what inspired him to make analysis and debate about Mao's continuing relevance more widely available. Fan's critique of post-1978 reform China is a simple one:

People had more dignity, higher social status and better welfare [...] In Mao's era, no one was out there alone; they always had a team to count on. If someone needed to build a house, he could turn to his workmates for help. But nowadays, it's all different.[37]

Far from being an era of rampant prosperity, the last 30 years in China have seen a growing army of those who have simply lost out or been sidelined by market liberalization and reform: those laid off from SOEs, those disenfranchised from the welfare system, those from rural areas who have had their land rights stolen from them by greedy officials. This list contains precisely the sort of people Mao is usually asserted as the champion of.

The Utopia website was blocked in April 2012, after it posted strong defences of Bo Xilai soon after his fall.[38] Attracting, on Fan's account, up to half a million visitors a day, it had become one of the most visited sites in the country. But defences of Bo along these lines made the leadership nervous:

> Bo's campaigns like 'Sing Red Strike Black,' 'Officials making poor friends,' 'Visiting the grassroots classes' after coming to power, and a series of actions like building low-rent houses, taking care of 'empty nesters' and left-behind children, narrowing the gap between the rich and poor, follow the constitution of CCP and the 'Serving the People' principle, and represent the people's wish for common prosperity. That's why I support him.[39]

The real enemy for Utopia supporters, among them nationalist bloggers and thinkers like Sima Nan, Liu Yang and Zhang Hongliang, were intellectuals who had argued vigorously for burying Mao once and for all – in particular Mao Yushi and Xin Ziling. Mao (no relative of the Chairman), over 85 when he wrote the blog entry for the news website Caixin Online in 2011, was to be rewarded with vitriol and anger. But his statements were straightforward enough. Just like Xi Jinping, he started by stating that Mao Zedong was a man, not a god. He continued:

Now, as more and more materials have come to light, we have been able slowly to return him to human form, a person of flesh and blood. But still there are those who regard him as a god, and who regard any critical remarks against him as a mark of disrespect. If you suggest that he committed errors, well that's something really not permitted.

Mao enumerated the standard list of problems: the Cultural Revolution, which he had directly inspired, and the great famines, stating that 'without a doubt, Mao Zedong was responsible'. Then Mao Yushi got personal: 'His [Mao Zedong's] thirst for power dominated his life, and to this end he went entirely mad, paying the ultimate price in his quest for power, even though his power was actually weakened as a result.' While Mao may have tried to cover his ambitions with class struggle, aimed at the bourgeoisie, the people he was really after were those he considered to be his enemies:

National unity, the interests of the people, all were given secondary importance. All the country's top leaders racked their brains about all day long was who benefitted [politically] from certain matters, and particularly what the [possible impact would be] on Mao Zedong's power and standing. No one dared give offense to Mao Zedong. All national matters became personal matters of the Mao family.[40]

According to *The Economist*, on 23 May a petition of 10,000 people opposing what Mao Yushi had written and asking for him to be prosecuted by the authorities was presented to a police station in Beijing. Comments on the article on the Caixin Online website brought out the worst in the online community: 'The whole nation is waiting for the dawn, the dawn of a day when Mao Yu-Shit [*sic*] and other anti-Mao reactionaries who vilify Mao are annihilated,' stated one.[41] A month later, the flames of the debate were reignited by Mao Yushi's review of fellow liberal Xin Zilin's book on Mao, *The Fall of the Red Sun*, in which he wrote on Caixin Online: '[Mao] is not a god, and he will be removed from the altar, divested of all the myth that used to shroud him and receive a just evaluation as an ordinary man.'[42] For this, Fan and his colleagues arranged a petition of 40,000 names, to be presented at the NPC demanding that both Mao and Xin be prosecuted for sedition. Calling both 'national traitors', six months later the Utopia website made Mao Yushi one of the top ten traitors to China, along with figures like jailed Nobel Peace Prize winner Liu Xiaobo. For Fan, the '3/7 theory' – the standard judgement on Mao as being 70 per cent right, 30 per cent wrong – and criticisms along the lines given by people like Mao Yushi, are wide of the mark:

> Who can really comment on Chairman Mao? The so-called 3/7 theory was only a temporary one. Looking back, many people's opinions are already changing. For example, war heroes like Chen Yun, Wang Zhen, Wei Wei, Ma Bin all agree the 'right' (achievement) part is underrated and the 'wrong' (mistakes) part exaggerated. On the other hand, some traitors in the Party betrayed Communism and created all sorts of rumors to attack Chairman Mao. There's a guy called Li Rui who claims to be Mao's ex-secretary and another one called Xin Ziling. Mao, in their eyes, is probably more like '70 percent wrong, 30 percent right,' if not worse.[43]

Despite this strenuous rhetoric about sticking up for the true national interest, almost all the Maoist sites, from Utopia to Mao Flag and Red China, were, by early 2014, shut down or inaccessible, inside and outside China. The domain for Redchinacn.com, the former home of Red China, was up for sale in early February 2014 for slightly more than US$ 1,000. Beyond the group around Utopia, there was a constellation of other Maoist-leaning individuals. There was the old left, mostly conservatives who stood by the command economy and Leninist ideology. Many of these worked in academia and figured among the 1,644 economists who signed the letter to Wen in 2012. There were also writers who focused on more cultural issues. One of these was Peking University's professor of sinology Kong Qingdong, who infamously branded the people of Hong Kong 'dogs of the British' in 2012, and who, in one of his blogs, aimed particular anger at Taiwanese director Ang Lee's racy *Lust, Caution* and spoke up for films with a stronger Maoist theme. Kong's aggressive attitude towards most forms of 'Western cultural imperialism' has extended to supporting the award of a Confucius Peace Prize (a deliberate attempt to create an indigenous equivalent of the Nobel Peace Prize) to Vladimir Putin in 2011, and commenting provocatively that North Korea has never suffered from famine.[44] Figures like Kong occupy the sort of territory that 'shock jocks' do in the United States – marginal but vocal, and representative of a specific sector of opinion in the new China. The menu of irritants for people like Kong ranges from Eurocentric views of the world to Orientalism, Western promotion of human rights despite the fact that, it is claimed, the West has neither the moral right nor the legitimacy to lecture China, talk of Enlightenment values and liberal democracy.

Fan explicitly referred to the *China 2030* World Bank report of 2012 and its liberal agenda as a provocation. The rumour that Utopia itself had been funded by the eminence of the left in China, Deng Liqun, author of a number of sour critiques of Jiang Zemin and Zhu Rongji's strategy towards SOEs in the 1990s and of a particularly virulent attack on Jiang Zemin's bringing entrepreneurs into the CCP in 2002, remains unproved.[45] But the issue of the left in China, and Maoist links to it, is an important one to think about. Figures as eminent as Deng Xiaoping had warned throughout the 1980s and into the 1990s that while rightism was an evil thing in China, the real danger was lurking on the left. Radical leftism is associated with all the great policy disasters of the post-1949 period and, although it was down, it was certainly not out. The threat of a leftist renaissance, therefore, was always a very uncomfortable one for the Party, and to raise the spectre of a return of the Cultural Revolution, as Wen Jiabao did when he obliquely attacked Bo Xilai in early 2012, was to summon up the real bogeyman of modern Chinese history.

DANGER FROM THE LEFT

Despite this, leftists have a powerful intellectual position, and the more sophisticated were able to offer some reminders of why there are incoherencies in the post-reform settlement in China. Wang Hui, a professor of Chinese literature at Peking University, is one of the most respected of these. In a series of essays over the last two decades he has presented a leftist critique of the polity of contemporary China that avoids the visceral and highly personalized simplifications of more populist Maoists like those associated with Utopia. For him, wholesale adoption of Western-style capitalism is a recipe for disaster. In an interview on the subject of modernity in China, Wang stated that 'modern Chinese thought is characterized by an anti-modern modernity. China's search for modernity began during the time of colonialism, so that its historical meaning involved a resistance against it and a critique of capitalism.'[46] How odd, therefore, that capitalism seems to run rampant in contemporary China. Wang's more penetrating remark was simply to acknowledge that under the veneer of consensus, both Maoist and post-Maoist China were riddled with political battles, which were 'inextricably linked to serious theoretical considerations and policy debate'.[47] At the heart of this was the question of what, in the end, the role of the Party was. At the time of Mao's death, the Party was a personal fiefdom, subject to the all-powerful Chairman's whims and tempestuous moods. Under Deng, however, it transformed into a sort of 'bureaucratic machine' (Wang's words), working and existing in a privileged space in society, but at least a delineated one. The Party's search for new sources of legitimacy resulted in its depending almost entirely on economic growth. It was the importance of this that became the mantra of leaders from Jiang Zemin onwards. Wang was rewarded by being enfranchised by the CCP establishment and becoming a member of the CPPCC, a body of about 3,000 individuals meeting once a year around the time of the NPC in Beijing and 'advising' them.

Wang's critique had a sting in its tail. What was the authentic voice of Chinese modernity that managed to escape the taunt of being

borrowed from or derivative of the West? This struggle to create something from within China's own intellectual traditions was a long-term
one, dating back to the final years of the Qing dynasty more than a
century before. The desire to have a viewpoint rooted in Chinese cultural identity was strong in the works of figures like Wang and some
of the other leftists ranged around him, such as fellow academics Pan
Wei and Qin Hui. These figures had political and social traction when
they fired back at the external critics of China during and after the
Beijing Olympics of 2008, arguing that after the financial crisis the
West had neither the moral nor the political right to start doling out
lectures to anyone else. The West, after all, had bullied, subverted and
cheated China throughout almost the entire period after the 1840s
and the First Opium War. To have the West, and in particular Europe
and the United States, reinvent itself as a supporter of universalist
values after its brutal colonizing history was nothing more than blatant
hypocrisy. For Wang and those sympathetic to him it was easier to see
the West not as some great exemplar, but, in a more complicated way,
as an unreliable, changeable partner that China had no choice but
to work with but did not need to have some vast cultural inferiority
complex towards. The antagonism towards purportedly Western values
and ideas by the Maoist radical leftists in China and their urging of
China to rely on itself have not, therefore, wholly evaporated since the
Cultural Revolution. Modern theorists, like Wang, simply articulate
these themes in a much more sophisticated and elegant way.

The images of Maoism are powerful: ecstatic students lovingly
looking at their great leader during his dawn appearances at the
great rallies of a million or more that filled Tiananmen Square in
the late 1960s – he was the red sun in people's hearts, a figure who
attracted religious levels of adoration. One of the seminal moments
of the Red Guard movement, the groups of anarchic revolutionary
students that were a characteristic of the era, was when student
Song Binbin pinned an armband with the characters representing
the name 'Red Guard' onto Chairman Mao's arm. This was taken
as a sign that Mao sanctioned the legitimacy of the movement. The
result was the unleashing of activism across the country. Almost half

a century later, in January 2014, Song Binbin, the daughter of Song Renqiong, one of the 'Eight Immortals' who had been instrumental in the foundation of the CCP and its rise to power, stood in a middle school in Beijing and apologized for her actions during the Cultural Revolution. In early August 1966 the group she had belonged to had beaten and then poured boiling water on the deputy head of their school, leaving the woman to die. 'I did not [intervene] but was unable to prevent the violence towards Principal Bian and other school staff,' Song stated. 'If we do not thoroughly understand and examine the mindset behind the entire Cultural Revolution era, similar incidents will happen again.'[48]

Song typifies a generation that is still recovering from the bittersweet ecstasy of Mao, and the intense love that many Chinese felt towards him during his life, along with the highly conflicted feelings they now have when confronted with increasing evidence of the terrifying costs of many campaigns he inspired and endorsed. A sledgehammer attack on Mao is unlikely to be helpful. He remains a contradictory and complex figure with whom historians inside and outside China will be wrestling for decades, if not centuries. But for those who invoke his name in the China of Xi Jinping, as this chapter has tried to make clear, there are no easy narratives and frameworks to fall into.

Broadly, Maoists who exist today can be divided into three groups. The first and most problematic are those who appeal to Mao as a great nationalist icon, a representative of a strong, vibrant China that would no longer be pushed around, and a restorer of the country's dignity who could tell the rest of the world to leave China to its own devices. This group of Maoists aims for the same kind of emotional mobilization and appeal as provocateurs anywhere. Its members love the Chairman's genius at image manipulation and his ability to speak directly to the agricultural grass roots of the country. They take great inspiration from Mao, and from his message to stand opposed to the West, with its bullying, manipulative, treacherous track record towards China, for the West to leave them alone and respect them. Those around Utopia are typical of this group.

Those in the second group are more ideological and have firm ideas about the role of the state and the command economy. For them, the real issue is the galloping inequality in China since reform, with the very people the revolution of 1949 was meant to serve – farmers, the proletariat and the underclass – being pushed even deeper into debt and deprivation, their social welfare decimated, as the state has disappeared from people's lives and left ordinary Chinese to fend for themselves. For this group, of which there are representatives right at the top of the CCP, the core mission is to support the role of the state and its political guidance by the CCP. The reformist language of someone like Wen Jiabao and his desire to liberalize the economy even further are anathemas to those in this camp.

The third group of Maoists contains those with a more political mission. For them, Maoist Communism has been a source of unity and strength for the Party, and without it China would be disunited and weak. The CCP therefore must maintain the unique role it had in society under Mao and not lose sight of its original political mission: to create a rich, strong, socialist country, a country where socialism serves China's mission to be stable and modern, but with the Party at the centre and its monopoly on power still uncontested. The political Maoists mix some of the elements of nationalism and ideology, but their focus is ultimately more Leninist – without control of power the Party is nothing, and without the Party China will fail.

For all their differences, there is one thing that the Maoists of modern China, whether they be supporters of Bo Xilai or radical grass-roots figures who support the Cultural Revolution, have in common: a desire to invoke the historic capital of the Great Helmsman and derive legitimacy from him. Despite all the changes in China over the last decades, this at least has remained the same. Mao remains as elusive a figure as he was during his life. The Red Guard groups during the Cultural Revolution, who fought hard to claim they alone represented his views and were acting according to his stipulations, differ little from the myriad of 'Maoists' who exist now, loudly stating that they are his real heirs. For outsiders, however, the spectrum that they cover, from those who assert they are supportive of true democracy to those who want a stronger dictatorship of the proletariat, and those who want more equality in society and greater social justice, remains bewildering. Mao's divisiveness and contentiousness therefore remain decades after his death, and his living legacy shows that he will continue to be as problematic a figure in the future as he was when he was alive.

For Xi, the Maoists are a threat because they are like subscribers to the old faith – people who have a rationale for opposing further marketization, and who speak to the resentments of a large constituency in China who feel that they have not benefited from the reform process. More dangerously, Maoists can appeal to the ways in which the former leader ran a Party that was largely clean: untainted by the temptation of wealth, and ideologically pure. Their critique of China as now being run by venal, self-interested bureaucrats who look after their own is, all too often, true. This gives the Maoist leftists moral and intellectual power. They exist therefore as the sole true pillar of opposition that the current leaders have to fight with great care. That a figure like Bo Xilai was able to stir up so much support and pose such deep problems necessitating extreme actions against him shows how potent this 'fifth column' in the Party is. If one of Xi's colleagues were ever to try to appeal to the Maoist inheritance, and succeed in gaining internal and public traction, then Xi would be in deep trouble.

ONLY CONNECT: WHAT JOINS THE LINKS

When we assemble the kinds of relationships around Xi, are we left with an ad hoc assembly of people whose sole connection to one another is that they just happen to know him, or do we find something cohesive and coherent? Perhaps the best way to try to answer this is to divide relationships for a politician into those that are emotional, those that are rational or functional, and those that are intellectual. Each has an important role to play. For Xi, his relationship with his wife Peng Liyuan is the most strongly emotional one. It is presented by state propaganda in that light, something unusual for contemporary Chinese leaders. In addition to this, she deals with what could be broadly categorized as 'soft' issues – either through her singing career, or through her support for humanitarian causes as a UN goodwill ambassador. Xi's relationships with low-key advisors and private secretaries are rational or functional in nature. With these people, he has a network of implementers, people who do his will and carry out his instructions, simply making things happen. But their role is not to initiate. That belongs to the intellectual allies – the people who think in ways that appeal to Xi and that have influence on his language, and on the policies into which he puts political capital. The final realm of relationships belongs somewhere between all of these: the political peers he works with, like Wang Qishan – people who have the most autonomy in some ways, but who need to be tied to Xi, and he to them, by bonds that override these issues of autonomy and self-directed action. Politicians have an emotional, rational and intellectual role. They are the most difficult to categorize. All of these relationship types are dynamic. Xi has the ability to harm these people, but they also have the power to harm him. He could manipulate the removal of his Politburo colleagues via anti-corruption probes. He could divorce or separate from Peng. He could dismiss his private secretaries. But in each case, he risks creating powerful enemies or damaging his own reputation. Power is always a two-way street.

The assets relationships provide are control, predictability and trust. Trust in an opaque system is a rare quality. The system itself lacks rules and processes. Things can be overridden by capricious human whim. The greatest problem with this is that it creates uncertainty for everyone, including the person overriding the rules who begins to believe the only reason they are obeyed is through fear rather than loyalty. Even Mao became corroded by paranoia and lack of trust towards the end of his career when the only rules seemed to emanate from him alone. Any politician is therefore on a constant quest to create more stability and certainty around him or her through forging alliances, obligations, debts and bonds based on more than just fear. Promises are made, alliances forged, debts incurred, patronage created. This at least sets in place some predictable bonds. Family relationships are among the most dependable because they are the hardest to walk away from – but they are also the most easy to exploit, and for that reason carry costs and danger. Like money in a financial system, trust is the currency of political systems, the common factor that needs to exist for transactions even to be possible. When trust disappears, the system seizes up.

There is little doubt that the CCP in recent decades has suffered from a trust deficit. Its edicts have not been believed. Its dramatic changes in policy and ideology before and after 1978 have necessitated constant explanation, yet have largely left confusion. The lack of openness about its finances and its personnel appointments has given the lie to its public professions of being a force for transparency. On top of all of this is the issue of its use of violence, particularly in 1989, to resolve issues on which it does not get its own way. In seeking to govern in a different way after the political and social costs of these old techniques have become too great, Xi has to deploy other methods. His most important step along this route is to create more trust, and from that loyalty – the most usable outcome of trust. Here, linking himself and his vocation or leadership role directly to the Party mission, for instance, is hugely helpful. Emotionally recruiting people to the long-term hope of creating a great nation that trumps their parochial, short-term aims is another method. Loyalty is the philosopher's stone in the Chinese system, something that the Party is on a constant mission to create. It makes the impossible possible, and the fiendishly difficult easy.

Many decades ago, just before he was felled in the 1950s anti-rightist purge, the great journalist Liu Binyan pointed out that loyalty is a double-edged sword.[49] It is a highly personal thing, and one of the few areas in which humans can truly exercise free choice and autonomy. We can be forced to comply, but loyalty has to come freely. And while forced compliance carries constant costs in terms of surveillance and discipline, loyalty's greatest attraction for a politician is precisely that it is given freely but has such strong bonds. The problem is that it is very difficult to acquire. There are many who would agree with the late Liu in feeling that the Party has wandered far from its original mission and the time when it was probably most trusted. It has become divorced from the simplicity of its founding beliefs. Worst of all, it has in the last 40 years become engorged with wealth, allowing its 'priesthood' to grow fat and arrogant and to lose its link with the people. What are people loyal to these days: the Party, or its wealth?

This gives the sense of emergency that Xi often speaks about some context. The Party must not only profoundly change its behaviour to gain this trust and loyalty, but also be seen to do so. It must undertake painful transformations, almost submitting itself to public flagellation, so that it looks worthy of people's loyalty. This is a lofty mission. But it makes some sense at least when one looks at the people ranged most closely around Xi. For Wang Qishan, for thinkers like Wang Huning and Liu He, reform means creating a sense of national purpose, a national mission. This might not offer the promises of a transcendent god and everlasting life, but it does at least give some succour and inspiration beyond parochial links and networks and the chasing of short-term gain. The CCP, the world's most successful creator of material wealth and prosperity in modern times, therefore, confronts a very old problem: how to try to create something new and ambitious while not jeopardizing what it already has. Finding a way to gain the 'higher kind of loyalty' that Liu Binyan wrote of is a very real issue. For Xi, the challenge is somehow to do this. Ideas for how depend on the close circle around him, the most representative figures of which I have described in this chapter.

4

THE POLITICAL PROGRAMME OF XI JINPING

> *When the Way prevails in your own land, count it a disgrace to be needy and obscure; when the Way does not prevail in your land, then count it a disgrace to be rich and honoured.*
>
> —***Analects*** **8.13**

In 1957, at a key moment in his rule, Mao Zedong issued his famous proclamation 'How to handle contradictions among the people'. China had already been under socialist rule for nearly a decade, yet the tensions between different forces in society remained. In some areas they had intensified. Looking back to ancient Daoist philosophy, Mao had dabbled with embracing the contradictions at the heart of his world outlook over most of the last two decades. Once in power, he could carry that contradictoriness into practice. It suited his mercurial nature.

Mao, however, was only contributing to a well-established tradition, one which took as its fundamental premise that China had problems which were soluble, and that an overarching strategic approach was the means to address these. If you nailed down the fundamental intellectual approach, then you could address the problems, and things could be cured. The idea that there was a political truth that the Party was pursuing and that would practically unleash the potential of the country was something that did not change even after Mao's death. Deng only formulated a different aspect of this truth, as did Jiang and Hu. They were making contributions to a great and continuing tradition. One day, the truth would be found. But until then, there was the continuing struggle, the pursuit, the aspiration to get better and better, daily, yearly, through each decade, and to continue seeking the 'perfecting' of modernity, with Chinese characteristics.

Locating Xi within this tradition helps us to understand the very programmatic nature of his 'political' mission. Modern Chinese leaders are not tied to electoral cycles in which parties come and go, and in which the terms of their rule can disappear in an evening once the electorate has spoken. They can inherit what previous leaderships have done, and then mould it according to their assessment of the new historic opportunities and challenges. Undermining and attacking the Party as it was before them is not in their interests. Claiming that they are evolving, developing, dynamically directing it to better deliver its core aims is what they have to do.

In his decade in power, Hu Jintao had talked increasingly about the need to pursue scientific development, and to create, by 2020, a moderately prosperous society, where per capita GDP would be double that of a decade before. This was one of the 'centenary goals' that Xi inherited. The question he and those around him have had to address is how best to achieve it. Unlike in democracies, where manifestos get produced before votes are cast, in modern China the leadership succession happens and then manifestos appear, though never as documents competing with other visions of what should be done. They are, instead, expressions of consensus among the elite, who have to take responsibility for their delivery and implementation. There is another way in which they also have to show consensus. They must remain consistent with the course of Party rule before, in the decades since it has been in power. The Party that was once one of disruptive revolution is now the servant of peaceful evolution.

THE THIRD PLENUM: WHAT XI STANDS FOR

The moments at which the Party declares its intentions to the world are usually National Congresses or plenums. These are its great set pieces, during which it can, as a body, speak of itself to itself and to others. Plenums, held yearly, when the Central Committee meets, articulate themes. They tell the story of the Party, and illuminate its intentions. Vestiges of the days when state planning was de rigueur, in the modern era they have become useful in the mission of informing Chinese, and the outside world, of the Party's core political programme. They have a strategic signposting function. Under Hu, they were used in a less intrusive way. But for Xi, the October 2013 plenum, the third under the National Congress that saw him appointed, had exploitable potential.

In December 1978, during the Third Plenum of a previous National Congress, cadres who had survived the bitter years of the Cultural Revolution gathered to sound, even if quietly, the death knell of Maoist idealism. Two years after the dictator's death, there was now enough space for them to declare a new direction. They did it in language so densely filled with the tone and rhetoric of the old period that it took a while for the rest of the world to understand what they had said. But within a few months, foreign capital started to flow into China, joint ventures with foreign enterprises were allowed, a market started to appear and entrepreneurialism was reborn. All of these would have been cause for severe punishment and state intervention only a few years before. Now they were tolerated, and even encouraged. But it was delivered without loud proclamations, in the dreary, sleepy language of a simple Party meeting. It happened with no one paying too much attention to it. In this way, the many who might have opposed it were, at least temporarily, taken by surprise. Deng was the master not of using exciting violence or mass campaigns to get his way, but of using stultifying boredom. It proved a devastatingly effective strategy.

REFORM: THE GOLDEN WORD

For Xi, evidently more of a showman than his predecessor, the precedent of the great Third Plenum more than three decades before was worth reminding people about and gaining some dramatic momentum from. The issue now was how to launch a new era of reform – a 'Chinese reform 2.0', as it were, where the Party, without the messy business of elections, would seek a new mandate. 'Only socialism can save China,' Xi wrote in his explanatory note for the Third Plenum statement after its conclusion, 'and only reform and opening up can develop China, socialism and Marxism.'[1] Deng in his Southern Tour in 1992 had said that there was reform or perdition. Everyone agreed that reform was still necessary. But as thinkers from the Central Party School in Beijing had pointed out in 2007, in a book setting out a blueprint for China's future, reform is a wholesome, good word, something everyone likes. It appeals to people's optimism, to their sense that things will get better and change, and that tomorrow will be better than today. The issue, as ever, was what kind of reform: where, how fast, and in what way. And reform always brought with it winners and losers. There was inevitably a cost to pay. Politics is often about trying to negotiate about who will pay, and how, spreading the risks and the burdens today, with the promise of returns sometime tomorrow, or in the future. Just as the Chinese government was forever investing in the fixed assets and infrastructure of the country, and Chinese people were saving vigorously because of their worries about the future and the need to one day pay for health care or deal with misfortune on their own, so reform showed that this faith was worth having, that it was something people could invest in. The hopes about the future are perhaps the Party's greatest asset, not the vast quantities of US currency in its central reserves.

China today, as Xi declared in his preamble to the explanatory note, is dealing with the challenges of 'unbalanced, uncoordinated and unsustainable development'. This was not a new criticism. Wen Jiabao had said as much in 2007.[2] China's growth model was high-maintenance. No country had ever managed to sustain this speed and extent of development. It was forever hungry: for resources, for energy, for people's labour and for natural assets. China's environment had paid a colossal price for the most epic industrialization the world had ever seen. And while the fruits of this model had been impressive – no starvation, rising levels of prosperity, manufacturing that sent exports flooding across the rest of the world and a vast machine of GDP growth that never seemed to slow down or rest – there was always the worry that one day this enormous juggernaut would stop. Then the Party would need something more than GDP. The magic growth figure needed to be replaced by other incentives. And the Chinese people would grow tired of investing forever in the future. They would demand some benefits now, for today.

Already, over 2012 and into 2013, the all-important GDP figure was creeping downwards. Kept above 8 per cent for most of the last two decades, it had acquired almost mystical importance. GDP was the figure that answered every criticism and word of dissent. Those wanting to criticize the Party or challenge its legitimacy had to face this down. The simple fact was that the Party had become the greatest wealth-creation machine the world had ever known. More formidable than a corporation like Apple, faster than the United States, the United Kingdom or Germany had ever been, outpacing even its ostensive models like South Korea, Japan or Taiwan, it now stood not as a place modelled on others but as a model in its own right. However, Party strategists knew well that the CCP had always to remain a step ahead of problems, pre-empting and keeping on top of emerging issues. This was one of its key functions: to be a risk-assessment entity, to try to map out scenarios for the future so that it had at least some ideas for dealing with issues as they arose. Provincial leaders, from whose training ground national elite leaders came, were predominantly crisis managers. There was no patience in Beijing, as previous chapters have shown, for people coming to say they couldn't handle what was thrown at them. Their priority was to bring only good news to the centre. China might say it is an innovation culture, but unlike truly innovative environments, it has no tolerance for failure. Far from being about reform or perdition, the CCP of Xi is much simpler: success or perdition.

In the final statement coming from the Third Plenum, Xi took the unusual step of issuing the aforementioned personal explanatory note, affixed to the main document with its 60 commitments to reform. This in itself is a remarkable sign of control and authority. Party documents under his predecessors stood on their own. They needed no parallel text explaining what it was they said. It was considered self-explanatory and needed no further elaboration. But for Xi, there was an opportunity to translate the Party's generic language into a more personal one, to show ownership over it. If there is a political manifesto for him, then this explanatory note provides that. It is a document produced from a mindset of conviction to inculcate conviction in those reading it. And going one better than Mao, whose 1957 proclamation about contradictions among the people had contained ten key points, Xi came up with 11 core areas.

1. THE MARKET

The market was once the most dangerous, the most outlawed of things in China. After the revolution of 1949, the state quickly and effectively moved into almost every area of the economy. By 1957, 99 per cent of economic activity was prescribed by the central state, and then controlled by its national and local agents. Those who kept small plots of land on which they produced goods either to sell or to give to neighbours in order to procure favours were therefore guilty of crimes. They were entrepôt capitalists, enemies of the state. Those who were accused of this suffered.

Central bureaucratic control of the economy was one of the main culprits behind the disasters of the Great Leap Forward and the famines that followed. Inefficiencies were omnipresent. Although China through the Maoist period maintained an annual growth rate of more than 5 per cent, it did so from a low base, and on the basis of terrible sacrifice and human suffering. The 1978 reforms embraced some marketization. They allowed farmers to sell surpluses back to the state. They allowed price reform, so that shops could buy from whomever they wanted. There were modest attempts to allow competition, with different kinds of companies set up. Gradually, over the 1980s, the role of the market increased. It became easier to set up private companies, and to secure different forms of loans, even if these were from underground credit sources. The grand work-unit system was slowly disbanded; SOEs were scaled back and prices liberalized. With the country's entry to the WTO in 2001, the market extended across sectors, and was so gargantuan that, more often than not, it made China seem like a vast haggling bazaar. People were able to buy and sell pretty much as they wanted, with prices determined by the market, not the state, except in core areas like utilities. Even so, the philosophical issues that marketization posed were ones that the more left wing in the Party and the elite kept returning to, as was explained in Chapter 3.

These leftist brickbats had little impact on the mainstream view, which was to accept the argument that the market remained the most efficient way to allocate resources, even though some restraints were placed on it. The state still ran some strategic SOEs, and set some prices. When necessary, it intervened, with control maintained over currency rates, interest rates and sources for loans. It was able to effect control through what economist Yasheng Huang called a 'political pecking order' whereby state companies were given beneficial treatment, had access to the best government procurement contracts and generally got a much more favourable deal.[3] China was a hybrid economy, one that showed some characteristics of a market, but in which the state still had a visible and prominent role.[4] The most obvious sign of this was in the production of Five-Year Programmes, macroeconomic documents plotting the key strategic directions and priorities for the Chinese economy in the coming years.

In the Party's narrative, China since 1978 had been engaged in building the 'primary stage of socialism'. The learning Party, as Hu and Xi had called it, was focusing on how to manage the relationship between the government and the market. Throughout the 2000s, the non-state sector had become increasingly prominent. By 2012, despite its continuing lack of real political enfranchisement (there were no representatives of non-state companies in 2012 on the Central Committee), it was the key ally for growth. More than half of GDP was from non-state entities. They were starting to send more investment abroad. They were among the few truly innovative

Chinese companies. They were employing rising numbers of people. They were, therefore, actors that could not be ignored in a period of falling GDP rates, where the Party could no longer be picky about where it wanted growth to come from.

To make the market figure not just preferential for growth, but essential, as the 2013 Third Plenum did, was a major ideological innovation. This statement had never appeared before, in any Party document. At the heart of this was a new vision of the relationship between government and the economy. 'It means,' Xi stated,

> that the main responsibility and role of government is to maintain the stability of the macroeconomy, strengthen and improve public services, ensure fair competition, strengthen market oversight, maintain market order, promote sustainable development, and common prosperity, and intervene in situations where market failure occurs.[5]

This can be called the basic contract between government and society that Xi was proposing. The other points flow from this ideological basis.

2. SMASH THE STATE ENTERPRISES

The market matters because it is the most neutral weapon against one of the greatest impediments to growth that Xi's China faces: the way that SOEs have been taken over by parasitical, selfish networks milking them for personal profit and in effect stealing from the state. Xi stated as the second prong of reform that the government will 'vigorously develop the mixed-ownership economy'. At the heart of this was a commitment 'to improve the state assets-management system'.[6] That involved the need to 'establish a system of professional managers', improve governance of state companies and strengthen investigations into their accountability, and ensure that the robbery of their profits ceases.

SOEs had been a target of reform since the Zhu Rongji era in the late 1990s, when more than 60 million of their employees had been laid off and many of their welfare functions reduced or abolished. For much of the early Hu period from 2002, they were put under greater competitive pressure by changes brought about by China's entry to the WTO. Grouped into 75 key conglomerates, state assets were managed by a central ministry. Through the lead-up to 2008, they seemed to become less important as the non-state sector grew in confidence and stature. But with the Global Financial Crisis of 2007–8, the SOEs made a remarkable comeback. While the rest of the world was reeling through falling growth and liquidation of assets, China's SOEs figured as a line of defence, one that produced dependable and increasingly strong growth, something extremely welcome as export markets collapsed and China felt the chill winds of the global recession. Figures like arch-conservative Wu Bangguo were emboldened enough to declare during the NPC in both 2010 and 2011 that the SOEs had been utterly irreplaceable for China during this period of crisis, and a proof that state control was always best. 'We do not do privatization,' he declared.[7]

SOEs are crucial for the Party state because of one quality: they produce the profits that bankroll it. Personal taxation and non-state and foreign-company tax receipts make up less than half of the overall fiscal revenue for the central government: SOEs contribute half on their own. Their bottom line, therefore, links so intimately to that of the government that they could almost be said to be one and the same. Their prosperity is shared. So too are their failures. SOEs are the central government's ATM. High profits from resource companies and major energy and finance entities have been politically as well as economically crucial. And for a few years from 2008, these profits were strong. A leader of China, beyond his political functions, has to be constantly mindful of the health of SOEs and their profitability. In that sense, therefore, Xi truly resembles a company CEO, not just the leader of a political party.

Despite this, SOEs have three major issues. The first is that their profits have been built on subsidies. They do not pay market rates for utilities or for land, and often avoid paying full rates for wages. SOEs are profitable because of the favourable conditions given to them not only in these areas, but also because they are protected from competition. They are destined to be profitable. Despite this, to come to the second issue, they have delivered less profit in the period from 2011 onwards. As China's growth rate has fallen, so have theirs, almost proving the suggestion made above that the state's and the SOEs' bottom lines are the same. Whereas the non-state sector produced 7 per cent profits on its turnover, the SOEs only managed a little more than 5 per cent in the first half of 2013.[8] Once net contributors to growth, they now figure as a drag.

Part of this drop in profitability might be due to inefficient deployment of capital and resources, or poor management. But, to come to the third issue, there is a more sinister side. SOEs have been a source of not just economic inefficiencies in recent years, but also political ones. They have become protectorates of vested interest, where vast off-balance profits have disappeared into the aether, some of them channelled through overseas offshore bank accounts, others going into the informal economy, and many of them into the hands of sections of the elite who have become parasites, feasting on these SOE profits at the same time as they erode them. This must rank as the largest golden goose in history ever to be slaughtered.

The man most closely associated with this process is a former Politburo Standing Committee member, Zhou Yongkang. Effectively head of domestic security from 2007 to 2012 through his chairmanship of a body called the Central Political and Legal Affairs Commission, Zhou had previously enjoyed a career in the state petroleum sector, which lasted for more than a decade and a half. Many of his associates were still within the broader energy sector, illustrating vividly the overly close relationship between those who were ostensibly regulators, officials and business people. Often these could occupy one body. Zhou was the emperor of this self-contained realm, one that was so overwhelmed by illicit money that some estimates put the embezzled amounts as high as almost US$ 15 billion.[9]

Zhou had added insult to injury by showing disloyalty during the fall of Bo Xilai in early 2012. He alone, according to some reports, had opposed the removal of his Politburo colleague. More egregious than this, he had even contemplated direct opposition to Xi. Rumours circulated that Xi's disappearance in September 2012 was due to a coup attempt. There were even more elaborate stories of a small insurrection occurring of groups loyal to Zhou. Whatever the truth of these, by 2014 Zhou himself was placed under formal investigation, and was then accused and found guilty of corruption and fornication. Open denunciation by the Party was remarkable: never before had a former member of the Standing Committee been investigated for corruption in this way. It was a remarkable testament either to Xi's faith in himself, or to his folly. He had basically set a new precedent, one that others could invoke in the future: even retired leaders can be targeted.

For all the drama around this issue, the market is the most powerful means of targeting the cancer at the heart of SOEs. Market discipline weans them off subsidies and prepares them for a brave new world where they will need, domestically and internationally, to stand on their own two feet. SOEs will have to become profitable and deliver better returns to the Party. The invisible hand of the market lies at the heart of this. And this invisible hand is the most neutral, apolitical tool to smash the vested interest that has clawed SOEs to its side and deprived them of their former prowess in profitability. The simple fact is that the market has to wean the venal networks off the drug of subsidies they have become addicted to. Market forces, therefore, are also strategic weapons, part of an armoury that Xi has called into action.

3. TAX THE RICH!

Tax is one of the ultimate expressions of state power: insidious, almost silent, and yet, as Benjamin Franklin pointed out three centuries ago, the only certain thing in life apart from death. But the equation 'taxation leads to representation' is one that worries the CCP. For as it seeks to modernize the tax base for the government, and reform its largely centralized fiscal system, it also has to contemplate a world in which the taxpaying private citizens of China will start to demand more for their direct payments to the government.

In the past, Chinese citizens' low wages were compensated for by free social welfare, housing, lifelong employment and a hundred other things, large and small. But reform has changed this. The state has withdrawn. Wages, however, have remained low, largely because of the government's obsession with investment. As stated earlier, the government has mobilized people through messages selling them access to a better future for themselves and their children in return for pain today. But as a number of nasty conflicts spreading across China that focus on wage settlements have made clear, it is an irrefutable fact that, these days, appeals to the greater social good and self-sacrifice are of little interest: Chinese people want to earn more for themselves, not see their contribution go into some vast collective pot.

The way the informal economy artificially raises the value of people's money keeps a lid on things at the moment. Cash reigns. Most goods are paid for without ever figuring on a tax spreadsheet. Many companies and enterprises pay for services in kind, precisely to avoid tax. Chinese, more than most, have a visceral dislike of seeing their money disappear into the pockets of unaccountable, strutting officials. But part of the pact of modernity is that private tax payment is on the horizon. And a new contract will need to be forged between the people and the rulers as this happens.

Part of this involves the fiscal distribution of power in China. The central government in the end calls many of the shots. This is the source of its authority. Provinces can go their own way on many issues, but on raising taxes, and in the payment burden to the central government, they are part of a tied system. In the recent past, cash-strapped local authorities could seek revenue from land sales, forcing low compensation on farmers they could then ship off, often with immense conflict and contention, to new cities. But land has limits, and most of it has been sold and developed. State banks at local level were another soft target, forced or induced to make vast, generous loans to local governments that often had no ability or intention of repaying them. But as government debt levels rose above 200 per cent, this avenue too was squeezed shut.

Local governments cannot be left high and dry in terms of funding. They, after all, are the frontline of the state. Their loathed officials are the ones who impose the most unpopular policies, for which they have been rewarded with some of the worst satisfaction and trust levels in the whole Chinese system. Xi knows these problems. After all, he started his career at the most basic level of government. In this respect, he is unique among his Standing Committee peers. As one official said to me in late 2014: 'Mr Xi knows the tricks of local-government officials, because he used to be one!' Responsible for increasing amounts of social welfare, in an attempt to keep a lid on a country becoming more contentious, where people have rising demands, local governments cannot fail. They need to be given a better fiscal deal. And the realistic means of doing this is raising taxes from the greatest current untapped source of these – the people. Tax levels in China for individuals, while high on paper, are in reality relatively depressed because wage levels are low, and many daily costs like utilities are subsidized.

The emergence of Chinese who pay higher and more representative rates of tax, and of fiscally more autonomous localities in China, is one of the most difficult issues the country now faces. Both potentially erode the powers of the centre. Chinese leaders go to great lengths to assert the unity of their country. Yet plenty have pointed out how it often looks more like a continent, rather than a unified nation state.[10] Fiscal unity is the greatest bond linking the provinces and autonomous regions. But the dynamics of China's different areas are radically different. Various models have been used over the decades, balancing the imperatives for control from the centre and the desire for regions to have more independence. But the elite stand by the formula that fragmentation equals weakness, and that they must guard against this with everything they have. Federalism, one of the possible ideas proposed to Chinese leaders, has become a dirty word. And among the most important lessons of the collapse of the USSR was that once the ideological glue holding a country disappears, governance starts to weaken and parts of a country break away. This is the price paid by those who cease to believe. Believers in Communism in China reap the rewards of strong, strategic, centralized leadership in the area that matters – resources and budgets. Non-believers have none of this, and follow a path to failure.

Provinces, with their different wealth levels, have varying arrangements with the centre. Some, mostly on the coast, are net tax contributors. But in the poorer western regions, they are revenue burdens. Subsidies and subventions flow their way. Tibet is a good example. A region of sparse population and low industrialization, it has one of the lowest GDP per capita rates in the country. Ma Rong, an expert on the region based at Beijing University, has argued that in 2008 more than 90 per cent of the autonomous region's government revenue came from the centre.[11] Other provinces, the most prominent of them Zhejiang, where Xi used to be Party secretary, encourage inward investment from their own enterprises into Tibet. Those who wander around Lhasa will see Zhejiang-linked construction sites. But they will also see many workers from neighbouring Sichuan Province. This is a mixed blessing. They come, work on the infrastructure projects and contribute to the economic development of the area. But they also tend to take away the profits and funds they receive when they return back to their homes, 1,000 or so kilometres to the south. In that way, the impressive sums of central money in fact tend to flow through the autonomous region, rather than staying there.[12]

Taxation is one of the fundamental powers of the central state. Allowing provincial leaders to have more influence in this area would be a big risk. It would create the sense for some that they were really independent, and embolden them. Some might argue about the ways in which they are net contributors to the central coffers, and start aggressively haggling for a better deal. 'The main aim of the reform,' Xi stated, 'is to clearly define authority of office, reform of the taxation system, make tax burdens stable and budgets transparent, and increase efficiency.'[13] Balancing the incentivizing element of taxation powers given to local governments with the danger that it might also create division and tensions is one of the most difficult challenges for Beijing.

But the current structure, in which budgets for very local issues are decided by bureaucrats in a surprisingly small central-ministry machine thousands of kilometres away, is probably the *least* efficient system. Estimates that perhaps no more than 1,500 officials in Beijing have the real authority to sign off on these disbursements demonstrate that beyond the Central Committee and the Party structures supplying the political mandate, substantial power is held by a small group of purse-string holders.[14] These people, in effect, fiscally run the country. And they too would have a powerful vested interest in defending themselves against any dilution of their powers. More than the corrupt officials, they are probably the most significant opponents to deep structural reform, because they would need to implement new procedures.

4. THE RISE OF URBAN CHINA

In its collective memory, for the overwhelming majority of its history China has been a country dominated by the rural areas. Up to as recently as the 1990s, more than 80 per cent of the population lived in the countryside. In the Mao period, they were people who had a separate residence status, holding a different *hukou*, and were allowed different kinds of social welfare and public goods.[15] Rural China caused the Mao revolution to succeed. It was from here that the CCP's early generation of leadership originally came, and where its army was recruited. Communism with Chinese characteristics is, in essence, a proletariat revolution fought and secured by rural, not urban, forces.

It is therefore a remarkable transformation that China is now on the cusp of being an urban country, where, according to the 2010 census, as many live in the new towns and cities as live in the hundreds of thousands of villages. This process will accelerate. For the new economy that Xi and his colleagues want, one in which consumption and services represent a higher proportion of GDP and from which a new kind of citizen will emerge, one who is homeowning and taxpaying, a stakeholder in the system who will defend it because of what he or she stands to lose if it ceases to exist, cities are the future.

In the years since 1978, China has probably built more cities more quickly than any other country that has ever existed. More than 260 cities have populations of over a million. Places like Beijing, Shanghai and Guangzhou link with neighbouring centres to create megacities. The 23 million residents in the 640 square kilometres of the Shanghai municipal area increase by half a million each year. The CCP might have been brought victory by the blood, sweat and tears of rural folk, but in its heart it has always been vehemently pro-urban. City residents did not suffer starvation in the great famines of the early 1960s. It was China's villages that bore the brunt of this tragic time. And cities were granted greater powers to open up to the out-side world during the first phase of the reform era. Rural areas only haphazardly got similar rights. As a sign of their powerlessness, rural areas of China were given the right to hold elections, because they mattered far less than the great conurbations. Four of the municipal areas – Tianjin, Chongqing, Beijing and Shanghai – have a status on a par with provinces.

It is clear that an urban China is where the Party's vision of modern-ity will be achieved. Accelerating the growth of cities is therefore a key priority. But this has never been tried before on such a scale and so quickly. By the end of 2030, perhaps long before, 70 per cent of China's people will live in cities. The social and political ramifications of this are immense. Societies will need to be created almost from scratch, and a sense of cohesion forged among people from different areas, different cultural backgrounds and different socio-economic groups. Far from being monuments to harmony, Chinese cities could become the vastest ghettos of contention and disharmony the world has ever seen.

Shanghai is an excellent example. Ten million lived in the city in 1990 when it was finally granted SEZ status, placing it on a par with Shenzhen and the other special zones. The Pudong area, once full of dreary warehouses and agricultural land, became the mighty line of skyscrapers that visitors can stand in awe of today. But assimilating an extra 13 million people in little more than two decades has been an immense undertaking. Whole swathes of the city's suburbia are taken up with endless rows of flats and villas. Finding sustainable jobs for this influx is an immense challenge, especially as so many of them have to be in services. The demand to drive cars and have an increasingly good quality of life has to be balanced against the sheer impossibility of accommodating these desires with the current municipal infrastructure. Shanghai's car number plates are jokingly referred to by locals as the most expensive pieces of metal in the world. They are priced this high as a means of controlling the number that can drive on the city's roads, but even so, many tens of thousands each year purchase cars that then join the other 2 million already running around, snarling up the central district and the routes into it. Air quality and water supply are all under critical pressure. Socially, too, the breakneck development of the last two decades has left people breathless. Families are separated from their rural networks, and divorces are rising to levels similar to those in the West. In 2012, the story of an elderly man who died and lay undiscovered in his apartment for a number of weeks illustrated how much in China has changed. In the most networked society in the world, where family is still one of the most reliable links, isolation like this was simply unimaginable a few years before. Ageing populations have only added to the sense that, for many Chinese, the future is one where they will be uprooted, isolated and unwanted.

Urbanization cannot be achieved at the expense of an impoverished, suppressed rural China. The Xi government has to bring modernity to the Chinese countryside. 'The overwhelming majority of farmers can participate in the modernization process on an equal basis and share the fruits of modernization,' Xi promised.[16] But this will be a huge task, and one that even the current government, with its limitless ambitions, has set a four-decade timescale to bring about. China's farmers still have a tough life. Many have sought better futures in the cities, but they suffer insecurity under the *hukou* system, a hangover of state control from the Maoist period, but one that has remained trenchantly in place despite all the other changes of the last few decades. China's farmers might have been relieved of much of their tax burden by the Hu–Wen government, but they are still the source of many of the protests and grievances that have fuelled the rise in mass incidents and petitions in the last few years.

Urbanization will take a further toll too on the country's physical environment. Cities are hungry places for fuel, water and resources. Skyscrapers produce as many greenhouse gases as factories. And shifting manufacturing from urban centres out to the peripheries doesn't deal with the fundamental problem of pollution, but just relocates it. Beyond all of these issues, there are the human costs: the changes in family structure and the rise of a totally different sort of lifestyle from the deeply networked one that sociologist Fei Xiaotong described in his work – a world in which everyone knew everyone else and was interlinked, visible and therefore bound by trust. The modern urban China is a place where trust is one of the most elusive qualities, and that is a problem for the Party and the government too, as already stated.

5. DEMOCRACY, WITH CHINESE CHARACTERISTICS

Democracy is not a word that Xi or his predecessors are frightened of, as long as it is said in the right way. Under Hu and Wen, there was a growing sense that the Chinese people needed to have more participation in decision making, and tactical moves were made to achieve this. The new Labour Law and Contract Law, introduced in 2008 and 2009 respectively, were devised after online and public consultations involving feedback from many millions of respondents. Some governments, like that of Chongqing under Bo Xilai, had experimented with inviting citizens to respond to specific policies.[17] The Party holds consultations all the time, sometimes even involving foreigners. The CPPCC, a body chaired now by Yu Zhengsheng, is meant to embody this, made up locally and nationally of a broad swathe of people who are representative of civil society, business and the eight 'patriotic' political parties (that is, other than the CCP itself) that were allowed to continue a predominantly symbolic existence after the PRC was established in 1949. It is regarded widely, however, as a toothless entity, one that has little real function apart from as window dressing – giving the impression of conferring legitimacy on the Party's and the government's decisions. It does not have veto power over laws, and has no significant scrutiny powers over budgets. Even the NPC, China's parliament, has little clout in this area. The CCP has the final veto power over the consultations it takes on board or rejects. In this way it has the best of both worlds, saying that people have had the chance to speak, that their words have been listened to and that its decisions reflect their views – even if they evidently do not.

The assumption has been that as a middle class arises – with property rights, a greater tax burden and a greater vested interest in the performance of the government – it will demand more of a say in how the country is run. The issue for Xi and his generation, however, is that they see no easy political model for how China might achieve this. It is too vast, its population too complex, and the creation of consensus over the best way to achieve this too difficult. The strategy in the past was simply for the Party to say it was the repository of wisdom and dictate what was going to happen. But in the emerging urban, service-sector-oriented, modernizing country, the most challenging thing for government is not people's fears, but their expectations and hopes. People want a say in their lives. They are not passive, and have higher expectations, demanding more from the state. It is in the Party's interests therefore to try to avoid this responsibility and such expectations, and to share the risks and blame with the public, rather than to sit imperiously in the driving seat waiting for the glory when things go right – and to risk being punished when they do not.

Liberal-democratic models do not appeal to the Party. Once, there may have been naive faith in a US- or British-style system. But the Chinese elite have watched these closely and seen just how messy they can become. They may sincerely believe that the United States has a great system for itself, but evidently don't see how it can be implemented in China. This is not just about preserving the monopoly in political power of the CCP. Like many, they see the dysfunctionality of the US system, and the fractious nature of its operations, its increasing hunger for patronage and money, and the ways in which it is often unable to confront hard issues and make decisions because of divisions within itself. They wonder how it could possibly operate in China, where there is no time to practise this sort of politics. Democracy, after all, is an expensive business. Taiwan and Singapore are often offered as possible political-development models.[18] But they have populations far smaller than China's, and much higher levels of development. For all the economic changes in the last decade, there has never been consensus on what political reforms should be implemented and in what order. This remains the case so far under Xi. It may change. In his period in power, Xi may feel that he can be bolder in allowing the development of elections to townships, or even to the Party. But he has so far shown no appetite for anything radical.

On the contrary, one of the characteristics of his period in power has been a clampdown on 'dissent'. The most infamous statement of this has been 'Document no. 9', issued in March 2013 to Party cadres, and briefly leaked online before being removed. This document sits as a parallel text against the soft tone of some of Xi's other public statements. It contains seven key points of attack. Many of these are consistent with the perceived problems during the Hu and Wen period a few years before. But it has a far more prescriptive feel, reportedly meant to lay down to academics and teachers what they could and could not discuss in their classrooms. Western constitutional democracy came in at number one, which covered things like divisions of power between the judiciary, executive and legislative, multiparty systems, universal franchise for elections, and so on. Together, these ideas are branded as a 'capitalist class theory', and accused of being a 'denial of the leadership function of the Party by Western political democracy' and an 'elimination of people's democracy'. They are presented as attempts to weaken China as a nation, bringing back memories of just how enfeebled the USSR was in the 1990s by the 'reforms' foisted on it by the West, at least according to mainstream Chinese interpretations. Adoption of 'universal values' and the 'propagation of civil society', the second and third taboos respectively, are also attributed to pernicious Western political interference, trying to deny China its own distinctive history and development path. Civil society might have flourished in the post-1978 period, but suspicion within the Party that it sometimes carried hidden political purposes and destabilizing intentions never disappears. Non-governmental organizations work under onerous approval regimes, with many that had strayed into contentious areas like ethnic rights having been closed down. 'Liberalism' was the fourth, covering a multitude of sins, from 'complete marketization and privatization' (somewhat contradicting the words on the market from the Third Plenum) to 'denying the state any role whatsoever in directing and managing the economy'. Fifth was the 'propagation of Western-style news management', allowing the media to publish what it liked without control from the Party. Sixth was 'denial of Chinese Communist Party history, and the history of new China', and the last 'denying praise to the Reform process and to socialism with Chinese characteristics'.[19]

It is true that some Chinese liberals have had a proclivity for idealizing Western models. In that sense, 'Document no. 9' was a 'falling out of love' letter, a notice of separation. However harsh its language, its main attitude seemed to be to affirm, however it could, that China could find its own way and had to stand for its own values. And there was something piquantly touching about a demand to hear praise from educators about how well reform had gone and how good the Party's achievements were. Even so, academics seemed mostly bemused by the idea that this was a workable pedagogical instruction. There was something inherently contradictory in telling students to liberate their thinking and seek interesting methods and new ideas, whether in China or elsewhere, but to do so in such a straitened context. As always with these documents, it seemed that the Party elite were caught talking rather wishfully to themselves. 'Document no. 9' outlined what they wanted to happen, but it wasn't something they felt easy about the rest of the world being aware of, and indeed Gao Yu, one of the journalists who leaked the document, ended up being harassed and punished.[20]

6. REFORMING THE JUDICIARY

Lauding Mao at the same time as talking about strengthening the legal basis of society, as Xi does, is another contradiction, given that the Chairman is most closely associated with the rule of man, not of law. The legal system under Mao was a bad fiction, with courts largely run as arms of the Party, their judges former military officers and their justice summary and brutal. In 1979, a concerted attempt was made to build up a set of laws, some taken from the Japanese, others from the German continental system. Since then, China has been on a legal roller coaster, passing hundreds of laws. Implementation has always been a challenge, however. Now the country has the statutes on its books, the challenge is to build confidence in the grand courts and the personnel filling them. This was the target not only of the Third Plenum, but of the fourth, a year later.

Justice matters in modern China, despite all the talk of doing things with Chinese characteristics. While the Party sets its face against ideas of universal values, because it argues that these are skewed to Western cultural and political standards, injustice seems to transcend boundaries. People know they have been victims because they feel it, and that feeling is as rotten and debilitating in rural China as it is in New York or London. Hunger for justice is what motivates the many millions making complaints to the central government. It is what clogs up courts from local up to national level throughout China, and causes people, in the words of Yu Jianrong, to be 'explosive' with anger.[21] Injustice, even in the most functional discourse, is a source of inefficiency, causing resentment and social anger that cost money to deal with. It takes from the bottom line. And it also undermines the greatest deliverer of social and commercial efficiency, which has been talked about above: trust.

Building up trust has been a theme Xi has returned to from the moment he became general secretary in 2012 – and trust between government and people in particular. Eroded by years of venality and brutality on the part of Party officials acting with impunity, it has been exemplified by video clips on Chinese social media of Party leaders

sounding off about the poor quality of people and how they only understand coercion – something one north-eastern cadre opined over a large
plate of crabs, unwisely not checking if he was being filmed.[22] Another
case saw an official who was denied boarding a flight to Kunming
being reduced to such rage that he trashed an airport gate.[23] Perhaps
the most infamous case in the period from 2012 to 2015 was that of
an air hostess who was savagely beaten by an army officer and his wife
after she tried to pass them instructions in a plane.[24] Accountability
either comes from Web lynching or more established procedures and
legal restraints. The latter are sustainable; the former is not.

Rule of law in China is a contentious issue because it involves
considering what areas the Party might tactically cede to the control
of others. However, the idea that the Party might be subjected to the
whims of a court is not currently on the menu. Courts are part of
the universe the CCP and its unified leadership embraces. They take
their mandate from the Party, and are not there to try to hold it to
account. That it has to do on its own. Justice, however, is important
for commercial and social issues. A decent legal system clears away
unpredictability. The opacity of decision making in China has been the
bane of companies and individuals, both Chinese and non-Chinese,
for a number of years. Finding the place where decisions are made, the
person who has the power to unlock the issue, is the source of endless
lobbying efforts, and the means by which consultancy companies have
been able to ask for fat fees. Rule by law, rather than rule of law, at least
mitigates some of this. It means that institutions and the individuals
in them have to observe some ground rules.

Xi states in his explanatory note from the Third Plenum that the
current legal system is 'defective' and 'suffers a lack of credibility'.[25]
It is a machine that needs to be improved, so that the inputs and
outputs are of better quality. Economically, injustice is a source of
inefficiency. Commercial laws for Chinese and non-Chinese companies create a more level playing field, without which the 'perfecting
of the market' in China – the core mission under this plenum – will
not succeed. But as GlaxoSmithKline (GSK), one of the world's
largest pharmaceutical companies, found out from 2013 into 2014,

the rise of law with Chinese characteristics is a double-edged sword. GSK has been working in China for decades, building up a lucrative business because of the power of its brand and the importance of its intellectual property. Its drugs for treating hepatitis B, a major problem in China, are one of the mainstays of its global business. However, there are plenty of Chinese officials who look at GSK, and the good profits it makes in their country, and feel resentful. Rule of law became important to GSK when, as with the mining corporation Rio Tinto a few years before, some of its senior managers, including its country chief executive, were accused of corruption and allowing illegal deals between hospitals and the company in which prices were set above market rates.

Such collusion is unsurprising. Medicine anywhere is a high-return business. And hospitals in China are famous for overprescribing because of deals between doctors and companies. A single such deal with a hospital authority can come to millions in RMB. These sorts of backhanders are a problem for the government, because Chinese people themselves are seen as paying into the coffers of a wealthy non-Chinese company. For GSK, however, there are thorny issues of how it can stop its executives getting dragged into collusion, just as, it was claimed, the Rio Tinto personnel were a few years earlier. Under pressure to achieve huge sales targets, and in an environment in which the perception is that it is not obeying the law that matters, but making sure you keep on the right side of those implementing and judging it, GSK got pulled into murky waters. Its chief executive was bribed with a secret film of him having sex with his girlfriend. One of the consultants pulled in by the company to investigate initial claims was himself accused of acting illegally and sentenced to jail in Shanghai. And an embittered former employee, taken on to do high-level lobbying, turned whistle-blower, causing the company huge damage. GSK itself admitted liability almost immediately, paid a fine and reshaped its business. But for a company like this, almost any price to stay in China is worth paying. The market is too important, and the levels of profitability there, even if reduced, are still enough to make it worth staying.

Was rule of law being promoted through the case of GSK? No one in the company dared say they were not being treated according to the laws of the locality they were working in. But their vulnerability to being used as a political tool was obvious. Chinese-government officials could argue they were doing precisely what the outside world wanted, and making an environment in which the regulations were clearer, the dangers of violating them more real and the implementation more transparent. Even so, for many investors China remained high-risk because of the fears of national treatment, and of perverse and arbitrary punishments. Courts were places to avoid, rather than to rely on. The *culture* of legality in China is still lacking, along with all sorts of other pressures, from protectionism to lack of transparency and lack of capacity.

Justice poses another issue for Xi: it is expensive. Courts need funding, and in the case of China most of this came from provincial governments. There were immediate conflicts of interest here. Employing lawyers was expensive, training judges challenging, and getting courts to function under the weight of rising levels of litigation difficult. The Fourth Plenum proposed a philosophy of law for China, but it also looked at the issues of training, funding and improving access to justice as part of an implementation strategy. More scrutiny of death sentences passed down by local courts was announced, supporting regulations from 2012 that removed a number of crimes from the capital-punishment list. China was once accused of executing thousands each year, but the country's figures have fallen dramatically. Even so, in 2013 it was still executing more people than the rest of the world combined.[26] Occasionally, public opinion has made a difference to cases. The harrowing story of Li Yan, who was sentenced to death for the murder of her husband in 2011, is symptomatic of this. Forced to endure years of demeaning, violent behaviour by her husband, she finally snapped, killing him with a knife. Her death sentence was overturned by a higher court after appeals for clemency inside and outside China in 2014. Courts had to show that in these cases they were listening.[27]

But for those wanting to take this as an opportunity to push back the boundaries of the state and attack the Party, there was less sympathy.

Xu Zhiyong, founder of the Open Constitution Initiative (OCI), a non-government group supporting stronger constitutional rule, was an academic in Beijing who had been harassed by the authorities since 2008 when he had been associated with Liu Xiaobo's Charter 08. Regarded as a moderate and a liberal, this did not stop him from being accused of subversion and handed a three-year sentence in 2014 after a number of months in detention. A number of other rights lawyers were also victimized, from Pu Zhiqiang to Teng Biao. Xi Jinping stated that judicial departments had to 'exercise their judicial and procuratorial powers according to law, improving the judicial power operation mechanism in which rights and responsibilities are clear, improving judicial transparency and credibility, and safeguarding human rights'.[28] But justice could still be tough in China when it needed to be.

7. CORRUPTION

Any discussion of corruption in China immediately hits definitional problems. For the OECD, the standard way of speaking about corruption is to see it as officials using public positions for private gain.[29] The United States, the EU and others have passed increasingly detailed legislation against bribery and corruption. Even in these developed legislatures, corruption is a problem that resists final eradication. For China, as Xi says in his explanatory note from the Third Plenum: 'Anti-corruption forces performing functions separately make it difficult to build up synergy, some cases are not dealt with resolutely, and the accountability system is too lax to handle reoccurring corruption cases.'[30] We are back on the terrain of efficiency, and improving the great machine of governance once more. In this context, corruption is not a moral issue. It is something that impedes the Party and government in their mission to bring better outcomes. On this basis, it needs to be addressed.

While Xi has made corruption a signature theme of his administration, it is also something he has spoken about before. More than many of his peers, he has shown an instinctive understanding of the political, and not just the economic, risks of corruption. In Fujian, he avoided being dragged into the massive Yuanhua company scandal of 1997–8, which lapped at the doors of serving Politburo members. Even before this, he spoke about the dangers of corruption, and the ways in which it can erode authority and credibility. Corruption attacks two sets of assets: the material and economic, and the reputational. It erodes not only the financial capital of the CCP, but also its moral capital. It is the latter that Xi has been keener to address.

Modern China is a place where there is definitely such a thing as corruption with Chinese characteristics. Never as blatant as in India, Indonesia or other places where corruption has been highly visible and problematic, and certainly not as brutal as in Russia or Central Asian countries, it is more of a subtle undercurrent, all-pervasive, often elusive, and something that provides a constant background buzz. Officials and those they collude with have become very accomplished at covering their tracks. But the real issue has been the ways in which corrupt monies and benefits have started to build up political loyalty and allegiances that erode those towards the Party. If Xi is on a mission to forge greater loyalty both between the CCP and its members and between the Party and the people, then corruption ranks as an impediment because it sets up an alternative patronage and incentive system.

Zhou Yongkang is the cause célèbre here. If we take the narrative of the Third Plenum and the manifesto therein, Zhou's crimes start to become much clearer. The fundamental mission of the Party is to build economic strength, because that will make China fulfil its destiny as a rich, strong country. With falling growth, however, chasing after raw GDP in the old way no longer works. The market needs to be more sophisticated and sources of growth more diverse, and efficiency is a key means of achieving this. SOEs are crucial. They have to be at the forefront of resource, labour and capital efficiency. They need to work under a more rules-based system in order to do this. Having corrupt networks within or associated with the state sector that are parasitical, antagonistic and antithetical to this mission, that run against this narrative, is akin to a human body trying to function normally while stricken by a malign tumour. Corruption erodes the power and authority of the Party. Once it was a cheap means for incentivizing and recruiting people, and could be tolerated. But now the fat years of easy growth are over, and with them the tolerance of corruption.

If there is no rule of law outside that sanctioned by the Party, however, how can this new environment of compliance be forged? How can the Party police itself, when it lets no one outside it scrutinize its standards and the ways these are implemented? Xi often talks of the need to change the culture of the Party, and to allow its cadres to internalize their role as one akin to that of a modern Communist priesthood: self-sacrificing, working for the good of the people and devoted to its cause. But this is a difficult belief for outsiders to maintain when elite leaders are seen to be operating according to different standards. More often than not, corruption is about perception. This is the way organizations like Transparency International (TI) tend to judge it. According to TI's 'Corruption Perceptions Index' for 2014, which ranks countries and territories based on how corrupt their public sector is perceived to be, with one being the least and 175 being the most corrupt, China comes an underwhelming 100th.[31] Xi the politician has to deal with the perception issue somehow. The first tactic has been to show, in Maoist fashion, that the 3,000-strong governing super-elite are being purged and cleaned up, so they can be a vanguard of proper behaviour.

Visiting the CDIC, the body mandated with this task, is an unsettling experience. Standing behind anonymous walls in western Beijing, it appears just like any other office block. But its actions have caused a sharp increase in the number of officials committing suicide since 2012.[32] Under Wang Qishan, a man described earlier as Xi's chief fixer and enforcer, the CDIC has become even more feared than before. Its unwelcome attention has fallen at the doors of former and current Politburo members, and reached the tops of ministries, provinces and SOEs. Even abroad, its officials have undertaken missions to Australia, New Zealand and Europe. Leaders of the past undertook sporadic clean-up campaigns, but Xi has mandated the most extensive and far-reaching campaign that the CCP has seen since 1978. Rumours that his zeal has unsettled even former leaders like Jiang Zemin and Hu

Jintao are hard to prove, but the fact that Ling Jihua, one of Hu's closest protégés, has been dragged into an investigation and subsequently
expelled from the Party shows just how far the net has been cast.

However unwelcome they are with officials, anti-corruption clamp-
downs are popular with the public. The fall in business for five-star
hotels and the drop in official junkets go down well. Seeing elite
politicians roughed up is always a pleasurable sight for the many
in society who carry the same disdain for officials that democratic
electorates do. But the tactics of Xi's campaign are also interesting.
The CDIC leadership, during its presentations to a foreign delegation in September 2014, on a sunny, atypically clear day in Beijing,
made it very explicit that it took seriously the pursuit of the four
evils of formalism, bureaucratism, hedonism and extravagance. And
their tactics were tried and tested, based partly on moral persuasion,
but much more on instilling fear. William Burroughs joked in his
novel *Naked Lunch* that, in law, one could either be just or arbitrary.
Teams from the 1,000-strong personnel employed at the centre in
Beijing are sent to provincial and sub-provincial levels of government
and SOEs to 'dig'. Operating according to a rubric that Xi himself
describes as 'innovative', these highly unwelcome provincial tours
usually pick on one or two random targets. Then the investigations
start. Everyone has something to hide, so there are always rich returns.
And as the pro-stability policy proves, making an example of one
or two people means that almost everyone else falls into line. Xi's
anti-corruption drive, very ironically, has ended up with the Party
practising stability-maintenance harshness on itself.

Wang Xiaofang's novel from the Hu era, *The Civil Servant's
Notebook*, describes the problem. A private secretary is dragged more
and more deeply into the world of vested interests and collusion in
which he has to work.[33] Officials do deals with business people and
other officials to protect themselves, building up discreet empires
where accountability is unwelcome, and looking after those who are
on your side is the key mission. Graft-busters coming into this territory
are met with denial and closed doors at almost every turn. Evidence
disappears, vast amounts of money vanish and people start to cover

their tracks. But bit by bit, the investigators can work through the patronage links, starting with the weak, getting closer to their target, the spiders sitting in the centre of the webs, often too fat on their illicit proceeds to move. Zhou Yongkang was perhaps the fattest of the most recent examples. The claim made against him was that he was continuing to receive benefits from the state petroleum industry even after he had ended his direct involvement with it and was put in charge of the powerful state security apparatus. This represented a huge conflict of interest because he was able to use the security services to enforce his will in the state commercial sector. His links covered his own militia, through his control of the PAP when he was the head of it in the Politburo. At this level, to whom is someone like Zhou loyal? Who has the final call on his allegiance? His wealth and influence become increasingly autonomous, at least from one angle. But a figure like Zhou miscalculated on one vital issue: the Party will always prevail when it is a question of self-protection. Mao instilled it with the best instincts for survival when it is pushed into a corner. In a play-off between the CCP and an individual, even one as insidiously successful as Zhou, the Party will win – because it has to.

8. THE WAR IN CYBERSPACE

Nobel Peace Prize winner Liu Xiaobo said presciently in 2006 that the internet was 'God's gift to China'.[34] From its early years in the 1990s, when it started to percolate through even to rural areas, China now ranks as perhaps the most digitally networked society on the planet. Social-media sites like Weixin and Weibo have almost a billion users between them. Tencent, an internet company started by a returnee from study in the United States, now has 750 million users alone. A few years ago, I visited the Facebook office in San Francisco as part of a small delegation. A map of their global penetration was spread across the wall. Everywhere, people were logging on to Facebook. The only blemish in this wall of global usage was the huge gaping hole where China should be. The 'Great Firewall' of China, created by academic

Fang Binxing, caustically called its godfather, may have been scoffed at in earlier days. But commercially and in terms of news management, it has proved remarkably effective. China has indigenized the internet and social-media companies, making sure the information – and, more importantly, the profits – stay under the Party's control. And while poster boys for Chinese entrepreneurialism like Jack Ma (Ma Yun) have managed to become immensely influential and rich by exploiting this sector, the whip hand remains within the Party.

The Party, Xi has said many times, must keep close to the people.[35] Ironically, the great symbol of openness, the World Wide Web, is in fact the best means to do this. Liu Xiaobo may be right in his statement that the internet was a gift, but it remains to be seen just who this gift is for – the government or the people. As long as the Party's thought management is efficient, as long as it remains one step ahead of everyone else in keeping control of the key messages, then the internet will allow it to penetrate into new areas and find out things that were not possible before. Some claim that Chinese leaders are able to surf the Web for an hour or so a day and find what previously had always been denied them – direct insights into the thinking, opinions and mood of the public. As in the past, before the internet age, Chinese leaders have tried to remain remote and inaccessible, creating an asymmetrical situation in which they can use the Web to see Chinese people and the outside world, but the outside world cannot pry too far into their business. From time to time people have managed to break through the physical barriers surrounding them, though it is never welcome. Liu Xiuli, who managed to get through to entreat Wen Jiabao directly in May 2012, was rewarded for her pains by being committed to a psychiatric hospital.[36] But this was regarded as a huge failure by the guards and watchdogs of the super-elite. For them, inaccessibility carries rich returns – mystique, an aura of power and the ability to keep away from the sharp end of troubling issues.

Whether they do surf the internet themselves, leaders like Xi certainly show a keen interest in the powers that the internet holds, some of which are favourable to them, some of which are threatening. In a speech to the Politburo at Beidaihe in July 2013, Xi reportedly admitted that the public were becoming more demanding, and that they no longer accepted things passively but were able to disseminate their demands through social media.[37] Leaders can directly assess the public mood by peeking into this material. Perhaps it is the only way they become liberated from their myriads of minders. In an odd way, the internet offers the super-elite in politics a new form of liberty too.

It also offers leaders like Xi a chance to take one more leaf out of the book of the great tactician, Mao. He had sidestepped the official media in Beijing in 1965, when the Cultural Revolution first began, by having an article published in the less controlled Shanghai press. He had sought means of bypassing the formal propaganda structures, with their ossified bureaucracy and deep conservatism, and speaking directly to the people. The same tactic served Deng Xiaoping well when his Southern Tour in 1992 was a hit in a press that at the time was slowly opening up, even if it initially figured very weakly in the *People's Daily* and other traditional state mouthpieces. One can only imagine the opportunities digital communication would have given to someone like Mao. For Xi, having this ability to go through social media to speak directly to as wide a public as possible is also a golden opportunity. This weakens the meddlesome interference of propaganda intermediaries who can often get things badly wrong. As with Mao, there often seem to be two versions of speeches Xi has made: one for public consumption and the other for internal circulation. The director of the Propaganda Department, Liu Qibao, reportedly erased words Xi made on constitutionalism on 5 September 2014, so that they did not appear in the *People's Daily* account of his talk. This necessitated a Xi loyalist, Huang Shenming, having to fight for the speech to be more faithfully recorded in other reports.[38] As in so many other areas, the internet and information management are a battlefield – a very crucial one, where tactics have to be deployed and advantage fought for. As an instrument of ideological control, the internet is a key component of any power dynamic in modern China. Xi is probably the first leader of the country who has had to have a clear, serious digital strategy. He has had to become president of virtual China as much as of physical China. As he opined in his explanatory note from the Third Plenum:

With fast growth in the number of users of micro-blogs, WeChat and other social-network services, and instant communication tools, which spread information quickly over wide areas and can mobilize large numbers of users, how to strengthen oversight within a legal framework and guide public opinion [...] have become pressing problems for us.[39]

Some of these problems have been dealt with by dextrous blocking of foreign sites. Others have been handled by employing many thousands of internet vigilantes to take down impure or problematic pages. And still others have been handled by the guerrilla tactics of operatives who, under concealed names, place government-friendly messages online. Mao fought his battles with real troops on real battlefields. For Xi, the conflict is in virtual space. But the tactics to secure victory – concealment, subterfuge, bluff – are remarkably similar.

9. A WORLD OF TROUBLES

For a country so exercised by worries about stability, one of the puzzles of recent years has been the lack of a body at the highest level of government that takes responsibility for coordinating security issues. The Politburo, up to a point, fulfilled this function. But during crises like the unrest in Xinjiang in 2009, or the riots two years later in Inner Mongolia, it depended on the general secretary at the time, Hu Jintao, taking charge, and getting the civil and military authorities to work together. Chinese leaders have grown good at crisis management. But over the years, events like SARS in 2003 or the Tibet uprising in 2008 have often seemed to take them by surprise. Turf wars between national and local security entities are common, along with fights over budgets. The US National Security Council has long been a proposed model, and was the one Xi chose to adopt in 2013. Needless to say, he was the inaugural chair. That means that a swathe of powers now resides directly under his control rather than being spread out over competing entities as they were before.

China's National Security Commission has its work cut out for it. Xi himself stated that its main responsibilities were 'to formulate and implement national security strategy, promote national security legislation, design principles and policies for national security work and discuss and resolve key issues concerning national security'.[40] That there is a ready market in China for worrying about instability and emerging forms of unrest is not in doubt. But who gets the budget, and the powers, to deal with these things is a huge issue. Zhou Yongkang had been the security tsar under Hu. But his indictment for corruption can also be read as sounding the death knell for this arrangement.

Hu might have faced the strife that occurred in Tibet and Xinjiang over 2008 and 2009 and at least pacified it. But these problems, and a host of others, have not gone away. Having an internal security strategy has never been more crucial. A series of events over 2013 and into 2014 showed this vividly. There was a whole taxonomy of protests in China, with a variety of causes and manifestations. A bomb attack by another unhappy petitioner on the local CCP headquarters in Taiyuan, Shanxi Province, in late October 2013 belonged to a group of what some experts on protests called 'desperate attacks'. So did the case of a disabled man who had tried to explode a self-made bomb at Beijing airport earlier in the year. Even more incendiary were those involving issues around ethnicity. Beijing saw a car attack in Tiananmen Square in November, linked to a disaffected complainant from the restive Xinjiang Province in the north-west, still populated by Chinese Muslims, known as Uighurs. But the most upsetting was a series of knife attacks by people connected with separatist groups in March 2014, which left more than 30 dead at Kunming railway station. In the following April and then May, car-bomb attacks in Xinjiang's capital, Urumqi, left dozens dead, prompting the central government to convene a number of meetings on how to handle the situation there. An added worry for the central government was the link between some local groups and international Islamic extremists. For Tibet, the situation remained more stable, even though self-immolations tragically continued throughout the year, exceeding 100 in the period up to early 2014. These are all issues where mismanagement can prompt things to spiral out of control. The Xi government, however, even with the new commission set up, was in no mood to listen to voices urging radical rethinking and even some ceding of strategic territory. Dr Ilham Tohti, a Beijing-based Uighur academic who had been highly critical of the central government's policies but never once attacked its legitimacy or defended the use of violence by dissenters, was detained while on his way to the United States in early 2014, and then given a life sentence later in the year for terrorism. The property and assets of his family members were also taken from them, leaving them destitute.

The function of a National Security Commission in Xi's China is to forge consensus on where the main threats are, and develop strategies to deal with them. But security in China has become big business. It gets huge budgets, has its own economy, and lots of vested interests have accrued around it. Removing items from the list of forbidden activities makes an impact on the personnel in the vast security apparatus who were once mandated with policing this area, making them lose influence and employment. Creating a new source of banned issues does the reverse. Twenty years ago, cyber-security was nowhere near as important as it is now, with almost no one working on the nascent internet and few resources going into it. Now it swallows vast amounts of money and personnel. Security is hugely political, and means balancing the viewpoints and interests of widely different stakeholders. Sometimes the biggest source of insecurity is the bitter turf wars and fights between the very agencies meant to maintain social and public safety.

In the shifting terrain of risk assessment and threats, the Chinese government cannot do everything and keep everyone happy. It has to prioritize. If it gets its assessments wrong and a problem arises that it cannot control, then the political impact could be vast. For Xi, holding all this power himself means that at least he can control things, instead of being helpless as he watches them unfold. But it carries one major risk: the buck stops with him. If there is a serious uprising, either in Xinjiang or in Tibet, or associated with justice issues in the rest of the country, and this spreads contagiously, he could suddenly fall from being China's godfather to being China's arch-criminal.

10. CHINA'S SILENT SPRING

If modern Chinese politicians are ever tempted to think that they are not warlords but magicians, then there seems to be one spell they have so far failed to cast. For weeks running from November 2013 into early 2014, and then from the same period in 2014 into the rest of 2015, a vast cloud of noxious smog hovered over the north-east and eastern side of the country. Inland cities like Lanzhou, Hohhot and Xi'an, with their heavy industry and coal, had become infamous for being world leaders in smog. But for Beijing and Shanghai, the two great showcase cities, it was demeaning to be wrapped in air so thick people in neighbouring tower blocks were not able to see each other. Central leaders might exist in rooms and buildings where air was conditioned and purified. But the people they said they wanted to forge a new relationship with and become closer to had to smother their mouths with gauze masks to prevent themselves being overwhelmed by toxic fumes.

This weather occurred with little deference to China's international reputation or its domestic needs. During the Beijing Marathon in October 2014, deep smog encased the route, meaning that all but the most foolhardy withdrew. Asked why he had decided not to participate, one runner told me it was like being asked to smoke 50 cigarettes over three hours. The air was associated with disease, flu and lung problems. And it was hanging over the most sensitive cities, ones where modernity was meant to be tangible and thriving.

During Xi's possibly mythical taxi ride in Beijing in early 2013, the driver had reported that the man who he felt looked so much like the newly appointed Party chairman had made comments about just how difficult it was to maintain growth but avoid pollution.[41] 'Improving China's natural-resource management', the tenth core area for the Third Plenum, tries to address this. Xi has used the phrase 'ecological civilization'. His words sound enlightened on this issue. In stark contrast to the environmental incoherence of many Western politicians, Xi is no climate-change denier. It is more that he is evidently hard-pressed to find an easy way to try to balance strong growth with protecting China's water, air and natural environment.

It may be that under his watch China will have to do what it most fears, and make a clear choice. An environmental catastrophe, or a pandemic associated with it, is the most likely crisis that could end the Communist regime's period in power and tear China apart. The issue has enough momentum to have prompted Xi to sign a major deal with President Obama just after the APEC summit in November 2014 and to follow this up with another deal when in the US in 2015, and support for the Paris Accord at the end of 2015. For the first time ever, on behalf of China, Xi committed to CO_2 emissions peaking by 2030. The Ministry of the Environment, while still very small, has been given enhanced status and powers. And both SOEs and non-state enterprises for the first time have much tougher regulations to fulfil, with fewer loopholes for them to evade authorities with. Even so, the most optimistic have to admit that China faces a truly gargantuan task in sorting out its environmental problems over the coming decades.

This leadership is pinning so much hope on innovation – preferably inside China, but possibly outside – leading to some magic cure. They look at the success the United States has had in exploitation of shale gas and the way this has helped it tame some of its emissions, and they have even cooperated with companies like Halliburton to try to exploit their own potential reserves in the south-west of the country. Even despite the Fukushima tragedy in Japan in 2011, China is still proceeding with the world's largest programme of nuclear-energy development. Energy efficiency is improving, alongside attempts to develop more wind power and renewable sources. Solar panels continue to glitter on the roofs of houses in the sun-blessed southern regions of the country. Efficiencies come from marketization, through the creation of a modernized and more effective national power grid (there used to be two, with set prices and little incentive for people to be sparing in their use of energy). Perhaps most crucially of all, officials are now being held to account for their ability to deliver ecological targets. Xi Jinping himself stated in a letter supporting the Eco Forum Global conference in Guiyang in July 2013 that 'ushering in a new era of ecological progress and building a beautiful China is an important element of the China Dream'.[42] But vested interests will be hurt as this proceeds. Some SOEs will see their manufacturing costs rise due to higher levels of compliance, and officials will risk being castigated for their inability to make their provinces greener. The problem is that the destination of the China Dream – a rich, strong country, with a prosperous middle class living in cities – is contradictory. With current technology, it cannot be achieved without taking yet more of a toll on the environment. Yet failure to clean up the environment will make the dream look more like a smoggy, dirty, polluted nightmare. The environment is the great battlefield of the CCP's ambitions to build a modern China, in rural and urban areas. And it is in the environment, rather than the complex cross forces of society, that the CCP will almost certainly meet its most formidable challenges.

NUMBER 11

Unlike Mao in his 1957 statement, Xi Jinping's explanatory statement covers one more major objective, an eleventh, added as a coda to the ten covered above. But this brings us back to the theme of this book – the nature and location of power in modern China. Despite the very diverse nature of the current and future developmental challenges facing China, whether implementing the market, reforming law, clamping down on corruption or reforming the fiscal and tax system, and the radical differences in how they need to be tackled and what policy measures or alliances in society might be needed in order to face them, there is a very clear message that Xi sends as he reaches his eleventh point. They will all need to be part of a unified plan of attack, and the central player in that plan is not the government, or society, or industry, but the Party. For Xi, the explanatory statement leads through its various announcements of sobering challenges towards a new social contract for the country: only the Party and the people together can overcome these huge issues. Without the guidance of the Party and its unified and unifying vision, China's problems will be insoluble. With it, there is a way forward. The body that Xi announces will do this – the Leading Group for Continuing the Reform Comprehensively – will be chaired by him. With one stroke of the pen, the power to direct, solve, delegate and propose comes directly to him.

This structural and institutional consolidation of power means that Xi sits at the heart of the body that directs government and Party policy across all areas where it confronts the diverse challenges outlined in the previous ten points. It ties the Party's leadership into the solution. The message is starkly simple: jettison the Party, and you jettison the hope of dealing with this grim menu of issues. In this simple committee, Xi has created a space in which he exists at the centre and understands and influences everything around him, like someone on a chair on a hilltop looking over the country around them. He has a great vantage point. With the announcement of this committee, the statement comes to look much more clearly what it was evidently intended to be – a manifesto not just for government and Party behaviour, but for Xi's directorship of it. But beyond the issues laid out in the explanatory statement, which are overwhelmingly domestic, there are also issues in the world beyond. It is to these, and Xi's role in them, that we now turn.

5

HOW DOES XI JINPING SEE THE OUTSIDE WORLD?

The Master said: To lead into battle a people that has not first been instructed is to betray them.

—*Analects* **8.30**

China has traditionally defined its diplomatic interests in ways that look like the same sort of concentric circles emanating from Xi described in Chapter 3. The United States is its top priority; the EU and its regional neighbours are its second-tier concerns, and then a number of other circles extend outwards, from Middle Eastern partners to Latin America and Africa. The further out these circles are, the less their interests overlap with China's. Importance in this framework is defined in terms of geopolitics, investment, economic relations, and energy and material resources. Seen in this way, China does not so much have alliances like the United States does, which are bound by treaties, similar worldviews and ideas that weld the partners together, but is attracted to mutual definitions and understandings of material interests that link with its own internal priorities: economic growth, the creation of a prosperous society and the construction of a rich, strong country. The final issue is proximity – China is most concerned about those partners that are in its regional strategic space, and this includes the United States. Partners in Latin America or Africa are more peripheral because of their distance. There is also the issue of how unified these partners are in their interaction with China. The

United States is highly cohesive in its interaction, whereas the EU, despite being a vast economic entity, is less so because of the divisions between its member states. China comes across in this setting as a pragmatic and realist power, looking to maximize its self-interest as it creates links and bonds internationally, using a number of instruments to achieve this. This is represented figuratively in the diagram on the following page.

SEEKING THE GRAND NARRATIVE

In the context of policy priorities, domestic reforms lead and foreign affairs take a peripheral role. China certainly doesn't seek a proactive international-leadership role. It is often berated for not being willing to stick its neck out on issues, either at the UN or elsewhere. With his grand domestic narratives – of reform, centennial goals and national regeneration – there does, however, have to be an international dimension to almost everything Xi says. After all, China's economic prosperity is married to its foreign trade partners, even while it seeks, in the words of Li Keqiang, to unleash sources of indigenous growth in activities like consumption and urbanization. The inner and outer are necessarily linked. And unlike in the era of Deng, Xi's China is now too large a player to hide behind feigned modesty and talk of 'keeping its capacities low and biding its time'. Its time is already here.

Xi's personal experience of the outside world is not as extensive as, for instance, that of Deng Xiaoping or Jiang Zemin, who both spent several years studying overseas, in France and the USSR respectively. Jiang spoke a number of languages well and showed a genuine curiosity about foreign literature and culture. For Xi, it seems his first encounter beyond China's borders was being part of a military delegation to the United States in 1985, when he famously stayed for a few days with a family in Iowa. He revisited them when in the United States in 2012. As a provincial official, and then as vice president and president, however, Xi has been a true globetrotter. His visits since 2013 have included Russia, Latin America, the United States, Europe, Australia,

CHINA'S RELATIONS WITH THE WORLD
The Four Ranks of Partnership

FIRST RANK

United States   very strong geopolitical and economic links, with close proximity and unity.

SECOND RANK

EU   strong geopolitical and economic links, particularly as a knowledge partner (China's best intellectual-property partnerships exist with EU countries), but with weaker proximity and cohesion.

Russia   strong geopolitical links because of a huge shared border; weaker economic links, mainly focusing on energy and resources; relatively high cohesion.

THIRD RANK

Association of Southeast Asian Nations (ASEAN) and Asia region   geopolitical and economic links, with strong proximity, but very weak cohesion.

Central Asian countries   moderate geopolitical and economic links (the latter strengthening through the construction of the 'new Silk Road'); strong proximity and, through the Shanghai Cooperation Organization (SCO), moderate cohesion.

FOURTH RANK

Africa and Latin America   weak geopolitical links compared to countries and groups above, but strong economic, resource and energy links, which are likely to get stronger in years to come; weaker proximity and cohesion compared to countries and groups above.

Middle East   moderate geopolitical and economic links (mostly energy); moderate proximity; low cohesion.

New Zealand, Fiji and Africa. One of the most glaring exceptions to this itinerary has been North Korea, the so-called close ally of China but one that apparently did not merit a visit by Xi up to the time of writing (April 2016), mostly due to Chinese irritation at the continuing nuclear ambitions of its small neighbour, and its continuing ability to cause diplomatic headaches.

How does Xi see the outside world? He inherits from his predecessors all the mess that China's history with its neighbours has left, and has to deal with the same problems in the region – a highly unenviable neighbourhood in which India, Pakistan and Afghanistan cover its western borders, Russia is to its north and North Korea is to its east; to the south are the contentious maritime territories that China disputes with Vietnam, Japan, the Philippines and others. That four of its neighbours have some nuclear capacity only adds to the complexity. Like Deng, Jiang and Hu, Xi has to walk a tightrope, ensuring he looks strong in front of his domestic support base on issues like Japan, or the contested border with India, while also trying to ensure that the country doesn't fall into a conflict that scuppers its hard-won stability and peace as it continues to build up its economy and make its people prosperous. Nationalism is a tempting card to play when things get tough at home. It is easy to blame foreigners for trouble in Hong Kong, as happened in 2014, for instance, or for tensions in the Taiwan Strait. But things can get out of hand quickly, with riots from 2005 onwards against Japan, and Chinese projects targeted by protestors in Vietnam in 2014. Xi talks of building a rich, strong nation, but that means different things to those outside China than to those within it.

One distinctive aspect of Xi as a diplomat is how he and his advisors have mapped out the concentric circles of relationships described above, and then tried to attach grand narratives to them. These cover, in particular: the idea of a new model of major power relations with the United States; civilizational partnership with the EU; and the 'new Silk Road' with Central Asia, the Middle East, Russia and maritime neighbours (called the 'Belt and Road' from 2014). The three models alone describe a new world order with Chinese characteristics.

THE UNITED STATES

The one characteristic that Wang Huning, Chen Xi and Liu He (Xi's three closest thinkers outlined in Chapter 3) have in common is that at some stage in their past they studied in the United States. Wang, Chen and Liu evidently have distinctive outlooks and come from very different backgrounds. But they share the experience of living in the United States and being exposed to its culture and intellectual climate. When they speak about that country, they do so from the perspective of personal encounter and engagement, something that is not true of any other country or region in the world.

The US relationship is critically important to China, and one that it privileges with an enormous amount of effort and attention. Xi Jinping himself broke with normal protocol by visiting Sunnylands in California to spend time with President Obama in mid-2013. Obama had been due to make a return visit to China after his underwhelming reception there in 2009, but the sense in Washington and Beijing that there had been too much miscommunication, and that the relationship was under strain, sanctioned this step outside diplomatic normality. During their time in the United States, the two presidents spent nine hours talking with each other. There can be few global leaders who speak to each other so much, and whose countries have so many overlapping areas of interest. The Strategic and Economic Dialogue (S&ED) ropes in almost every major ministry on both sides when it convenes annually. The United States and China are necessary partners, but ones with real underlying issues. For all their cooperation and joint interests, the two countries represent different visions of the world. Underneath their harmonious language towards each other there is implicit disharmony and latent competition.

For many in China, the United States has embarked on a mission to make the rest of the world subscribe to its values and become increasingly like it. In the past, there were naive beliefs about the superiority of the US governance system. But George Bush Junior scuppered these with his messy first election and then the ways in which he ran roughshod over the US constitution in order to prosecute his 'war on terror'. According to some Chinese analysts of foreign affairs, Obama has been viewed by the Chinese leadership as a weak president. But the 'pivot' to Asia sponsored by his first Secretary of State Hillary Clinton only deepened the narrative in Beijing that there was a campaign of containment under way.

It is easy to see why foreign-policy thinkers in China may believe this. Wherever they look, America seems to get involved. It has treaty alliances running in a great wall across the Pacific, from Japan to South Korea and down to the Philippines, Australia and New Zealand. While China dislikes the obligations that these treaty links bring, it does appreciate, as Henry Kissinger has explained, the way they at least create more strategic certainty for countries that sign up to them, making it clear who their friends are.[1] But things get worse. America is linked to India, Pakistan and Afghanistan, and has made significant diplomatic alliances with partners even as historically complex for China as Vietnam and Myanmar. Wang Hui, a Beijing-based academic, can well sigh that the borders of the United States come right up to those of China, in view of the fact that 'there is nowhere in the world that is not a US frontier'.[2] But the United States also fills so much ideological and cultural space, its films infiltrating China despite restrictions, its Apple products ending up in the hands of even the first lady, Peng Liyuan, and its elite universities educating people like the daughters of Xi Jinping and Li Keqiang (even if they were reportedly summoned back when Xi's new leadership came to power). If there were ever a love–hate diplomatic relationship, then that between China and the United States is it, with many American political leaders' zealous distaste for the one-party system undermining all the appreciative words they say about how well China has done since 1978, when it partially bought into global economic and developmental norms.

China's search for some space in this relationship has been a long-term task. Deng Xiaoping created a framework in which China made sure that it kept close to the world's sole remaining superpower, no matter what. Even after Tiananmen, the two continued working with each other, despite symbolic spats. Over the years, these spats have become serious: the bombing of the Chinese embassy in Belgrade in 1999 was a particularly bad moment. But with 9/11 in 2001, the United States became distracted with its problems in the Middle East and with Islamic fundamentalism. Jiang Zemin saw this as offering a moment of strategic opportunity for China, during which it would have a little more space to develop itself and promote its actions in the region. During the Global Financial Crisis in 2008, China felt even more emboldened. But it probably overplayed its hand, pushing its neighbours around over the maritime border disputes in 2009 into 2010, and creating too much bad feeling. The net result of this 'assertiveness', as some described it, was that China was lonely and bereft of real friends. Its soft-power efforts have achieved less allegiance diplomatically than hoped. Chinese foreign outward investment and the Confucius Institute (a non-profit organization based in universities throughout the world that aims to promote Chinese language and culture), along with the other paraphernalia of soft diplomacy and its attendant symbolism, have not gained China international trust and respect. This has been the cause of deep frustration, something that is especially well articulated by thinkers like Qinghua University's Yan Xuetong, who states that China needs now to use its own indigenous philosophical traditions in order to create a moral basis to appeal to the outside world and gain its trust and loyalty. 'The goal of our strategy,' he proposed, 'must be not only to reduce the power gap with the United States but also to provide a better model for society than that given by the United States.'[3]

The conundrum for Xi since coming to power therefore has been to create more space for a frustrated China while at the same time avoiding confrontation with a United States that can be a bad enemy. Wherever Xi looks, he can see places where the United States will become irritated quickly if he makes a misstep. Two of the thorniest areas are over Taiwan and Hong Kong. Both are places that China claims are not foreign-affairs issues but domestic ones. But both are places where the outside world, led by the United States, sees that it can legitimately express interests and become involved. And both have been frontiers for challenge and evolution in US–China relations, proving Wang Hui's observation that the border between the two countries is not so

much a physical as an ideological and symbolic one, coming right up
to the edges of China and, in the case of Hong Kong, deep into it.

Hong Kong is of current interest because it represents a battle of
wills between two systems. The colonial legacy in the city has turned
out to be a half-hearted one. Britain left with some decorum in 1997,
following reams of written agreements that were distilled in the 1984
accord with China, which paved the way for reversion of sovereignty,
and the later Basic Law, the constitution of the Hong Kong Special
Administrative Region. These documents, however, had an airy abstrac-
tion, and in 2014, 17 years after the handover and only a third of
the way into the 50-year period during which Hong Kong had been
promised a high level of autonomy, the time came for China to spell
out in more detail the ways in which more self-governance would be
possible for the city.

The central government did this partly by issuing a hard-nosed
white paper as a statement of official opinion on the matter in May
2014, only a few days before premier Li Keqiang went to the United
Kingdom and was granted an audience with the Queen. The symbolism
of this was not lost on many, who saw China taking a cool revenge
on its old colonial tormentors. The white paper stated categorically
that supreme power for Hong Kong rested with the NPC in Beijing.[4]
As this institution is famously under the control of the Politburo,
few were misled. Xi and his Party colleagues were calling the shots.
But this was a preamble to the real announcement, which came in
September, when, after months of tepid consultation, the Hong Kong
government issued its proposal. It amounted to something far short
of what the democrats in the city had expected: a selection committee
of around 1,500 would screen candidates and reduce the list to two
or three, who in 2017 would then be offered to the 5 million-strong
electorate for their final decision. For Beijing, this was a significant
move forward. But for students and academics in Hong Kong it was
incendiary. Their anger was not appeased by the hapless serving chief
executive C. Y. Leung, who betrayed his businessman past by simply
stating what everyone knew but no one wanted to hear: this was the
best that Beijing (who really had the final say, whatever the appearances)

was going to allow the Hong Kong government to offer, and it was not going to back down. Protests on the streets led to gridlock in the central area of the city. These were not fully moved until mid-December. The bright yellow of the 'umbrella revolution' marked a politicization of Hong Kong's people that had never been seen before.

The United States, with the United Kingdom behind it, was immediately blamed by the more popular Chinese media for being the instigators of this unrest. This echoed a narrative that had already been used by Russia against the United States in Ukraine, and in other trouble spots. The United States was somehow imputed with the power to turn people out onto the streets of a city thousands of miles from its borders. It is unlikely that Xi or his closest colleagues believed this, but it served a useful purpose in showing that the Chinese people needed to be wary of its great powerful friend.

A similar issue came up with Taiwan. Under President Ma Ying-jeou, in office since 2008, Taiwan had managed a series of confidence-building measures and new trade links with the mainland, which culminated in the first ever meeting between the presidents of the two countries in Singapore in November 2015. But attempts to push through a service-sector accord in early 2014 led to unrest and the 'Sunflower Movement'. As in Hong Kong, students took to the streets, and even managed to storm the parliament's Legislative Yuan building. Ma's popularity fell to less than 10 per cent. His own KMT party was wiped out in local elections held later in the year. The accord was stopped. Once more, many in China claimed that the United States was hovering in the background, as its links with the island are politically and militarily strong.[5]

Xi has particular links with Taiwan. During his 16 years in Fujian Province he was part of a provincial leadership that embraced investment across the Strait, and he built up a good record of relating to Taiwanese business people. This was pragmatic, because they brought the wealth and GDP growth that he, as a local official, depended on for promotion at that time. But over the Taiwan issue since 2012, Xi has shown increasing ambition, stating to former Taiwanese vice president Vincent Siew at the APEC congress in 2013 that the two could not put off talking about political issues forever. In 2014, even as the turmoil was unfolding in Hong Kong, he referred to the 'one country, two systems' rubric as a perfectly usable one for Taiwan, and one that it should consider, something that was almost immediately rebuffed by Ma, despite their having now personally met.[6]

Taiwan and the associated issue of Hong Kong remain the thorniest of 'international policy' issues for Xi because they are ones that he and his circle could consider domestic, but which the United States and the outside world feel they have a direct interest and involvement in. The United States, in particular, has legal commitments through the Taiwan Relations Act of 1979, which stipulates that the executive seek congressional advice should any security issue arise over the island. A powerful constituency in the United States feels ideologically committed to doing whatever it needs to defend Taiwan, particularly as it is now a democracy. The potential for real US–China conflict therefore comes to its most intense point in this area. It hovers behind much Chinese thinking about the United States, and is a major reason why so many Chinese policy makers feel that America continues to interfere illegitimately in its affairs.

How does Xi claim more diplomatic space and status, therefore, without incurring unwelcome suspicion from its most important, but in many ways most problematic partner? The idea he proposed in 2013, while on US soil, was a grand, abstract one. Stating at a press conference after the summit with Obama that the Pacific was big enough for both countries, he then went on to talk of a new model of major power relations. He didn't get down to specifics, but the formulation at least worked.[7] It accorded the United States high status, but also showed that China felt it now needed to be accorded some equality. China could defend itself by saying that this was only in accordance with the United States' talk a few years ago of China becoming more of a global stakeholder. It also, very subtly, made clear that China wanted a suitable role for its economic importance in the geopolitical realm.

Under this new rubric, China and the United States have the power to do much good in the world. They vividly illustrated this when, during the 2014 APEC meeting, hosted by China in Beijing, Obama and Xi stole the show by inking in a new climate-change agreement – resolving to cap their emissions by the end of the next decade and work together more closely on environmental challenges. As the world's largest and second-largest users of energy and green-house-gas emitters, this was a huge breakthrough. It also shows that when their interests align, they are able to do major deals despite all their differences. Despite Xi's new meta-narrative, however, both countries internally lack a coherent view of each other. For the Chinese, the United States is either the great spoiler or big brother they are always seeking approval from. For the Americans, China is either an alien political system trying covertly to steal up on them and take away their dominance, or a country it is worth making every effort to convert to their way of thinking, bringing it over to what President Clinton called during his visit to the PRC in 1998 'the right side of history'.[8]

And for the outside world, the US–China relationship is one, under Xi, that is jealously guarded, where both sides spend much of their time in locked rooms with each other, and only sporadically let the rest of the world interrupt their adult conversations. However fractious and discordant they are with each other, anyone else who tries to slip into this intense dialogue risks being given short shrift. The Chinese remain flattered by their great access in the world's capital, Washington. And the United States only takes so much autonomy from their allies on China policy before muscular intervention. Before Xi ever appeared on the scene, the EU's attempts to lift an arms embargo in 2005 with China were knocked back by an angry Washington. Both sides deny vehemently that there is such a thing as a 'G2'. But much of their behaviour seems to suggest there is. Perhaps, though, with his talk of a new model of major power relations as a way to understand the links between the United States and China, Xi was showing awareness that the only thing more fearsome than the United States' hate is its love. Preserving at least some space and distance is the name of the game, and that, at least, he achieved by 2015 – a fact reinforced by his state visit to America in September.

THE EU: THE SECOND CIRCLE

If the United States is the great yin of the modern Chinese geopolitical world, then the yang resides in the EU. Whatever the United States is, the EU is not. The United States has hard power, political unity and something approaching a policy towards China. The EU is the reverse: little hard power, not much political unity and no real policy on China. But that doesn't mean that it is negligible for Beijing. It is the biggest provider of good-quality technology, and a massive export market. The EU also figures in Chinese thinking fleetingly as a counterbalance to the United States, before it reminds Chinese leaders that it ranks as one of the most infuriating and annoying partners the world has ever known.

Part of this is the proclivity of the EU for offering nasty surprises. Diplomatic recognition between the two was first forged in 1975, when what is now the EU was merely the European Economic Community (EEC) and had nine members. Things are different now. Membership has expanded to 28, and the EEC has long been replaced by the union set up in 1992 as part of the Maastricht Treaty of that year. Even worse, what was once a purely trade-related relationship has now changed, largely at the behest of the Europeans, into a more complex political and strategic one, including more than 80 dialogues across areas from science to the environment, but also embracing thorny political and rights issues. In 2002, the State Council produced a white paper on policy towards the EU, making the EU the first of China's diplomatic relations to be awarded this accolade. But 12 years later, on the eve of Xi's own visit to the capital of the EU, Brussels, a new paper was issued. This mapped out the pent-up frustration China had been feeling.

On Tibet, Taiwan and human and social rights generally, the EU has a tendency to become very preachy towards China. This is the source of its particular ability to irritate Xi Jinping. Since 1992, it has encoded a larger number of value propositions in its constitution. And while avoiding the zealotry of the United States, the EU can come across sometimes as promoting the idea that it wants China to join the 'end-of-history' crowd and change its political system to fit in. This is something that has figured in every main policy document that the EU has issued on China since 2006, when it has increasingly talked about working with China to achieve reform and change within its own political and governance system. For Xi's visit, therefore, China's accompanying second white paper was a subliminal admission that a decade of 'strategic partnership' had led to much disappointment. The arms embargo imposed after Tiananmen had not been lifted. The EU had failed to grant China market-economy status because of the large role of the state in its industries. And it had continued to push on Tibet, human rights and other issues in ways that Chinese leaders found increasingly frustrating. On top of this, the eurozone crisis from 2009 had undermined the EU's economic prowess. On these issues, the white paper pulled no punches. The EU, it stated prescriptively, 'should lift its arms embargo on China at an early date'.[9] On Taiwan:

> the Chinese side appreciates the commitment of the EU and its member states to the One China principle and hopes that the EU will respect China's major concerns regarding the Taiwan question, oppose 'Taiwan independence' in any form, support peaceful development of cross-Strait relations and China's peaceful reunification and handle Taiwan-related questions with caution.

On Tibet:

> the Chinese side appreciates the position of the EU and its member states of recognizing Tibet as part of China's territory and not supporting 'Tibet independence'. The EU side should properly handle Tibet-related issues based on the principle of respecting China's sovereignty, independence and territorial integrity and non-interference in China's internal affairs, not allow leaders of the Dalai group to visit the EU or its member states under any capacity or pretext to engage in separatist activities, not arrange any form of contact with officials of the EU or

its member states, and not provide any facilitation or support
for anti-China separatist activities for 'Tibet independence'.

This sat alongside very clear calls for stronger cooperation in finance,
counterterrorism and technology partnerships. The paper stated
grandly:

> China and the EU, the world's most representative emerging
> economy and group of developed countries respectively, are two
> major forces for world peace as they share important strategic
> consensus on building a multi-polar world. The combined
> economic aggregate of China and the EU accounts for one
> third of the world economy, making them two major markets
> for common development. Being an important representative
> of the oriental culture and the cradle of Western culture and
> with a combined population accounting for a quarter of the
> world's total, China and the EU stand as two major civilizations
> advancing human progress. With no fundamental conflict of
> interests, China and the EU have far more agreement than
> differences. Both sides are at a crucial stage of reform and
> development and China–EU relations face new historic oppor-
> tunities. Deepening the China–EU Comprehensive Strategic
> Partnership for Mutual Benefit and Win–win Cooperation will
> provide impetus to the development of China and the EU and
> contribute to peace and prosperity of the world.

The clue in this piece was in the appeal to partnerships between two
major but very different entities, one a collection of countries, the
other a unified single state, and the ways in which both of these sides
in their different ways were dealing with reforms. Xi himself, in a
speech made at the College of Europe in Bruges only a few days earlier,
during the first ever visit by a Chinese head of state to Brussels and
the European Commission headquarters, was to focus on this idea of
partnership and multifaceted links. In the past, this had largely been
left to the premier. Wen Jiabao had nurtured it during his ten years in

the hot seat, no doubt finding that it was often a thankless task. That Xi has taken a direct interest and involvement suggests that China–EU relations have been upgraded, but is also an admission that foreign policy needs to be holistic these days.

The reference by Xi to EU and China being civilizational partners is important.[10] There are a number of attractions to this term. Firstly, it neatly avoids the messiness of equating a singular sovereign state like the PRC with a collection of separate states like the EU. A concept like 'civilization' is abstract enough to cover both. But it does flatter the EU with at least some semblance of cohesiveness, and shows willingness on Xi's part to grant it some parity with China. This assertion of parity must have placated many in China who feel that, for all its good points, the EU is insufferably self-righteous about its values and what it represents. This is at least one way of showing that there is no reason to be so sniffy towards a country that has as rich and diverse a history and culture as its own (Xi made the attributes and characteristics of Chinese history and achievement clear in his speech). Finally, Xi was able to pursue one of the themes that Wen Jiabao had warmed to during the final phase of his premiership while observing the instability within the EU and the looming potential implosion of the euro. Xi could report that the EU, like China, needs to embrace reform and to change itself. These must have been sweet words for China, as one of the foremost targets of European sanctimoniousness over the previous few decades.

THE NEW SILK ROAD

On the road leading out of Xi'an, there is a large sign: 'Beginnings of the Silk Road', it grandly states, with a picture above of a statue of merchants dressed in ancient-style clothes, some on foot, some riding highly stylized camels laden with goods. Those seeking the romance of the old merchant routes into Central Asia, through to the Middle East and beyond, have to wrestle with the current demotic state of suburban Xi'an, and the historical issues of what the Silk Road was.

Historians argue that it may have been no more than a band of territory, a variety of routes used by travellers, rather than one single road. In his history of the Tang dynasty, Mark Edward Lewis calls them 'silk roads'.[11] These routes have maintained their romance, however, just like the Orient Express or Route 66. And they make tangible the ways in which earlier Chinese dynasties were open to the outside world, both formed by and extending trade and cultural interaction.

In the twenty-first century, around China's vast western border, there are a number of countries that it has to maintain good relations with in order to secure its energy supplies, to ensure regions like Tibet and Xinjiang are secure, and to guarantee the integrity of its borders. The previous chapter discussed the premium that Xi and his prede-cessors have placed on stability. There is a strong, historic memory of problems always coming from the west, and the inner-Asian region. As recently as 1962, China fought India over borders that remain disputed. Analysts like Robert Ross from the United States and Wang Jisi from China argue that the country has always predominantly been a land power, and, for Wang, needs to maintain this position in the twenty-first century, looking to forge a zone of legitimate influence in the central and southern region of the Asian continent.[12]

This region is characterized by cultural, political, religious and lin-guistic diversity. And it is one that China has only tentatively built rela-tions in. Security issues, around Xinjiang in particular, and then ener-gy-security ones, promoted the establishment in 1996 of the Shanghai Five, a loose grouping of China, Russia, Kazakhstan, Tajikistan and Kyrgyzstan; following the inclusion of Uzbekistan in 2001, this trans-formed into the Shanghai Cooperation Organization (SCO). Regarded warily by the United States and others during its formative years as an attempt to create alliances that excluded the world's policeman in areas that mattered to it, as the 2000s went on it informally embraced Iran and more diverse powers, and became one of the key forums in which Russia and China undertook structured discussion.

Along the Central Asian belt, however, there are big differences in the ways countries relate to China. Some are major energy and resource suppliers. Russia is a much more formidable ally and competitor, a country that China had enjoyed complex and sometimes very acrimonious relations with (they last clashed militarily in 1969).[13] Expanding beyond the SCO, there are partners like Pakistan, one of China's closest allies, but one that is also problematic and fickle, combining espousals of eternal friendship and fidelity to its huge eastern neighbour with attempts to extort investment and technology out of it. During the last decade of its implosion, Afghanistan has also posed problems of stability and commitment, with the withdrawal of US troops in 2014 intensifying rather than lessening the dilemma of China's security commitment there. With India, the ongoing border dispute was raised once more during a visit Xi made to the country in 2014, which happened to occur just at the time of reports of a major skirmish provoked by Chinese troops along the disputed border.

All of these countries are united by the fact that they want to capitalize more on economic opportunities arising from links with China. Staggeringly, since 1992 trade has increased 100-fold between Central Asia and its vast eastern neighbour. The PRC is the largest trade partner of all the countries in this region, except Uzbekistan, where it lies second. In 2012, the total value of this came to US$ 46 billion. Even with Uzbekistan, in 2013 trade climbed to US$ 2.87 billion, a 60 per cent increase on the year before.

The big money in these trade flows is all related to energy. Kazakhstan is oil-rich, with the second-largest reserves among the countries of the former USSR. In September 2013, during his state visit to the region, Xi Jinping signed a US$ 15 billion oil deal. This supplemented the US$ 4.2 billion deal between state-owned oil company Sinopec and PetroKazakhstan in autumn 2005. The 1,300-kilometre Kazakhstan–China pipeline will be at the heart of this agreement, a joint venture with another of China's main state-owned oil companies, China National Petroleum Corporation (CNPC). In addition to this is a further deal that Xi signed with his counterpart, President Nazarbayev, for a major oil pipeline to be completed in 2015, granting an 8 per cent share in the vast Kashagan oilfield. Xi also signed a deal for investment in a new gas pipeline to run from the south-west to the south-east of Kazakhstan from 2015. Kazakhstan is not alone in receiving Chinese largesse. Turkmenistan has received investment from CNPC in the Central Asia–China gas pipeline, running from what is currently the second-largest gas field in the world. The pipeline will eventually create a network not just throughout the Central Asian states, but into Afghanistan, tapping into the largely unexploited resources that exist there. And to underline how important having good logistics and infrastructure is, in 2006, through the China Road Company, there was an investment of US$ 300 million in the Dushanbe–Chanak toll road. In terms of shoring up its security position, China held anti-terrorist joint exercises involving more than 1,000 Chinese military personnel in Kazakhstan in 2010, and joint terrorist drills in Kyrgyzstan in 2013 involving almost 500 police. These exercises in 2010 and 2013 were held under the auspices of the SCO.

On the surface, everything looks to be going well between China and its north-western neighbours. The sort of win–win outcomes that Beijing constantly says it is seeking seem to be eventuating, with Chinese state investment pouring into Central Asia, and Beijing offering itself as a security partner. But there are also clear risks for the countries involved. For Beijing, there is the constant shadow of instability in its new-found allies. Central Asian countries are beset with governance and corruption issues, with many of them being poor on observance of rule of law and human rights. The possibility of future unrest is therefore never far away, with the spectre of an uprising like that of February 2014 in Ukraine ever-present. Beijing's strategy to diversify its energy supply and not become over-reliant on one partner is sensible. The taps could be switched off very quickly.

The great asset of the new Silk Road (going under the more prosaic name of 'One Belt, One Road' since 2015) is that, like the old, it is marvellously vague. No one is quite sure where it starts and where it ends. But it puts to the fore the primacy of mutually beneficial trade relations, and appeals to self-interest in the softest, most indirect way. It also hints at a long prior history of Chinese engagement in regions to its west, showing how stable and well established these links in the economic, cultural and social realm are. Xi's talk since 2013 of this new Silk Road has been embraced by countries throughout the region, become the theme of conferences and trade fairs, and supplied the third of the troika of overarching external narratives for Xi's China.

The image of the new Silk Road is also one that has traction far beyond China's borders. It gets mentioned in the Middle East, and even in Eastern Europe. At a conference in Lithuania in late 2014, I was intrigued to see the concept raised there, as it related to opportunities between this region and one so far away. In Poland, too, the Silk Road seems to have some links. But perhaps most extraordinary of all is the concept of a 'Maritime Silk Road' running through the whole of South East Asia, even down to the coast of Australia. This glorious idea achieves the seemingly impossible: it dresses up straightforward material and commercial interests into something pioneering, ennobling and romantic. But behind it is one powerful urge, best summarized by a sign seen in Europe in 2014: 'We love RMB.'

THE REST OF THE WORLD: A NEW GLOBAL POWER

And iterations of that sentiment are what, in essence, capture the rest of the globe. For Xi Jinping, the great irony is that just as he is trying to wean Chinese people off addiction to pure money and money-making, and to encourage them to think about more complex and nuanced social outcomes to strive for, the rest of the world seems to have fallen deeply in love with Chinese money. From the east coast of Africa to the suburbs of Sydney, from the sophisticated financial centres of Zurich and New York to the shanty towns of Latin America and the farms of Indonesia, or the oil fields of the Middle East – the one thing linking all these diverse areas in the second decade of the twenty-first century is a desire to get access to some of the trillions in Chinese money that are swishing around the world. The philosopher Nietzsche may have been right when he declared at the end of the nineteenth century that God was dead: but in the modern era God has been replaced by another three-letter word – RMB.

And RMB figures almost everywhere. Chinese investment out of the country was almost as great as that into it in 2014. This more than anything else was the aspect of the grand narrative that everyone, inside and outside, understood. Chinese money is dreamed about and fantasized over. It figures in the planning of grand corporations and right down to that of small enterprises. The greatest impediment to its global dominance is its non-convertibility. The 'Great Currency Wall' of China is regarded by leaders as one final protection from the vagaries of a world outside that can do things as idiotic as the Global Financial Crisis of 2008. But, bit by bit, this wall is being breached, with RMB hubs created in London, Hong Kong and Sydney. There are many reasons to think that the sole reason the central leadership tolerates the endless hassle of Hong Kong politics is the city's importance as the frontline of this engagement between RMB and the world outside – more than 60 per cent of Chinese outward investment goes through Hong Kong.

Xi Jinping wrestled with the best kind of language to engage with this wider world. The partners that were most difficult to capture in friendly narratives were the closest – Japan, South and North Korea, and then Vietnam, Malaysia and Indonesia. The closer they were to China, the more wary they were of warm embraces and seductive words. Since 2009 they had complained of Chinese assertiveness over maritime borders, made sharper by the fact that these now clearly had exploitable resources. Pragmatic deals that shelved the almost irresolvable issues of sovereignty were put forward, but this occurred against a background of constant sniping and ill feeling. In 2014, a vast 'seabed exploration' apparatus was shifted into contested waters by China, causing a huge diplomatic backlash in Vietnam. Clashes over the Diaoyutai/Senkaku islands continued, with provocation on both sides, and neither the Japanese leader Shinzo Abe nor Xi Jinping seemed keen to see the other partly for fear of looking like they were weakening in front of domestic constituencies. Only at APEC in Beijing in November 2014 did a hilariously surly encounter take place between the two, one that inventive netizens compared to a downbeat-looking Xi as Winnie-the-Pooh meeting Abe as Eeyore.

Xi might have felt that with Japan, Vietnam and other neighbours there were serious issues to discuss. But from what little he did or said about North Korea, it looked very much like his primary feeling was contempt. His predecessor Hu had maintained robotic seriousness about China's impoverished, unstable northern neighbour, stressing their adherence to Marxism and at least maintaining regular visits. But as North Korean defector Jang Jin-sung pointed out in his memoirs, while everyone is transfixed by the 38th parallel and its political demarcation between the South and the North, for him the more important barrier was that between China and the Democratic People's Republic of Korea (DPRK), which he described as an 'ideological demarcation line'. 'The country Kim Jong-il hates most is China,' he told bemused Chinese interlocutors when he finally managed to abscond.[14] Breaking all previous protocol, Xi himself visited South Korea in 2014, but showed no signs of wanting either to take the hour-long flight east to Pyongyang, or to receive Kim Jong-il's son Kim Jong-un at home. Rumours circulated that China had simply turned off energy supplies to its dependent neighbour. Xi seems not to have inherited his predecessors' weakness for North Korean blackmail and Machiavellian manipulation. This too was good populist politics in China, where most regarded the North Koreans as embarrassing, parasitical and contemptible.

Beyond China's region, however, things get easier, at least on the surface. A visit to African countries by premier Li Keqiang in early 2014 maintained the drumbeat of how politically straightforward China was as an economic and diplomatic partner compared to the endlessly complicated, plotting West. China came, too, with limited historical baggage, and with an appetite to work with Africans, to develop their infrastructure and build their markets. In July 2014, Xi attended the BRICS summit in Brazil, searching like everyone else for a meaningful link between these five totally different entities (Brazil, Russia, India, China and South Africa). He seems to have achieved at least something tangible by proposing the establishment of a joint bank, based in Shanghai, where capital would be pooled for developmental projects. A similar principle lies behind his support for an 'Asian Infrastructure Investment Bank', something that was opposed by the United States, who tried to convince Australia not to join, despite clear evidence that it was in their interests to do so. Australia was reviewing this decision in March 2015 when the United Kingdom, France, Germany and a number of other countries confirmed that they did intend to join, despite US opposition.

But it is in places like the Middle East, at the edges of the new Silk Road, where the challenges of being an emerging superpower with interests that stretch across the world are most intense. Xi's predecessors built up a series of alliances in the Arab world that cover almost every country. China has managed to sidestep most of the issues of commitment to one side or the other in conflicts involving Iraq, Libya, Egypt, Syria and Iran. It has managed to sit neutrally between Israel and the Palestinian authorities, being friends to both but avoiding unwelcome claims of being hypocritical and unprincipled. The old standpoint maintained since the 1950s of 'non-interference in the affairs of others and respect for their sovereignty' isn't something Xi looks like he is willing to change.

China's dependence on the Middle East for half its imported oil is symptomatic of just how strained it is going to find maintaining its non-committal pose. The region, in that sense, is a test bed for China's diplomacy in its new role as the world's second-largest and most dynamic economy. Increasingly, Iran and other countries are building investment and political links with Beijing, something that has captured the keen interest of the United States and made the language about 'new model of major power relations' look more ominous than it originally appeared. Is China trying to build up a series of alliances in the region, ones that could be mobilized against the United States when it chose to do so? Is China really prepared, or willing, to be brought into the politics of the Arab world with all its complexity and danger? China has no choice but to defend its interests in the region. But with its own internal struggle against Islamic fundamentalism in the Xinjiang area, this region carries real challenges for China, ones it is hard to see it maintaining lofty distance from for too long. So far, Xi has yet to capture the right meta-narrative for this. In the Middle East, Xi's smiling diplomacy and sweet-sounding flattery fall against hard, geopolitical reality, where words are never enough and actions are always being demanded to demonstrate support and alliance.

THE CHINA MODEL

The most enthusiastic propagators of the idea of a replicable 'China model' are usually not Chinese. Figures like Joshua Cooper Ramo and Martin Jacques are the ones who speak up for this idea.[15] But figures in Beijing were more interested in stressing China's exceptional nature. There is a China model, and it applies to China. The rest of the world is a different issue.

For Xi, though, the calculation is a simple one. On its progress towards achieving its all-important centennial goals, he and his circle of policy makers appear to accept that benign relations with the rest of the world, and in particular their region, are rational. The wisdom of the Deng worldview of being at peace with the rest of the planet while you make yourself strong within is backed up by 30 years of benefits from trade and other forms of international relationship. This has been a big success.[16]

Diplomacy, however, is never solely about logic. It always has an emotional angle. It involves status, honour and pride.[17] One Western theorist has talked of the way geopolitics is about appetite, hunger and the desire to be recognized and seen by others, with the associated cultural signifiers of this.[18] Just as Xi has had to prosecute campaigns to engage the emotions of Chinese people domestically, speaking to narratives and themes in a different language to that of his predecessor, so externally he needs to take the lead in explaining his country to a world that is either confused by or antagonistic to its political difference to their systems, or that is wary of China, or simply irritated by it and the disruption that its prominence now poses. Previous iterations like 'peaceful rise' no longer seem to work well. Now there is the more urgent task of coming up with phrases and ideas that are seen as realistic but also tactful – phrases that resonate in China and appeal to the strengthening sense there that the country is finally receiving the credit and recognition it merits, but that do not spook the rest of the region and the wider world.

Despite this, for tactical reasons Xi doesn't want his country to be dragged into heavy commitments that will impede it. It looks at the alliance and treaty system of the United States half with envy, half with contempt. Pragmatic engagement based on clear recognition of mutual self-interest seems to be the fundamental philosophy guiding China's international engagement. The problem is that this is an unappetizing and somewhat unexciting message with which to try to win the hearts and minds of foreigners. As Robert Cooper said, the good thing about friends, with their loyalty and predictability, is that they are far cheaper than enemies. Having a world of friends contributes to the bottom line of China Ltd. Enemies are cost centres.[19]

One tactic that Xi has tried, through ideas like the new Silk Road, is to refer to China as a cultural entity, a place with a long history of civilization that has contributed immensely to humanity and through which it can be understood even today. He refers in speeches to figures like Xunzi, Confucius and Mencius, and in addition to Admiral Zheng He and great classical poets like Du Fu and Li Bo from the Tang dynasty, as well as China's history as an innovator, inventor and a creative culture. Confucius Institutes have figured as means of trying to promote this, though with occasionally awful own goals.[20] Will the world outside accord China respect for its culture, and link the country that exists now with those of the past that Xi is appealing to? Will they start to understand China better, and see it as an ally and not a threat, as somewhere offering a softer diplomatic future, a final counterbalance to US zealousness? All of these issues depend to a great extent on just how successful Xi is as the face of China. Hu Jintao was regarded as a disaster on this front, barely able to register in the consciousness of Western audiences. Xi has to do better. And for someone with the fearsome menu of domestic challenges listed in the previous chapter, the fact he still visits places as disparate as New Zealand, Central Asia, Brazil and Fiji shows that he takes this external task very seriously.

6

WHAT DOES XI WANT IN THE NEXT TWO DECADES?

The Master said, Do not be ready to speak of it, lest the doing of it be beyond your powers.

—*Analects* **14.21**

How do China's current leaders see the future? What is it that Xi Jinping and his colleagues mean when they talk about the 'China Dream'? We know the importance of the first centennial goal of creating a middle-income country by 2020 because of the amount of time Xi and his colleagues spend talking about it. But what about the world beyond 2020?

Chinese leaders are different to those in democracies because of their ability to work within a longer time frame. Elected political leaders need to focus on delivery of short-term goals dependent on their electoral cycle. It is rare for them to think three years ahead, let alone 20. Chinese leaders are not the servants of electoral or party politics. The assumption is that this allows them to aim for longer-term policy goals, such as the Five-Year Programmes. They have more space to pursue the future.

There is also a philosophical question sitting alongside this. Chinese leaders believe in scientific progress, and since 1949 have set out dynamic visions for the future of their country based on this faith. For Western leaders, it is often more about maintaining the good things developed economies have, where the status quo is seen as being preferable to any future radical rupture. This breeds complacency about policy, seeking to preserve but not to transform. Changes, when they happen, are best if incremental. For post-1949 China there was a clear dissatisfaction with the levels of poverty and low development that the country had sunk to, as well as a revolutionary emergency agenda. While China now is a different place to that of 1949, the desire remains for constant reform, and for achieving a tomorrow that is better than today. Chinese leaders still talk of the 'perfecting' of the socialist system and the achievement in the future of a 'perfect market'. 'Perfection' is almost a taboo word for administrators working in risk-averse democratic political systems. It is left to mystics, technology impresarios and the entertainment sector. The best that can be hoped for is 'improvement'. In market socialist China, even today there are few qualms about considering 'perfection' as a legitimate goal.

Despite this common framework, ideas about the future have changed since 1949. During the leadership of Mao Zedong and Deng Xiaoping, an aim was sometimes posited 15 years in the future (such as the aim declared in the Great Leap Forward of 1956 to overtake the United Kingdom in steel manufacturing, or, as in the Cultural Revolution from 1966, to radically reconfigure society so that it achieved perfect socialist goals). For Deng Xiaoping, the aim was to achieve socialist modernity in China, and triple GDP within three decades, a benchmark that ended up taking only a decade to achieve. The utopian goals of the Mao period were replaced from 1978 by ones in which the hunt for specific, raw GDP growth was given highest priority. One can say therefore that the future for Chinese leaders changed after 1978. Before this point, they attempted to achieve idealistic outcomes, but ones whose implementation turned out to be divisive and socially destructive, where equality and commonality among all people were the key objectives, no matter what the costs in terms of productivity, dynamism and sustainability. After 1978, it was all about becoming wealthier and better off, even if that meant living with social differences. In essence, this can be understood as a transition from ideological to material goals. In a single sentence, that is the story of the great transformation of 1978.

China is a more complicated place now, and we can see this in the way that its current leaders talk about the future. What in fact do Xi and his colleagues want for China? Can they be said to have a vision, and if so, how can we understand it? In what ways does the outside world figure in this vision? What do Chinese leaders say their own people want in the next ten to twenty years, and how do they act to bring this about? This set of questions is worth considering because the current Chinese leaders are the ones most able to control outcomes. They have the main levers of control at the moment. They may lose them one day. But from the position of the present, we can say that the people most able to deliver the China 2035 vision are sitting in Zhongnanhai at this very moment.

THE 'BENCHMARK VISION'

Conquering the future is important, but there is no neat 'manifesto for the future' that Chinese leaders have produced. No single document exists that sets out what it is they are driving at for the next two decades. In abstract terms, however, the future does haunt their pronouncements, either as a place of challenge, of fundamental change, or of the final delivery of the aspirational goals they often talk about. We can therefore say that the elite have articulated a benchmark vision through the pronouncements of people like Xi. This is a notion that the current Chinese government locates within the parameters set out by Deng Xiaoping in the early 1980s, which remain the framework within which it sees the future to this day. In this vision for the future, there are three phases. In the first, ten-year period of reform, the goal is to provide adequate food and clothing for China's population and to fulfil the basic material demands of the country. Chinese leaders would say that this has already been achieved. In the second phase, the plan is to build a moderately prosperous country by 2020, with a per capita GDP of around US$ 13,000 calculated in terms of purchasing parity. This phase is ongoing. The final phase, running from 2020 to 2050, is to complete the modernization of both the rural and urban parts of China.[1] This has yet to be achieved, and constitutes the second of Xi's centennial goals.

These three phases are necessarily very broad. The landmarks that constitute their core achievements vary and become more abstract as we proceed from the first to the third. The road map to achieving the second phase by 2020 is starting to figure in planning for the 12th and 13th Five-Year Programmes, running from 2011 to 2020, and there are targets set in key Party declarations from the Third Plenum statement of late 2013, the Fourth Plenum of 2014 and other key leadership speeches over this period. However, the achievement of the third phase figures very little in current government baseline objectives. If there is a long-term vision that Chinese leaders spell out for China, it is best captured by the phrase '*fuqiang guojia*' ('rich, strong, powerful country'), a term with currency going back over almost a century, and one that sets out the China Dream that Xi Jinping has frequently talked about since early 2013.

THE FOUR MAJOR RISKS TO XI'S CHINA

In conceptualizing China's future, we have to deal with the four great 'ifs' of its medium- to long-term stability and development. These can be categorized as social questions around the country's continuation as a stable and unified country, domestic political questions involving the continuation of its current political model, geopolitical questions involving the impact of the outside world, and economic questions involving the issue of maintaining sustainable, good-quality GDP growth. These four areas map out the terrain of risk: any of them could completely derail Xi Jinping's leadership.

Social issues involve the unity of China. The country's unity is recent, and its borders new, settled mostly in the period from 1949 to 1980.[2] This involved negotiations over more than 20 contested areas. The issue of Taiwan remains unresolved, and the autonomous regions of Tibet, Xinjiang and, to a lesser extent, Inner Mongolia, all border regions, which make up almost 50 per cent of the current country's land mass, are continuing causes of potential instability. The search for a sustainable solution to their long-term governance is therefore ongoing. The current government policy framework of maintaining ethnic unity, preserving social stability and encouraging economic development, articulated most recently in the 2014 meetings on Xinjiang held in Beijing, are unlikely to be effective in the long term. Under Hu Jintao and now Xi, there has been a debate about, for instance, a 'new generation of ethnic policies' by scholars like Hu Angang of Qinghua University and Ma Rong of Beijing University. These figures are already raising serious questions about current policy parameters. This is not just an ethnic matter: China's social cohesion, with rising strife between the winners and losers of the reform process over the last three decades, is also a major issue. Control over these issues is a major part of the thinking of contemporary leaders.

Everything in this book has made clear that in the thinking of Xi and his colleagues, the leadership of the CCP is central to the successful governance of modern China. The role of the Party in creating a framework for government policy and assessing outcomes of policy remains uniquely powerful and uncontested. In the short to medium term, this looks unlikely to change. The CCP is the sole unifying element in a society of increasing diversity, and is the only entity that believes it has the legitimacy and capacity to articulate and deliver an holistic social, economic and political vision. But no Communist party with a monopoly on power has lasted more than 74 years (this record is still held by the Communist Party of the former USSR). Because of this, the CCP is highly aware of its vulnerability. In a meeting with foreign scholars held in Beijing in September 2014, vice president Li Yuanchao, someone closely linked to Xi, spoke of the need for political reform in view of the Party's long continuation in power, and of its necessarily having to refresh its narrative with the people of China. However, beyond statements of the need for political reform, and declarations (such as that made by Xi while marking the 60th anniversary of the NPC) that Western models are not workable in China, as yet there has been no clear, detailed road map for how the CCP sees the development of the country's political reform, beyond reform within the Party itself. The shape, velocity and direction of the modernization of China's administrative and political system remain major sources of uncertainty. In this area, we broadly know what Chinese leaders don't want for the future. But we don't really know what they do want.

When it comes to external, geopolitical issues, we see the concentric circles of relationships that matter to China described in Chapter 5, and the need for the country to maintain its alliances. In terms of supply chains, sources of growth, export markets, resource supply and security, China is a uniquely global actor. It is impacted by and impacts on the rest of the world due to its size and location. Bordering 14 countries, it is part of a region that contains almost half the world's population, and its current investment links spread to almost every area of the globe. This is only likely to increase in the coming two decades, and carries as much risk as opportunity. The 2008 Global Financial Crisis threatened to impact dramatically on China, and was only averted through huge fiscal stimulus, its protected capital and current account. Since the era of former paramount leader Deng Xiaoping from the late 1970s to the early 1990s, China has largely had a benign international context in which to grow its own economy. But it is a country with a history of others interfering in its internal affairs, at least in modern times, with unresolved borders with India and on its maritime front, and with nascent nationalist tendencies (particularly regarding Japan and the United States). For this reason, economic or political deterioration in the international environment will have an adverse effect on China, just as a deterioration of China's internal situation will impact on the world.

Finally, there are economic issues. Producing GDP growth has been the core source of legitimacy for the Party since the reform process under the post-Maoist government started in 1978. Over the last three decades, China has managed to achieve a little less than 10 per cent GDP growth each year, although since 2012 this has fallen to 7.5 per cent, with a drop to under 7 per cent for 2015. The era of double-digit growth has come to an end, with the Xi Jinping leadership speaking of more modest growth and the need to seek more efficiency. Even so, a strong, positive growth rate for the next 15 years is still necessary. In almost every leadership statement, from former president Hu Jintao's speech at the 17th National Congress in 2007 to the Third Plenum statement under Xi Jinping in late 2013, producing economic growth has been placed at the core of the Party's function, and the most powerful source of its legitimacy. But in statements made at the same Beijing meeting referred to above, Li Yuanchao made it clear that the Party's failure to continue delivering a good material standard of living for people would result in its falling from power. This awareness of the demands of a population with a rising rights-aware, assertive and urban middle class is behind much of the Party's talk since late 2012 of better service to the people, addressing corruption and delivering good-quality administration. Satisfying this constituency has increasingly become the objective of government policy.

HOW XI'S LEADERSHIP SEES THE FUTURE

While Chinese leaders have not spelled out specifics for the future in a single place, there are core sources which supply information about the kind of framework within which they envisage the management of the four great risk areas outlined above and what they want to achieve. This 'vision', I would argue, is set out in four different places.

The first is in a report issued by the World Bank and the Development Research Centre of the State Council (DRC) in China in February 2012, called *China 2030: Building a Modern, Harmonious and Creative Society*. This demonstrates in some detail targets for the next two decades. Interestingly, many of its core policy recommendations – about deepening the market, extending the reach of the non-state sector and moving to more sophisticated ways of assessing GDP that take into account people's well-being – figured prominently in the Third Plenum of 2013. For this reason, the report can be taken as a semi-official declaration of intent in China for the longer-term future.[3] *China 2030*, with its vision of the country becoming a 'modern, harmonious, creative and high-income society', provides the core outline of what China might look like in 2035, and which policies it will use to get there.

The second is in official documents, which have been dealt with in some detail elsewhere in this book. The 60-point statement issued by the Party in October 2013 at the Third Plenum, especially, stands as a manifesto, a statement of political intent by the new leadership. In particular, it states that government policy needs to shift away from production of raw GDP growth to a 'fast, sustainable model' that will need to be more efficient and more reliant on perfecting marketization in China. As the main leader with macroeconomic responsibility, premier Li Keqiang has also outlined the structural changes necessary to deliver the continuing modernization of the Chinese economic model. These embrace increasing consumption, raising the service component in the economy, reducing government investment in fixed assets and accelerating China's urbanization. We can divine from this document what sort of future it might be driving towards.

Because the official material available is largely very careful, or highly circumscribed, in what it says about political change, we have also to look at semi-official material written by those within the Party and government apparatus, which speculates about political change in ways that elite leaders might support. Written by two scholars from the Central Party School in Beijing, Zhou Tianyong and Wang Changjiang, and a serving official, Wang Anling, *Gong jian* (Storm the Fortress) of 2007 develops a clear vision of where China's political reform might need to focus. It spells out internal reform for the Party while preserving its unified rule, devolving powers to China's provinces and allowing higher levels of participation in decision making to ensure that rule is stable, prosperity is delivered and China is politically, economically and socially sustainable. Authored by key officials for the Party's main think tank, this document is still highly relevant as a carefully worked out official view of how to change China's fiscal and administrative system within the parameters of one-party rule.[4]

Finally, there is material from international data bodies collated over the past. Simply put, the best predictor of the future in China is the past, though of course it can be treacherously hard to interpret which parts of the past to look at for clues to future growth. For core areas, from demographics to economic growth, historical trends do offer a basis for understanding how the future might develop if current policy and the aspirations of the material above are observed. These are easily searchable, and come from such bodies as the United Nations, World Bank and IMF.

THE THINGS THAT ARE EASIEST TO PREDICT

Recent historical patterns can give some idea of the most likely trends for the following core areas: demographics, energy usage, GDP growth rates, productivity and composition of the economy. Based on the size of China's population today, the fertility rate over the last decades and the composition of the population in terms of gender and urban/rural levels historically, there is a relatively high standard of predictability about China's demographics. The trends one can discern suggest that gender composition will remain stable, population size will increase (while remaining manageable) and the largest foreseeable challenge will be a steep rise in median age, and dependency of people over the age of 60. These predications can be adversely affected by a pandemic, unforeseen rises or falls in fertility rates, social policy (which could either encourage or discourage childbearing) and medical care for the elderly. A relaxation of the one-child policy, something that in fact was formally announced in October 2015 at the Fifth Plenum in Beijing, when it was declared that couples could now have two children, might lead to a rise in population. Conversely, a pandemic, such as a major outbreak of bird flu, might lead to a fall in population. But it is clear that the likeliest challenges will arise neither from the population size nor from its age and gender composition, but from the policy tools with which to deal with an ageing population and its social welfare and health needs. Policy failure here could have huge implications. It is also clear that the response to the rise in obesity, and the chronic illnesses associated with it, will be increasingly important in the decades to come.

The use of resources, energy and environmental indicators are also crucially important. Again, based on today's levels and historical trends, there are plenty of possible scenarios to consider, some more likely than others. But there is less predictability about this area than with demographics. The adverse factor here is environmental collapse; the most likely positive factor will be the creation of new, energy-efficient technologies that better address China's energy needs and repair its environmental degradation. Economic indicators can also be projected from the past into the future, figures over the last decade in particular. We can get an idea from these of annual GDP growth rate, GDP per capita (gross and purchasing-power parity), unemployment rate, wages, inflation, the balance of trade between imports and exports, foreign direct investment, government spending and debt, car registrations, consumer spending, disposable personal income, personal savings and taxes. These help build a picture of the likely future shape and health of the economy. The GDP growth rate is taken as impacting on all the other indicators.

CHINA 2035: 'A MODERN, HARMONIOUS, CREATIVE AND HIGH-INCOME SOCIETY'

In 2035, if the current Chinese leadership sticks to its main parameters, China will remain unified, GDP growth will be strong and the CCP will remain in power. The Chinese government will be able to maintain a high level of control over political, social and economic policy levers. It will experience limited external disturbance and a largely benign international environment. For this to happen, the world will have maintained an annual growth rate over the previous two decades of 3.3 per cent, falling to 2.3 per cent by 2035. The benign and stable economic environment will have continued, with no major downturn in the previous two decades. Demographically, while China's population will have aged, the changes to the one-child policy announced in October 2015 and proactive internal migration campaigns, along with a raising of the retirement age, will have made the impact of ageing on the population and of gender imbalance manageable and by 2035 the situation will have mostly stabilized, aided by efficient social-welfare costs and effective pension reform. Environmentally, China will have addressed its air quality, water pollution and sustainability issues, and shifted from the 70 per cent dependence on fossil fuels of 2014 to levels closer to 45 per cent, with highly renewable, more nuclear-based and more diverse sources of power. In terms of productivity and the composition of its economy, by 2035 China will be a high-income, high-service-sector, high-consuming country. It will be reliant on indigenous sources of growth and on export levels similar to those of the United States in 2014, with more goods and services being generated within China.

In terms of economic structure, marketization will have continued, meaning that, by 2035, two-thirds of the economy will be in the hands of non-state-owned companies with an entrepreneurial culture. These companies will have flexible access to capital, and will be investors abroad. The service-sector-working urban population of China with a higher component of GDP in consumption will be well established. The urban middle class will make up three-quarters of the Chinese population. The number of those who have tertiary-level education will have increased to 40 per cent, with Chinese universities ranking among the best in the world because of the high sums put into research and development over the previous 20 years. China's energy usage will have diversified, becoming much more energy efficient, with a coherent national grid, the marketization of utility prices and, through innovative technology, a much lower reliance on fossil fuels and the emergence of robust renewable sources of energy. Car usage will have been curbed by excellent infrastructure in cities, the creation of electricity-powered cars and deeper urbanization. From a society of great inequality in 2014, with a Gini coefficient of close to 0.5,[5] the Chinese government – through a redistributive tax system, and the development of the western and less developed areas of China – will have created a more equal society with a diamond-shaped structure, in which there are relatively small numbers of wealthy and poor, and most are middle class. The 150 million living in poverty in 2014 will have been reduced to around 20 million, with malnutrition and other chronic signs of inequality largely extinct.

By 2035, the provinces and autonomous regions of China will have been entrusted with the full fiscal powers to raise and spend more than 60 per cent of their own revenue and expenditure. While some responsibilities will remain in the hands of the central state, provincial powers will have increased dramatically. China will have assumed a proactive and powerful role in the Asian region, with a naval force and power projection sufficient to protect its major interests. It will have managed its relations with its neighbours, with the DPRK likely to be under a wholly different political system by then, and the issue of Taiwan resolved either by a federal arrangement in which Taiwan becomes part of China with a high degree of independence, or through the recognition of Taiwanese independence. China's army will be one of the largest and most modern in the world, but it will have assumed some of the responsibility to protect and to undertake regional peacekeeping and intervention that the United States has exercised over the previous century.

By this time, there will be controlled development of rule by law, which will operate in the fields of commerce and society, but will not subject the CCP itself to restraints of legal scrutiny. The Party will maintain its extra-judicial standing, even though legal procedures will be developed in society; there will be better-trained judges, more separation of powers and greater predictability for the economy. Civil law will also be more strongly established, serving social stability. Officials will be paid highly in order to offset corruption, with a more depoliticized, professional cadre of local and national officials, many of whom will not be Party members.

The urbanization and development of western regions through pro-growth strategies will have occurred. Inequalities between western, central and coastal provinces will have been addressed by more decentralization of fiscal powers, but with strong central political control. The western area will be assisted by the development of infrastructure. China will shift away from a capital-intensive, investment-reliant economy; there will be more non-state-sector companies and a stronger role for them in government procurement, with the SOEs largely made more efficient by market forces and restricted to key areas. Energy and resource companies are likely to be split up, made more international and diversified in their ownership. Consumption will rise with increased wage levels. Civil society will be given a firmer legal foundation and a stronger role in services once supplied by the government. Educational improvements will have occurred through the reform of universities to encourage innovation, with more Chinese attending university than ever before, and the quality of universities improving. For this reason, more Chinese students will remain in China to study, and there will be a significant rise in China's internationally accepted research output. National innovation plans will have prioritized technological and science areas, and in these investment will have produced world-class centres and a proper intellectual-property regime to protect them. The Party will grant wider means to consult with the emerging middle classes, in order to tap their knowledge and involve them in the development of their society. Elections at township and prefectural level will exist on the same model as that introduced for villages in the 1980s and 1990s. These will involve multiparty candidates.

Over this period, technological breakthroughs will mean that Chinese technology companies will be global leaders, with proprietorial intellectual property particularly in bioscience, computer science and automotive technology. China will lead the world in clean technologies, and will have made breakthroughs in areas relating to clean fuel and renewables because of targeted government support. A national system for social welfare financed by an insurance fund into which Chinese taxpayers contribute will be created. China will be largely self-sufficient in foodstuffs, and will have a sustainable water-management system.

Good-quality free-trade agreements with other countries will exist, with China having signed agreements and enjoying balanced trade with most of the world's major economies. In particular, it will be the key trading and technology partner of African and Latin American countries. There will be deeper investment abroad, searching for better capital returns: China will be the world's largest outward investor, and a major source of capital. Shanghai will rank as the world's largest international finance hub, largely through its unique position as the interface between the domestic finance market and the rest of the world.

Labour mobility will be encouraged through the reform of the *hukou* system: there will be complete mobility for Chinese citizens in China, with more than 70 per cent living in cities through incremental and manageable increases over the previous 20 years. The Chinese countryside will be modernized, with the agriculture sector consolidated and mechanized. Revenue for cities and provinces will be revised so that some taxation can be raised locally. With technological breakthroughs, the national innovation plans of 2006 will have created a stronger innovation culture within the non-state sector, and there will be better and more efficient deployment of capital through the creation of a more rules-based, predictable and regulated finance and lending sector. China will be a major deployer of funding for research and development. It will have developed its own avionics, engineering and shipbuilding capacities. There will be efficiency in the use of capital in finance reform; a strong regulatory framework guaranteed by law and creating accountability both in government and enterprise; banks that are open to competition and are international in their operations; a capital account that is open, and where the Chinese currency is one of the key global currencies next to the US dollar. Domestic consumption will have risen, alongside wage rises in the last two decades, which will cause a rise in disposable income, in particular for urban homeowners, who will have the rights to 200-year leases for their property, better inheritance laws and more financial products, domestically and internationally, within which to invest. China's enterprises will largely be in the hands of the non-state sector, with private companies given a strong voice on the Central Committee of the Party. With their election as local leaders, either as Party or non-Party affiliated members, non-state entrepreneurs will become increasingly politically prominent in society. Non-state companies will constitute China's strongest innovators, supported by legal protections and by full access to government procurement. The state will only control key strategic assets, such as defence and nuclear, and have controlling shares in energy and resource companies, which will be partially marketized.

In terms of energy efficiency, the government will support incentives through the 13th, 14th, 15th and 16th Five-Year Programmes and will control emissions from cars via the construction of more efficient urban and rural transport structures. Solar power will be used in most urban areas to account for the energy use in the majority of buildings. Tax incentives will be used to promote higher use of renewables, and China will have benefited from the use of imported Russian and locally sourced gas.

WHAT IF?

This is an approximation of the world as it will be in 2035, if we take what Xi and the leaders around him say. There are, of course, a million things that could go wrong. Social unrest could get out of hand; the unity of the country could collapse; war with Japan or the United States might erupt over maritime borders or Taiwan; or, more likely than any of these, a food contamination crisis or pandemic could bring the country to its knees. China's tragic history of crisis is one of the worst in the world. It is a country that has known bitter, bitter failures.

There are many other potential scenarios. One of them would put China in a situation similar to that of the USSR, with the Party simply collapsing and oligarchs rising like warlords, running separate parts of the country, with the coastal regions jettisoning the central and western regions, which are left to stagnate or implode. The economy might collapse, with sources of growth closing down. The finance sector might simply become unstuck; debt could overwhelm SOEs and the local and central government. Then China would suffer its own massive financial crisis, and the rest of the world would have to decide whether to intervene. China's water poverty might impede the great drive to urbanize, with cities proving unsustainable and some of the newest abandoned. China already has ghost cities. As drought spreads, it might end up with ghost provinces. The environment is already at breaking point as a result of the last three decades of unprecedented industrialization. At any moment, it might break down altogether, affecting food supplies and air quality and creating massive weather events that decimate large areas of the country. A pandemic could spread quickly, overwhelming China's health-care system, causing a breakdown in social order. Then the old chaos of the past will come again. The mighty CCP of today might very suddenly look a weak and vulnerable thing.

These are not the outcomes that the CCP wants. By 2035, if it can have a sustainable, urban, green, high-status country, then the dream will be well on the way to fulfilment. But here is the great quandary for the rest of the world. For all our qualms about the CCP, about its history and its difference from us, when we look at the future, and at the vision expressed in what Chinese leaders now say, it is one that most of us could easily live with. We are hoping for the same thing. We want a world where Chinese and non-Chinese live sustainably, more equitably and peacefully. We want stability. For this reason, Xi's Party becomes our best bet to get there. Very ironically, in this context we are all supporters of Xi's CCP.

CONCLUSION

WHO IS XI?

> *The Master said: When everyone dislikes a man, enquiry is necessary. When everyone likes a man, enquiry is necessary.*
> —*Analects* 15.27

In 2014 a major global leader, only a couple of years into his job as head of an entity containing more than a billion people but whose governance and leadership had been beset by crisis and confusion in recent years, gathered together his chief decision makers and delivered an unequivocal series of devastating criticisms of them. Berating them for problems arising from 'the pathology of power' and 'narcissism', he said that they had come to act like 'lords and masters', building 'walls and routines around themselves' and losing their connection with the very people they were meant to serve. He listed their problems: cliquishness, careerism, acquisitiveness, competitiveness and indifference to others, losing sight of what really mattered in their work to 'restrict themselves to bureaucratic matters'. He reserved particular scorn for those who had succumbed to 'the terrorism of gossip' and who stood ready to 'slander, defame and discredit others'.[1]

As the newly installed leader of almost a billion Catholics globally, Pope Francis is in charge of an organization with a history centuries longer than the CCP's. But his battle to instil a renewed sense of mission into a Church that has lost touch with its spiritual roots, tarnished its legitimacy and become consumed by material power so that its leadership fails to live up to its critical current tasks is eerily similar to that of Xi with the CCP. The parallels don't end there. Just as with Francis, Xi has looming over him members of previous leaderships, some of whom are still alive. As with Francis, he has to forge some sort of reconnection with a membership that endured several years of cerebral, largely detached top leadership prior to him – a leadership that created the impression that the organization had been dozing while the rest of the world accelerated into the future.

Xi may lack the Pope's florid language in tackling the issue. But his meaning is the same. His words on 15 November 2012, when he first emerged from behind a screen in the Great Hall of the People in Beijing to address the world as Party leader, were clipped and to the point: 'In the new circumstances our Party faces many severe challenges as well as many pressing issues within the Party that need to be addressed,' he said. Then he directly described the most pressing of these: 'corruption, being divorced from the people, and being satisfied with going through formalities and bureaucracy on the part of some Party officials'.[2] Replace 'Party officials' with 'priests', and the same sentence would not look amiss coming from Pope Francis.

Parallels between the Catholic Church and the CCP have been noted before. They have even been observed in China, where in the past the Central Party School in Beijing has looked in some detail at how the Church has managed to maintain cohesiveness and ideological control over such a disparate global community of the faithful. What perhaps most appeals to the cadres in Beijing is the 2,000-year success of the Church in managing to survive, despite its many trials and challenges. The CCP, of course, lacks one great advantage that the Church has: it does not promise those who follow and believe in it eternal life or the remission of sins, nor does it appeal to a supreme being whom it serves, despite the extraordinary claims made about Mao at the height of his powers. This lack of spiritual resources is something that nags at China's current leaders, and prompted them to establish an 'Office for Spiritual Civilization' some years ago, which was headed by Liu Yunshan. Even so, the Party has in recent years used language that creeps more and more towards a message to Chinese people that the Party is on a mission to make them not just rich and materially better off, but satisfied and fulfilled.

WHO IS XI: CHINA'S GODFATHER?

For the writer Yu Jie, there is another template with an Italian theme that Xi might fit into: that of godfather to a Mafia clan. Yu, who produced an equally critical treatment of the avuncular Wen Jiabao while still based in China, one for which he was rewarded with beatings and expulsion from the Party, is now based in America. He penned a book on Xi in 2014 that addressed the question of what sort of leader he was, making his starting point the valid enquiry into how someone who had only got onto the Central Committee in 1997 by the skin of his teeth, and who had shown no real skill as a provincial leader, could become the dominant political figure in China.[3] Yu's chief thesis is that Xi and his sent-down generation have zero real understanding or sympathy with democracy, because they were so effectively formed by the Yan'an spirit that infused their formative years and shaped their worldviews. Maoism is the only systematic, comprehensive and accessible body of ideas that Xi would have had access to over this period.[4] Yu contrasts Xi's warm words about this period of rustication with the real consequences for his family. He describes how Xi's mother reportedly wrote to premier Zhou Enlai in 1972 begging for Xi's father's case to be reviewed and for him to be released, and the sense of insecurity that his family break-up must have instilled in him. Yu then asks how it is possible that someone who grew up in this climate of fear could not but have a mindset in which he would try, once in power, to reinforce his position in any way he could as a practical psychological defence against such horrible times ever returning.[5] With Xi's emotional commitment to Maoism, Yu poses the question of whether, in fact, he still stands by his father's influence and memory in view of how conflicted his relationship was with the Chairman, and whether the best way to understand Xi might be to look at him as someone who places fidelity to ideology above everything else.[6]

Pope or godfather? Both these models have a dramatic punch. But perhaps the truth about Xi is more prosaic. The easiest way to locate him is through the public positions he occupies, and what they say about the varieties of power available to him. Xi is, in the end, the general secretary. This was the first position he secured, and the most important. Without that, the presidency and even leadership of the army are worth little. To appreciate truly the significance of this role, we have to work through what the Party itself is as an organization, what its history has been, how it describes its current function and what kind of entity it has become after more than 60 years in power. When we grapple with the questions of who Xi is, what he wants to do and what the nature of his power is, we inevitably have to think about the Party he stands at the head of, to which he owes everything and through the ranks of which he has risen to be in the position he is now. The idea that Xi is some kind of strongman has to be circumscribed and qualified by this focus on the Party, and how it limits and enhances his powers. In answering this, we realize that without the Party, Xi is no one. But the Party, with or without Xi, has to continue. The Party is the power in China, and Xi is only powerful through it, operating within the limits it sets. On this basis, he is no Mao.

The power of the Party is often misunderstood. Most treatments look at it from the standpoint of its organizational strengths and attributes. They look at it as a social entity: at its hierarchy, its internal governance, the ways in which it has attempted to build intellectual consensus and enforce discipline. One of the most common mantras is that it is pragmatic, driven by outcomes, realistic and hard-nosed in the way it goes about its business, and solely focused on staying in power. Its ideology is seen in this framework as at best a quaint hang-over from its foundational phase, and at worst plagued by irrelevance that it has never had the courage or sense of purpose to eschew. The things that matter are its ability to incentivize people with economic goodies, and its efficiency.

I have argued in this book, however, that the power of the Party led by Xi is precisely in its belief systems, in the link its most influential leaders see between the ideology they have developed over its

90 years in existence and 60 years in power, and the delivery of their idea of perfect modernity – a strong, rich, stable China, one that is prosperous, respected and powerful. This is not a simple message to deliver. Nor is it inconsistent. It reaches beyond parochial issues of personal networks and temporary enrichment to something that runs across the complexity of Chinese society and appeals to almost everyone. The emotional power of this 'goal', and the ways it is linked to the organization of the Party as well as, more importantly, to its ideas and ideals, is the greatest power asset that Xi Jinping has. It is no longer through the gun, or through uniform terror and repression in the style of Mao, that he can enforce discipline. Xi's core message is that the country will reach its great goal, restore itself to the nation it once was and rectify the injustices of history – these are things that are really worth striving for. And these are the things that he has become a servant of.

This is a game of high stakes. Things could go wrong. Rumours on the US-run Boxun website in early 2015 spoke of an attempted military coup in Beijing by disgruntled army personnel hit hard by the anti-corruption campaign. There had been similar rumblings in early 2012 around the time of the fall of Bo Xilai. We can likely dismiss these as fantasies, and they may never have happened. But we should not be complacent about the insecurity at the top end of Chinese politics. Luck can come and go within a few seconds. Figures like Xi, who look strong and secure today, can suddenly find their networks become cold around them, and people can turn against them. It could easily go badly for Xi – the Politburo is a merciless, unsentimental place, and if enough people around the table start worrying that Xi is taking things in the wrong direction, then all the rules and protocols that prevailed before will be worth naught. As one official stated in 2014, the first law is survival. Everything else stems from that. It is unlikely, but not unthinkable, that people in the United States or Europe will switch on their TVs one morning and see reports of Xi being unceremoniously removed from power by a palace coup. As he himself said, it is a hard thing to govern a country like China. And it is a very easy place to make enemies.

If he does succeed in surviving, and even prospers, then the rewards are limitless. There are ways in which he could easily extend his mandate beyond 2022. Constitutions, after all, are things that can, with enough support, be rewritten. This is precisely what Putin did in Russia. And if Xi delivers on his programme of a confident, wealthy, sustainable country by 2021, when his Party position ends, then the public may well prefer that he stay around. Power is the most challenging drug to wean oneself off.

As the last chapter shows, if Xi's government does achieve its goals, then the Party has to think harder about its role. Do we see in this distant perfection of modernity in China some moment of alignment and mystical unity, whereby the Party withers away, true to its Marxist roots, and somehow China, transformed, renewed and strengthened, has some other governance appropriate to its new state? These questions into the deep future are not ones that Xi and his fellow leaders are willing to address. To them, everything is about the path to nirvana, not what happens when the country attains it. To deny that the Party and Xi as its current leader have this spiritual dimension to their words and their exercise of power is to misunderstand and misinterpret them. It lingers palpably behind almost everything they say.

Looking at Xi outside the context of the Party, therefore, means that you are looking at something that in a sense doesn't exist. Xi, unlike Mao, never grew into the Party, but always belonged to it. He has no existence separate from the culture of the Party, and no autonomy from it. The ideas of him being a godfather or a new Mao, as Yu Jie states, take him from the current context into one that, if it ever existed in the past, is no longer relevant.

His skill, as I have attempted to demonstrate in this book, is in being an instinctively good reader of the Party's interests: someone who can steer and direct it in the treacherous phase that is often talked about, as it strives to achieve its millennial goals by 2021. Looking into the eyes of Xi Jinping, you look into the eyes of the Party itself – the personification of its ambition and spirit, its most faithful and truest servant, and someone like Pope Francis, who, for all his outward exemplification of influence, persuasion and force, would almost certainly object to the claim that he is pursuing his own interests and indulging the narcissism of power. The truly powerful, as history proves time and time again, locate their power far away from themselves. And for Xi Jinping that is in the ideals, beliefs and passions of the world's final Communist party, holding a monopoly of power over a colossal country.

NOTES

All URLs given in the notes and bibliography were accessible as of 11 November 2015 unless otherwise stated.

PREFACE

1   See Robert Lawrence Kuhn, *How China's Leaders Think: The Inside Story of China's Past, Current and Future Leaders* (rev. edn; London: John Wiley, 2011).
2   Simon Leys, *The Hall of Uselessness* (Collingwood: Black Inc., 2012), p. 260.
3   It is astonishing how resilient the myth of the Great Wall being visible from the moon still is. It originated through a simple single entry in the US *Ripley's Believe It or Not* cartoon strip in the 1930s, and remains with us today, despite the fact that there is not a shred of evidence it is true.
4   All but one of the quotations are taken from *The Analects*, trans. Arthur Waley (London: Everyman, 2000). The exception is the epigraph to Chapter 2, which is a quotation attributed to Confucius as given in the *Chambers Dictionary of Quotations* (1997).

INTRODUCTION

1   Yasheng Huang, *Capitalism with Chinese Characteristics* (Cambridge: Cambridge University Press, 2008), pp. 175–6.
2   Chinese leaders have been arranged into 'generations': the first under Mao, the second under Deng, the third under Jiang Zemin, the fourth under Hu Jintao and the fifth, the current one, under Xi Jinping.

3   Cheng Li, *China's Leaders: The New Generation* (Boulder, CO: Rowman & Littlefield, 2001), p. 3.

4   Personal communication with someone who was on the US delegation to China in 1972, September 2012.

5   Jeff Mason and Steve Holland, 'Obama says China's Xi has consolidated power quickly, worrying neighbors', Reuters [news agency] (4 December 2014). Available at http://www.reuters.com/article/2014/12/04/us-usa-china-obama-idUSKCN0JH21420141204.

6   Yu Jie, *Zhongguo Jiaofu* [China's godfather] (Hong Kong and New York, NY: Open Books, 2014).

7   On Singaporean former leader Lee Kuan Yew's assessment in May 2009 of Xi Jinping, see 'Deputy secretary Steinberg's May 30, 2009 conversation with Singapore minister mentor Lee Kuan Yew', WikiLeaks [website] (4 June 2009). Available at https://wikileaks.org/plusd/cables/09SINGAPORE529_a.html. Lee's words have proved prescient: 'Xi is a princeling who succeeded despite being rusticated. When the party needed his talents, Xi was brought in as Shanghai Party secretary. Xi is seen as a Jiang Zemin protege [*sic*], but in another three and a half years Jiang's influence will be gone. The focus now is on maintaining the system. There are no more strongmen like Deng Xiaoping. Jiang did not like Hu, but could not stop him, because Hu had the backing of the system and he did not make mistakes.'

8   'Singapore founding father Lee Kuan Yew says Xi Jinping is in Mandela's class', *South China Morning Post* [website] (7 August 2013). Available at http://www.scmp.com/news/asia/article/1294831/lee-kuan-yew-says-xi-jinping-mandelas-class?page=all.

9   Tania Branigan, 'China needs political reform to avert "historical tragedy"', *Guardian* (14 March 2012). Available at http://www.theguardian.com/world/2012/mar/14/china-political-reform-wen-jiabao.

10   Mobo Gao, *The Battle for China's Past* (London: Pluto Press, 2008), p. 87.

1   THE HUNT FOR POWER IN MODERN CHINA

1   The biography that best describes the psychological toll of this trauma is Alexander V. Pantsov and Steven I. Levine, *Mao: The Real Story* (New York: Simon & Schuster, 2012).

2   For Yu Keping's take on this, see his opening chapter in Kenneth Lieberthal, Cheng Li and Yu Keping, *China's Political Development: Chinese and American Perspectives* (Washington DC: Brookings Institution Press, 2014).

3   For these pillars, see CCP Party History Office, *Zhongguo gongchandang lishi 1949–1978* [Chinese Communist Party history 1949–1978] (Beijing: Zhonggong Dangshi Chubanshe, 2011), and Jonas Kallio, *Tradition in Chinese Politics: The Party-State's Reinvention of the Past* (Helsinki: Finnish Institute of International Affairs, 2011).

4   Rana Mitter, *China's War with Japan 1937–1945: The Struggle for Survival* (London: Allen Lane, 2013).

5   'Constitution of the People's Republic of China, adopted 4 December 1982'. Available at http://en.people.cn/constitution/constitution.html.

6   Denial of this narrative, for instance, figures in the sixth of the 'seven political perils' outlined in the CCP communiqué of March 2013 that became known as 'Document no. 9', which forbids 'promoting historical nihilism, trying to undermine the history of the CCP and New China'. The prescription goes: 'The goal of historical nihilism, in the guise of "reassessing history," is to distort Party history and the history of New China. This is mainly expressed in the following ways: Rejecting the revolution; claiming that the revolution led by the Chinese Communist Party resulted only in destruction; denying the historical inevitability in China's choice of the Socialist road, calling it the wrong path, and the Party's and new China's history a "continuous series of mistakes"; rejecting the accepted conclusions on historical events and figures, disparaging our Revolutionary precursors, and vilifying the Party's leaders. Recently, some people took advantage of Comrade Mao Zedong's 120th birthday in order to deny the scientific and guiding value of Mao Zedong thought. Some people try to cleave apart the period that preceded Reform and Opening from the period that followed, or even to set these two periods in opposition to one another. By rejecting CCP history and the history of New China, historical nihilism seeks to fundamentally undermine the CCP's historical purpose, which is tantamount to denying the legitimacy of the CCP's long-term political dominance.' For the full text, see 'Document number nine: a ChinaFile translation', ChinaFile [website] (8 November 2013). Available at http://www.chinafile.com/document-9-chinafile-translation.

7   Cary Huang, 'How leading small groups help Xi Jinping and other Party

leaders exert power,' *South China Morning Post* [website] (20 January 2014). Available at http://www.scmp.com/news/china/article/1409118/how-leading-small-groups-help-xi-jinping-and-other-party-leaders-exert.

8   See Evgeny Morozov, *The Net Delusion: How Not to Liberate the World* (London and New York: Penguin, 2011).

9   Li Tuo, 'Wang Zengqi yu xiandai Hanyu xiezuo – jiantan Mao wenti' [Wang Zengqi and modern Chinese writing – and a discussion of "Mao-style prose"'], Douban [Chinese social-networking website] (18 September 2009). Available at http://www.douban.com/group/topic/8051808/.

10   For a very good discussion of this see Norman Fairclough, *New Labour, New Language?* (London: Routledge, 2005) and Geremie Barmé, 'New China newspeak', *The China Story* [website] (2 August 2012). Available at http://www.thechinastory.org/lexicon/new-china-newspeak/.

11   This is analysed in Kerry Brown, *Hu Jintao: China's Silent Ruler* (Singapore: World Scientific, 2012).

12   The text of this speech was published as Liu Yunshan, 'Anzhao goujian shehui-zhuyi hexie shehui yaoqiu shenhua tuozhan chuangxin xuanchuan sixiang gongzuo' [Based on the requirements of constructing socialist harmonious society, deepen, expand in scope and innovate propaganda of ideological work], *Qiushi* [Chinese journal] 19 (2005).

13   See Perry Link, *An Anatomy of Chinese* (Cambridge, MA: Harvard University Press, 2013) for a comprehensive overview of this.

14   The text of this interview is published in Xi Jinping, *The Governance of China* [English version] (Beijing: Foreign Languages Press, 2014), p. X.

15   Published ibid., p. 68.

16   Robert Lawrence Kuhn, 'Xi's tenet of comprehensive governance', *China Daily* [website]. Available at http://www.chinadaily.com.cn/opinion/2015-08/05/content_21502358.htm.

17   Despite Xi's strictures against the threats of the internet, given later, he himself has been reportedly an active user of the internet and the first to see the value of using blogging and online resources. See Yang Hengjun, 'Xi Jinping, China's first "blogger"', *Diplomat* [website] (12 September 2014). Available at http://thediplomat.com/2014/09/xi-jinping-chinas-first-blogger/.

18   For a unique overview of just how this internal surveillance system worked, see Michael Schoenhals, *Spying for the People: Mao's Secret Agents 1949–1967* (Cambridge: Cambridge University Press, 2013).

19   See for instance 'The erotic carnival in recent Chinese history', in Liu Xiaobo, *No Enemies, No Hatred*, ed. Perry Link, Tienchi Martin-Liao and Liu Xia (Cambridge, MA: Belknap, 2012), p. 150 onwards.

20   Xi Jinping, *Governance*, pp. 181, 183.

21   Ibid., p. 181.

22   The definition can be found in *Convention on Combating Bribery of Foreign Public Officials in International Business Transactions* (Paris: OECD, 2011), p. 7: 'Each Party shall take such measures as may be necessary to establish that it is a criminal offence under its law for any person intentionally to offer, promise or give any undue pecuniary or other advantage, whether directly or through intermediaries, to a foreign public official, for that official or for a third party, in order that the official act or refrain from acting in relation to the performance of official duties, in order to obtain or retain business or other improper advantage in the conduct of international business.' Available at http://www.oecd.org/daf/anti-bribery/ConvCombatBribery_ENG.pdf.

23   See Andrew Wedeman, *Double Paradox: Rapid Growth and Rising Corruption in China* (Ithaca, NY: Cornell University Press, 2012).

24   Timothy R. Heath, *China's New Governing Party Paradigm: Political Renewal and the Pursuit of National Rejuvenation* (Farnham: Ashgate, 2014) is a particularly good example of this.

25   Martha Nussbaum, *Political Emotions: Why Love Matters for Justice* (Cambridge, MA: Harvard University Press, 2013), p. 2.

26   See in particular Michel Foucault, *Power: The Essential Works of Michel Foucault 1954–1984*, vol. 3, ed. James D. Faubion (London: Penguin, 2002).

27   China's two 'centennial goals' are designed to mark, respectively, the 100th anniversary of the CCP's foundation in 1921 and the 100th anniversary of the establishment of the PRC in 1949. The first goal is for China to become a 'well-off society' by 2021. The second is for China to become a fully developed nation by 2049.

2   XI THE MAN

1   Cheng Li, *China's Leaders: The New Generation* (Boulder, CO: Rowman & Littlefield, 2001), p. 10.

2   Xi Jinping, *The Governance of China* [English version] (Beijing: Foreign Languages Press, 2014), pp. 481, 483.

3   Li Taohua and Hu Lili, *Xi Jinping dazhuan* [Biography of Xi Jinping] (Deer Park, NY: Mirror Books, 2013), p. 15.

4   Ibid., pp. 32–3.

5   Michel Bonnin, *The Lost Generation: The Rustication of China's Educated Youth (1968–1980)*, trans. Krystyna Horko (Hong Kong: Chinese University Press, 2013), p. xvii.

6   Xi himself has referred to this loneliness and bitterness in a brief recollection of this period, written in 1998, titled 'Wo shi huang tudi de erzi' [I am a son of the yellow earth]. It is referred to in Li Taohua and Hu Lili, *Xi Jinping dazhuan*, p. 68.

7   Ibid., p. 92.

8   The drama of the Cultural Revolution in Qinghua is treated at length in Andrew G. Walder, *Fractured Rebellion: The Beijing Red Guard Movement* (Cambridge, MA, and London: Belknap, 2009), p. 38 onwards.

9   For a description of this period, see Ezra F. Vogel, *Deng Xiaoping and the Transformation of China* (Cambridge, MA, and London: Belknap, 2011), pp. 51–5.

10   Nancy Lin, 'Architecture', in Chuihua Judy Chung, Jeffrey Inaba, Rem Koolhaas and Sze Tsung Leong (eds), *Great Leap Forward* (Cambridge, MA: Harvard Design School and Taschen, 2001), p. 245.

11   Personal source, 1998.

12   See Barry Naughton, *The Chinese Economy: Transitions and Growth* (Cambridge, MA: MIT Press, 2007), p. 242.

13   See Chen Guidi and Wu Chuntao, *Will the Boat Sink the Water? The Life of China's Peasants*, trans. Zhu Hong (New York: PublicAffairs, 2007). On village- and township-level challenges, see Linda Jacobson, 'Local governance: village and township elections', in Jude Howell (ed.), *Governance in China* (Oxford: Rowman & Littlefield, 2004).

14   Li Taohua and Hu Lili, *Xi Jinping dazhuan*, p. 148.

15   Ibid., p. 162.

16   See Deng Xiaoping, 'June 9 speech to martial law units', Tiananmen: The Gate of Heavenly Peace [website]. Available at http://www.tsquare.tv/chronology/Deng.html.

17   Jianjun Zhang, *Marketization and Democracy in China* (London and New York: Routledge, 2008). P. 146 onwards describes the Wenzhou development model well.

18   The title of Zhang's article was the unequivocal 'We must make it clear that private business cannot be enrolled in the Party', particularly

NOTES TO PAGES 73–93

unfortunate as this is precisely what happened a few months afterwards. It had, as we can now see, no impact on Zhang's career. See Willy Wo-Lap Lam, *Chinese Politics in the Hu Jintao Era: New Leaders, New Challenges* (Armonk, NY, and London: M. E. Sharpe, 2006), p. 131.

19 For an outline of this history, see Chen Jie and Bruce Dickson, *Allies of the State: China's Private Entrepreneurs and Democratic Change* (Cambridge, MA: Harvard University Press, 2010).

20 Li Taohua and Hu Lili, *Xi Jinping dazhuan*, p. 199.

21 Robert Lawrence Kuhn, *How China's Leaders Think: The Inside Story of China's Past, Current and Future Leaders* (rev. edn; London: John Wiley, 2011).

22 For a detailed discussion of the highly technical issue of division between local- and central-government fiscal responsibilities and budgets, see Yang Guangbin, 'Decentralization and central–local relations in reform-era China', in Kenneth Lieberthal, Cheng Li and Yu Keping, *China's Political Development: Chinese and American Perspectives* (Washington DC: Brookings Institution Press, 2014), pp. 254–82.

23 Mark W. Frazier, *Socialist Inequality: Pensions and the Politics of Uneven Development in China* (Ithaca, NY: Cornell University Press, 2010), deals with this issue in some detail: 'It may come as a surprise to many readers that the most expensive function of the Chinese government is not urban construction, infrastructure or national defence but, instead, the provision of public pensions' (p. 2).

24 Michael Ignatieff, *Fire and Ashes: Success and Failure in Politics* (Cambridge, MA: Harvard University Press, 2013).

25 Bo Zhiyue, *China's Elite Politics: Governance and Democratization* (Singapore: World Scientific, 2010) offers the most detailed breakdown of membership categories in the Central Committee.

26 See 'All the parities in China', *The Economist* (24 February 2011). Available at http://www.economist.com/node/18233380.

27 Wang Xiaodong, Song Shaojun, Huang Jilao and Song Qiang (eds), *Zhongguo bu gaoxing* [China is not happy] (Nanjing: Phoenix Publishing and Jiangsu People's Publishing Company, 2009), p. 13.

28 Rana Mitter, *A Bitter Revolution: China's Struggle with the Modern World* (Oxford: Oxford University Press, 2004), p. 40.

29 Jamil Anderlini, 'Bo fallout threatens China's security chief', *Financial Times* (20 April 2012). Available at http://www.ft.com/intl/cms/s/0/f978ce9c-8ae6-11e1-b855-00144feab49a.html.

30   Xi Jinping, *Governance*, p. 479.

31   Max Weber, *The Vocation Lectures: Science as a Vocation, Politics as a Vocation*, ed. David S. Owen, Tracy B. Strong and David Livingstone (New York: Hackett, 2004), pp. 34–5.

32   Yuval Noah Harari, *Sapiens: A Brief History of Humankind* (London: Harvill Secker, 2014), p. 112.

33   Ma Jingshun, *Xi Jinping neibu jianghua* [The internal talks of Xi Jinping] (Hong Kong: Guangdu Shuju Publishing, 2014).

34   Ibid., p. 52.

35   Xi Jinping, *Governance*, p. 15.

36   Ibid., p. 18.

37   Ibid., p. 29.

38   Ibid., p. 43.

39   Ma Jingshun, *Xi Jinping neibu jianghua*, p. 106.

40   Xi Jinping, *Governance*, p. 193.

41   Ibid., p. 196.

42   Ibid., p. 200.

43   Li Taohua and Hu Lili, *Xi Jinping dazhuan*, p. 324.

44   Michael Forsythe, Shai Oster, Natasha Khan and Dune Lawrence, 'Xi Jinping relations reveal fortunes of elite', Bloomberg [website] (21 June 2012). Available at http://www.bloomberg.com/news/articles/2012-06-29/xi-jinping-millionaire-relations-reveal-fortunes-of-elite.

3   XI, HIS ENEMIES AND HIS FRIENDS

1   There always needs to be a word of caution when trying to plot relationships in China, however. It is not a science and has a high failure rate. A good example is to look at the question of Xi's possible links as seen by Alice Miller, one of the finest analysts of Chinese elite politics, in 2010. Of the long list of potential connections that Xi made through his career that are listed in Miller's report, almost none have figured much since his becoming general secretary in 2012. Relationships in China, like anywhere else, come and go. Plotting out the ones that really stay important is a precarious business. This is offered as a caveat to all that follows. See Alice Miller, 'Who does Xi Jinping know and how does he know them?', *China Leadership Monitor* 32 (spring 2010). Available at http://media.hoover.org/sites/default/files/documents/CLM32AM.pdf.

2   Fei Xiaotong, *From the Soil: The Foundations of Chinese Society*, trans. Gary G. Hamilton and Zheng Wang (Berkeley, CA: University of California Press, 1992), p. 30 onwards.

3   'Heirs of Mao's comrades rise as new capitalist nobility', Bloomberg [website] (27 December 2012). Available at http://www.bloomberg. com/news/articles/2012-12-26/immortals-beget-china-capitalism-from-citic-to-godfather-of-golf.

4   Tom Philips, Michael Moore and Sam Marsden, 'The mop-haired British entrepreneur soon to become an official part of China's first family', *Daily Telegraph* (28 October 2012). Available at http://www.telegraph. co.uk/news/worldnews/asia/china/9639027/The-mop-haired-British-entrepreneur-soon-to-become-an-official-part-of-Chinas-first-family. html.

5   Kentaro Koyama, 'Red aristocrats: Xi mother laid down the law on business practices', *Asahi Shimbun* (22 October 2012). Available at http://ajw.asahi.com/article/asia/china/AJ201210220002.

6   See Michael Forsythe, Shai Oster, Natasha Khan and Dune Lawrence, 'Xi Jinping relations reveal fortunes of elite', Bloomberg [website] (21 June 2012). Available at http://www.bloomberg.com/news/articles/2012-06-29/ xi-jinping-millionaire-relations-reveal-fortunes-of-elite.

7   Li Taohua and Hu Lili, *Xi Jinping dazhuan* [Biography of Xi Jinping] (Deer Park, NY: Mirror Books, 2013), pp. 440–2.

8   Ibid., p. 450.

9   Xi Jinping, *The Governance of China* [English version] (Beijing: Foreign Languages Press, 2014), p. 496.

10   Sara Carty, 'Now we know who really runs China', *Daily Mail* (13 November 2014). Available at http://www.dailymail.co.uk/news/ article-2832346/Now-know-REALLY-runs-China-Lady-Peng-Liyuan-tell-husband-Chinese-leader-Xi-Jinping-wave-crowd-one-stern-look. html.

11   Ke Lizi, *Yinxiang Xi Jinping de ren* [The people who influence Xi Jinping] (Deer Park, NY: Mirror Books, 2013), pp. 112–4.

12   Jamil Anderlini, 'Wang Qishan, China's anti-corruption tsar', *Financial Times* (5 August 2014). Available at http://www.ft.com/intl/cms/s/0/ bb14b9c4-1bce-11e4-9db1-00144feabdc0.html#axzz3SWtueu6H.

13   James Char, 'A turning point in China's anti-graft campaign', *Diplomat* [website] (11 January 2015). Available at http://thediplomat. com/2015/01/a-turning-point-in-chinas-anti-graft-campaign/.

14 Personal communication, October 2014.

15 For this, see Kerry Brown, *The New Emperors: Power and the Princelings in China* (London: I.B.Tauris, 2014).

16 On Yu's background, see Cheng Li, 'Yu Zhengsheng, one of China's top leaders to watch', Brookings John Thornton China Study Center [website]. Available at http://www.brookings.edu/about/centers/china/top-future-leaders/yu_zhengsheng.

17 Ke Lizi, *Yinxiang Xi Jinping de ren*, p. 163.

18 'Xi names low-key outsider as personal secretary', *South China Morning Post* [website] (25 July 2013). Available at http://www.scmp.com/news/china/article/1290050/xi-names-ding-xuexiang-personal-secretary.

19 Ke Lizi, *Yinxiang Xi Jinping de ren*, pp. 173–4, and 'Secret seven: inside Xi Jinping's low-key brain trust', *Want China Times* (13 June 2013). Available at http://www.wantchinatimes.com/news-subclass-cnt.aspx?id=20130613000121&cid=1101. See also Bo Zhiyue, 'Xi Jinping's advisors' [East Asian Institute Background Brief no. 847, September 2013].

20 Ke Lizi, *Yinxiang Xi Jinping de ren*, p. 185.

21 Ibid., p. 190.

22 David Bandurski, 'Busy bee, President Xi', China Media Project [website] (27 October 2014). Available at http://cmp.hku.hk/2014/10/27/36702/.

23 Willy Lam, 'Members of the Xi Jinping clique revealed', *China Brief* xiv/3 (7 February 2014). Available at http://www.jamestown.org/programs/chinabrief/single/?tx_ttnews%5Btt_news%5D=41933#.VOujVnysWSo.

24 Ke Lizi, *Yinxiang Xi Jinping de ren*, p. 29.

25 Xiang Jiangyu, *Xi Jinping tuandui* [The groups of Xi Jinping] (Deer Park, NY: Mirror Books, 2013), pp. 419–30.

26 Jeremy Page, 'The wonk with the ear of President Xi Jinping', *Wall Street Journal* (4 June 2013). Available at http://www.wsj.com/articles/SB10001424127887323728204578513422637924256.

27 Bob Davies and Lingling Wei, 'Meet Liu He, Xi Jinping's choice to fix a faltering Chinese economy', *Wall Street Journal* (6 October 2013). Available at http://www.wsj.com/articles/SB10001424052702304906704579111442566524958.

28 Ke Lizi, *Yinxiang Xi Jinping de ren*, p. 220.

29 Ibid., p. 38.

30 Chris Buckley, 'Chinese president in waiting signals quicker reforms', Reuters [news agency] (7 September 2012). Available at http://www.reuters.com/article/2012/09/07/us-china-politics-xi-idUSBRE8860BI20120907.

31 Ke Lizi, *Yinxiang Xi Jinping de ren*, pp. 31–4.

32 World Bank and Development Research Centre of the State Council, *China 2030: Building a Modern, Harmonious, Creative Society* (Washington DC: World Bank, 2012). Available at http://www.worldbank.org/content/dam/Worldbank/document/China-2030-complete.pdf, p. 17.

33 Ibid., p. 17.

34 See David Barboza, 'Family of Wen Jiabao holds a hidden fortune in China', *New York Times* (25 October 2012). Available at http://www.nytimes.com/2012/10/26/business/global/family-of-wen-jiabao-holds-a-hidden-fortune-in-china.html?pagewanted=all&_r=0.

35 For a concise statement of this, see A. Greer Meisels, 'Lessons learned in China from the collapse of the Soviet Union' [University of Sydney China Studies Centre Policy Paper no. 3]. Available at http://sydney.edu.au/china_studies_centre/images/content/ccpublications/policy_paper_series/2013/Lessons-learned-in-China-from-the-collapse-of-the-Soviet-Union.shtml.pdf.

36 Quoted in Cary Huang, 'Mao Zedong granddaughter on rich list, prompting debate', *South China Morning Post* (9 May 2013). Available at http://www.scmp.com/news/china/article/1233208/mao-zedong-granddaughters-addition-rich-list-prompts-debate?page=all.

37 Robert Foyle Hunwick, 'Utopia website shutdown: interview with Fan Jinggang', Danwei [website] (14 April 2012). Available at http://www.danwei.com/interview-before-a-gagging-order-fan-jinggang-of-utopia/.

38 At the time of writing (April 2016) this site remains offline, with visitors to the address referred to http://www.wyzxwk.com/ and the website of the bookshop (http://www.wyzxsd.com/) where there is active content.

39 Quoted in Hunwick, 'Utopia website shutdown'.

40 Mao Yushi, 'Returning Mao Zedong to human form', Caixin Online (26 April 2011). Available at http://cmp.hku.hk/2011/04/28/11944/.

41 Quoted in 'Boundlessly loyal to the great monster', *The Economist* (26 May 2011).

42   Quoted in Ed Zhang, 'A Maoist utopia emerges online', *South China Morning Post* (26 June 2011). Available at http://www.scmp.com/article/971754/maoist-utopia-emerges-online.

43   Quoted in Hunwick, 'Utopia website shutdown'.

44   Jonathan Watts, 'Chinese professor calls Hong Kong residents "dogs of British imperialists"', *Guardian* (24 January 2012). Available at http://www.theguardian.com/world/2012/jan/24/chinese-professor-hong-kong-dogs.

45   Despite strenuous lobby, Deng was never voted onto the CCP Central Committee because of widespread dislike of his ideas in the Party. He died in March 2015.

46   Wang Hui, *The End of the Revolution: China and the Limits of Modernity* (London: Verso, 2009), pp. 77–8.

47   Ibid., p. 6.

48   Tom Philips, 'Red Guard apologies for first murder of Cultural Revolution', *Daily Telegraph* (14 January 2014). Available at http://www.telegraph.co.uk/news/worldnews/asia/china/10568280/Red-Guard-apologises-for-first-murder-of-Cultural-Revolution.html.

49   Liu Binyan, *A Higher Kind of Loyalty* (London: Methuen, 1990).

4   THE POLITICAL PROGRAMME OF XI JINPING

1   Xi Jinping, *The Governance of China* [English version] (Beijing: Foreign Languages Press, 2014), p. 77.

2   'Premier: China confident in maintaining economic growth', Xinhua [news agency] (16 March 2007). Available at http://news.xinhuanet.com/english/2007-03/16/content_5856569.htm.

3   Yasheng Huang, *Selling China: Foreign Direct Investment During the Reform Era* (Cambridge: Cambridge University Press, 2005), p. 79 onwards.

4   Hence the reason the EU has refused to grant China market-economy status.

5   Xi Jinping, *Governance*, p. 85.

6   Ibid., p. 86.

7   Quoted in 'The long arm of the state', *The Economist* (23 June 2011). Available at http://www.economist.com/node/18832034.

8   Ryan Rutkowski, 'Why China's state enterprises want to diversify their business', *Peterson Institute for International Economics: China*

Economic Watch [blog] (22 July 2013). Available at http://blogs.piie. com/china/?p=2994.

9   Benjamin Kang Lim and Ben Blanchard, 'China seizes $14.5 billion assets from family, associates of ex-security chief: sources', Reuters [news agency] (30 March 2014). Available at http:// www.reuters.com/article/2014/03/30/us-china-corruption-zhou-idUSBREA2T02S20140330.

10 See Odd Arne Westad, *Restless Empire: China and the World since 1750* (London: Bodley Head, 2012).

11 Ma Rong, *Population and Society in Contemporary Tibet* (Hong Kong: Hong Kong University Press, 2011), p. 170.

12 For an excellent discussion of this see Emily T. Yeh, *Taming Tibet: Landscape Transformation and the Gift of Chinese Development* (Ithaca, NY, and London: Cornell University Press, 2013), p. 98 onwards.

13 Xi Jinping, *Governance*, p. 89.

14 See Alfred M. Wu, 'Searching for fiscal responsibility: a critical review of the budget reform in China', *China: An International Journal* xii/1 (April 2014), pp. 87–107.

15 A *hukou* is a household-registration document, issued at birth, which divides Chinese citizens into urban or rural residents and grants them different rights in terms of social welfare and so on. Introduced in the 1950s, the *hukou* operated as an internal passport before being liberalized from the 1980s. But it still has an impact on where people can live in the long term and on how much tax they pay.

16 Xi Jinping, *Governance*, p. 90.

17 See Gerard Lemos, *The End of the Chinese Dream: Why Chinese People Fear the Future* (New Haven, CT, and London: Yale University Press, 2012) for an account of how this kind of consultation is done.

18 See Bruce Gilley, *China's Democratic Future: How It Will Happen and Where It Will Lead* (New York: Columbia University Press, 2004) for a discussion of some of the possible scenarios.

19 Ma Jingshun, *Xi Jinping neibu jianghua* [The internal talks of Xi Jinping] (Hong Kong: Guangdu Shuju Publishing, 2014), pp. 148–53. The quotations from 'Document no. 9' in this section have been translated by me, but for a full English version of this text see 'Document 9: a ChinaFile translation', ChinaFile [website] (8 November 2013). Available at http://www.chinafile.com/document-9-chinafile-translation.

20 Celia Hatton, 'Chinese journalist Gao Yu faces trial for leaking state secrets', *BBC News: China Blog* (20 November 2014). Available at http://www.bbc.com/news/blogs-china-blog-30125635.

21 Yu Jianrong, 'Social conflict in rural China', *China Security* iii/2 (spring 2007), p. 7.

22 The official was named Liang Wenyong. The video can be accessed at http://world.time.com/2013/09/17/chinese-official-pigs-out-at-lavish-banquet-disses-countrymen-gets-fired/.

23 'China official Yan Linkun's airport rampage goes viral', *Daily Telegraph* (25 February 2013). Available at http://www.telegraph.co.uk/news/worldnews/asia/china/9892547/China-official-Yan-Linkuns-airport-rampage-goes-viral.html.

24 See 'Chinese flight attendant claims military official beat her', *chinaSMACK* [blog] (2 September 2012). Available at http://www.chinasmack.com/2012/stories/chinese-flight-attendant-claims-military-official-beat-her.html.

25 Xi Jinping, *Governance*, p. 92.

26 Leila Haddou, 'Death penalty statistics country by country, 2013', *Guardian* (27 March 2014). Available at http://www.theguardian.com/world/datablog/2014/mar/27/death-penalty-statistics-2013-by-country.

27 'Chinese Li Yan's death sentence overturned in landmark decision', Amnesty International [website] (10 July 2014). Available at http://www.amnesty.org.uk/li-yan-death-sentence-overturned-landmark-decision#.VQEPZBtDGUk.

28 Xi Jinping, *Governance*, pp. 92–3.

29 See Chapter One for the full OECD definition.

30 Xi Jinping, *Governance*, p. 93.

31 See the page containing data for China on the Transparency International website. Available at http://www.transparency.org/country#CHN.

32 Didi Kirsten Tatlow, 'Spate of suicides tied to drive against graft', *New York Times* (11 September 2014). Available at http://www.nytimes.com/2014/09/12/world/asia/suicide-cases-across-china-tied-to-drive-against-graft.html?_r=0.

33 Wang Xiaofang, *The Civil Servant's Notebook* (Beijing: Penguin, 2012).

34 See Liu Xiaobo, 'God's gift to China', *Index on Censorship* xxxv/4 (2006), pp. 179–81.

35 Ma Jingshun, *Xi Jinping neibu jianghua*, p. 165.

36 See 'Petitioner sent to mental hospital,' Radio Free Asia [website] (18 May 2012). Available at http://www.rfa.org/english/news/china/petitioner-05182012113540.html/.

37 Ma Jingshun, *Xi Jinping neibu jianghua*, p. 192.

38 Ibid., pp. 206–9.

39 Xi Jinping, *Governance*, p. 94.

40 Ibid., p. 95.

41 This is recounted in Kerry Brown, *The New Emperors: Power and the Princelings in China* (London: I.B.Tauris, 2014), pp. 12–13.

42 Xi Jinping, *Governance*, p. 233.

5 HOW DOES XI JINPING SEE THE OUTSIDE WORLD?

1 Kissinger does this by comparing the ways in which the Chinese board game of Go is focused on controlling space, whereas chess is more about achievement of linear strategic objectives. See Henry Kissinger, *On China* (New York: Penguin, 2011), pp. 22–32.

2 Wang Hui, *The End of the Revolution: China and the Limits of Modernity* (London: Verso, 2009), p. 132.

3 Yan Xuetong, *Ancient Chinese Thought, Modern Chinese Power* (Princeton, NJ, and Oxford: Princeton University Press, 2011), p. 99. This earned him the response from Yang Qianru of Peking University that China's problem, 'both now and far into the future, is to guarantee our own survival, development and security, not lead the world' (ibid., p. 153).

4 See 'Full text: the practice of the "one country, two systems" policy in the Hong Kong Special Administrative Region', Xinhua [news agency] (10 June 2015). Available at http://news.xinhuanet.com/english/china/2014-06/10/c_133396891.htm.

5 See Zachary Keck, 'China claims US behind Hong Kong protests', *Diplomat* (12 October 2014). Available at http://thediplomat.com/2014/10/china-claims-us-behind-hong-kong-protests/.

6 Lawrence Chung, '"One country, two systems" right formula for Taiwan, Xi Jinping reiterates', *South China Morning Post* (27 September 2014). Available at http://www.scmp.com/news/china/article/1601307/one-country-two-systems-right-formula-taiwan-xi-jinping-reiterates?page=all.

7 Office of the Press Secretary, the White House, 'Remarks by President

Obama and President Xi Jinping of the People's Republic of China after bilateral meeting', White House [website] (8 June 2013). Available at https://www.whitehouse.gov/the-press-office/2013/06/08/remarks-president-obama-and-president-xi-jinping-peoples-republic-china-.

8   Bill Clinton, 'Why I'm going to China', *Newsweek* (29 June 1998). Available at http://www.washingtonpost.com/wp-srv/newsweek/why.htm.

9   This and the following quotations from the white paper are taken from 'China's policy paper on the EU: deepen the China–EU comprehensive strategic partnership for mutual benefit and win–win cooperation', Ministry of Foreign Affairs of the People's Republic of China [website] (2 April 2014). Available at http://www.fmprc.gov.cn/mfa_eng/wjdt_665385/wjzcs/t1143406.shtml.

10   'President Xi's speech at the College of Europe', China Internet Information Center [website] (1 April 2014). Available at http://www.china.org.cn/world/2014-04/04/content_32004856.htm.

11   Mark Edward Lewis, *China's Cosmopolitan Empire: The Tang Dynasty* (Cambridge, MA: Belknap, 2009), pp. 3, 159.

12   See Andrew Small, *The China–Pakistan Axis: Asia's New Geopolitics* (New York: Hurst, 2015) and Robert S. Ross, *China's Security Policy: Structure, Power and Politics* (London: Routledge, 2009).

13   For a concise overview of this history, see Lo Bobo, *Axis of Convenience: Moscow, Beijing and the New Geopolitics* (Washington DC: Brookings Institution Press, and London: Chatham House, 2008), particularly ch. 2, 'The burden of history', pp. 17–35.

14   Jang Jin-sung, *Dear Leader: From Trusted Insider to Enemy of the State, My Escape from North Korea*, trans. Shirley Lee (London: Rider, 2014), pp. 260–1.

15   See Martin Jacques, *When China Rules the World: The Rise of the Middle Kingdom and the End of the Western World* (London and New York: Allen Lane, 2009) and Joshua Cooper Ramo, *The Beijing Consensus* (London: Foreign Policy Centre, 2004). Available at http://fpc.org.uk/fsblob/244.pdf.

16   Rosemary Foot and Andrew Walter, *China, the United States, and Global Order* (Cambridge: Cambridge University Press, 2011), p. 65, has a good illustration of this regarding the need for financial reform in China and the ways WTO entry assisted this.

17 See in particular Richard Ned Lebow, *A Cultural Theory of International Relations* (Cambridge: Cambridge University Press, 2008), ch. 2, 'Fear, interest and honour' (pp. 43–121), for a good account of this.

18 Dominique Moïsi, *The Geopolitics of Emotion: How Cultures of Fear, Humiliation and Hope Are Reshaping the World* (New York: Doubleday, 2009).

19 Robert Cooper, *The Breaking of Nations: Order and Chaos in the Twenty-First Century* (London: Atlantic, 2003), in particular p. 116.

20 Perhaps the most infamous case was the demand by Hanban, the entity that runs Confucius Institutes, that a notice for the Chiang Ching-kuo Foundation in Taiwan be removed from conference papers for an event held in Portugal in 2014. See 'EACS to protest Hanban's academic meddling: source', *Taipei Times* (31 July 2014). Available at http://www.taipeitimes.com/News/taiwan/archives/2014/07/31/2003596335.

6   WHAT DOES XI WANT IN THE NEXT TWO DECADES?

1 These objectives were reiterated in the era of the new leadership by vice president of China Li Yuanchao to a meeting of international scholars in the Great Hall of the People on 3 September 2014.

2 See M. Taylor Fravel, *Strong Borders, Secure Nation: Cooperation and Conflict in China's Territorial Disputes* (Princeton, NJ: Princeton University Press, 2008).

3 World Bank and Development Research Centre of the State Council, *China 2030: Building a Modern, Harmonious, Creative Society* (Washington DC: World Bank, 2012). Available at http://www.worldbank.org/content/dam/Worldbank/document/China-2030-complete.pdf.

4 Zhou Tianyong, Wang Changjiang and Wang Anling, *Gong jian, Zhongguo zhengzhi tizhi gaige yanjiu bao gao, shi qi da hou* [Storm the fortress: a report on the reform of China's political system after the 17th Party congress] (Xinjiang: Xinjiang Production Corps Publication House, 2007).

5 The Gini coefficient is a measure of inequality based on income distribution, on which zero represents perfect equality (that is, where income is equal throughout a society) and one represents maximal inequality (such as where a small group of people hold all the wealth and the majority have none).

CONCLUSION

1   Eamon Duffy, 'Who is the Pope?', *New York Review of Books* (19 February 2015), p. 11. Available at http://www.nybooks.com/articles/archives/2015/feb/19/who-is-pope-francis/.
2   Xi Jinping, *The Governance of China* [English version] (Beijing: Foreign Languages Press, 2014), p. 4.
3   Yu Jie, *Zhongguo Jiaofu* [China's godfather] (Hong Kong and New York, NY: Open Books, 2014), p. 3.
4   Ibid., p. 15.
5   Ibid., p. 20.
6   Ibid., p. 72.

BIBLIOGRAPHY

Barmé, Geremie, 'New China newspeak', *The China Story* [website] (2 August 2012). Available at http://www.thechinastory.org/lexicon/new-china-newspeak/.

Bo Zhiyue, *China's Elite Politics: Governance and Democratization* (Singapore: World Scientific, 2010).

——— 'Xi Jinping's advisors' [East Asian Institute Background Brief no. 847, September 2013].

Bonnin, Michel, *The Lost Generation: The Rustication of China's Educated Youth (1968–1980)*, trans. Krystyna Horko (Hong Kong: Chinese University Press, 2013).

Brown, Kerry, *Hu Jintao: China's Silent Ruler* (Singapore: World Scientific, 2012).

——— *The New Emperors: Power and the Princelings in China* (London: I.B.Tauris, 2014).

CCP Party History Office, *Zhongguo gongchandang lishi 1949–1978* [Chinese Communist Party history 1949–1978] (Beijing: Zhonggong Dangshi Chubanshe, 2011).

Chen Guidi and Wu Chuntao, *Will the Boat Sink the Water? The Life of China's Peasants*, trans. Zhu Hong (New York: PublicAffairs, 2007).

Chen Jie and Bruce Dickson, *Allies of the State: China's Private Entrepreneurs and Democratic Change* (Cambridge, MA: Harvard University Press, 2010).

Chung, Chuihua Judy, Jeffrey Inaba, Rem Koolhaas and Sze Tsung Leong (eds), *Great Leap Forward* (Cambridge, MA: Harvard Design School and Taschen, 2001).

Confucius, *The Analects*, trans. Arthur Waley (London: Everyman, 2000).

Cooper, Robert, *The Breaking of Nations: Order and Chaos in the Twenty-First Century* (London: Atlantic, 2003).

Fairclough, Norman, *New Labour, New Language?* (London: Routledge, 2005).

Foot, Rosemary, and Andrew Walter, *China, the United States, and Global Order* (Cambridge: Cambridge University Press, 2011).

Foucault, Michel, *Power: The Essential Works of Michel Foucault 1954–1984*, vol. 3, ed. James D. Faubion (London: Penguin, 2002).

Fravel, M. Taylor, *Strong Borders, Secure Nation: Cooperation and Conflict in China's Territorial Disputes* (Princeton, NJ: Princeton University Press, 2008).

Frazier, Mark W., *Socialist Inequality: Pensions and the Politics of Uneven Development in China* (Ithaca: Cornell University Press, 2010).

Gao, Mobo, *The Battle for China's Past* (London: Pluto Press, 2008).

Gilley, Bruce, *China's Democratic Future: How It Will Happen and Where It Will Lead* (New York: Columbia University Press, 2004).

Han Fei Tzu, *Basic Writings*, trans. Burton Watson (New York: Columbia University Press, 1967).

Harari, Yuval Noah, *Sapiens: A Brief History of Humankind* (London: Harvill Secker, 2014).

Heath, Timothy R., *China's New Governing Party Paradigm: Political Renewal and the Pursuit of National Rejuvenation* (Farnham: Ashgate, 2014).

Hibbard, Peter, *The Bund: Shanghai Faces West* (Hong Kong: Odyssey Books, 2007).

Huang, Yasheng, *Selling China: Foreign Direct Investment During the Reform Era* (Cambridge: Cambridge University Press, 2005).

——— *Capitalism with Chinese Characteristics* (Cambridge: Cambridge University Press, 2008).

Ignatieff, Michael, *Fire and Ashes: Success and Failure in Politics* (Cambridge, MA: Harvard University Press, 2013).

Jacobson, Linda, 'Local governance: village and township elections', in Jude Howell (ed.), *Governance in China* (Oxford: Rowman & Littlefield, 2004).

Jang Jin-sung, *Dear Leader: From Trusted Insider to Enemy of the State, My Escape from North Korea*, trans. Shirley Lee (London: Rider, 2014).

Kallio, Jonas, *Tradition in Chinese Politics: The Party-State's Reinvention of the Past* (Helsinki: Finnish Institute of International Affairs, 2011).

Ke Lizi, *Yinxiang Xi Jinping de ren* [The people who influence Xi Jinping] (Deer Park, NY: Mirror Books, 2013).

Kissinger, Henry, *On China* (New York: Penguin, 2011).

Kuhn, Robert Lawrence, *How China's Leaders Think: The Inside Story of China's Past, Current and Future Leaders* (rev. edn; London: John Wiley, 2011).

Lam, Willy Wo-Lap, *Chinese Politics in the Hu Jintao Era: New Leaders, New Challenges* (Armonk, NY, and London: M. E. Sharpe, 2006).

Lebow, Richard Ned, *A Cultural Theory of International Relations* (Cambridge: Cambridge University Press, 2008).

Lemos, Gerard, *The End of the Chinese Dream: Why Chinese People Fear the Future* (New Haven, CT, and London: Yale University Press, 2012).

Lewis, Mark Edward, *China's Cosmopolitan Empire: The Tang Dynasty* (Cambridge, MA: Belknap, 2009).

Leys, Simon, *The Hall of Uselessness* (Collingwood: Black Inc., 2012).

Li, Cheng, *China's Leaders: The New Generation* (Boulder, CO: Rowman & Littlefield, 2001).

Li Taohua and Hu Lili, *Xi Jinping dazhuan* [Biography of Xi Jinping] (Deer Park, NY: Mirror Books, 2013).

Lieberthal, Kenneth, Cheng Li and Yu Keping, *China's Political Development: Chinese and American Perspectives* (Washington DC: Brookings Institution Press, 2014).

Link, Perry, *An Anatomy of Chinese* (Cambridge, MA: Harvard University Press, 2013).

Liu Binyan, *A Higher Kind of Loyalty* (London: Methuen, 1990).

Liu Xiaobo, *No Enemies, No Hatred*, ed. Perry Link, Tienchi Martin-Liao and Liu Xia (Cambridge, MA: Belknap, 2012).

Lo Bobo, *Axis of Convenience: Moscow, Beijing and the New Geopolitics* (Washington DC: Brookings Institution Press, and London: Chatham House, 2008).

Ma Jingshun, *Xi Jinping neibu jianghua* [The internal talks of Xi Jinping] (Hong Kong: Guangdu Shuju Publishing, 2014).

Ma Rong, *Population and Society in Contemporary Tibet* (Hong Kong: Hong Kong University Press, 2011).

Mitter, Rana, *A Bitter Revolution: China's Struggle with the Modern World* (Oxford: Oxford University Press, 2004).

—— *China's War with Japan 1937–1945: The Struggle for Survival* (London: Allen Lane, 2013).

Moïsi, Dominique, *The Geopolitics of Emotion: How Cultures of Fear, Humiliation and Hope Are Reshaping the World* (New York: Doubleday, 2009).

Morozov, Evgeny, *The Net Delusion: How Not to Liberate the World* (London and New York: Penguin, 2011).

Naughton, Barry, *The Chinese Economy: Transitions and Growth* (Cambridge, MA: MIT Press, 2007).

Nussbaum, Martha, *Political Emotions: Why Love Matters for Justice* (Cambridge, MA: Harvard University Press, 2013).

Pantsov, Alexander V., and Steven I. Levine, *Mao: The Real Story* (New York: Simon & Schuster, 2012).

Ross, Robert S., *China's Security Policy: Structure, Power and Politics* (London: Routledge, 2009).

Schoenhals, Michael, *Spying for the People: Mao's Secret Agents 1949–1967* (Cambridge: Cambridge University Press, 2013).

Small, Andrew, *The China–Pakistan Axis: Asia's New Geopolitics* (New York: Hurst, 2015).

Vogel, Ezra F., *Deng Xiaoping and the Transformation of China* (Cambridge, MA, and London: Belknap, 2011).

Walder, Andrew G., *Fractured Rebellion: The Beijing Red Guard Movement* (Cambridge, MA, and London: Belknap, 2009).

Wang Hui, *The End of the Revolution: China and the Limits of Modernity* (London: Verso, 2009).

Wang Xiaodong, Song Shaojun, Huang Jilao and Song Qiang (eds), *Zhongguo bu gaoxing* [China is not happy] (Nanjing: Phoenix Publishing and Jiangsu People's Publishing Company, 2009).

Wang Xiaofang, *The Civil Servant's Notebook* (Beijing: Penguin, 2012).

Weber, Max, *The Vocation Lectures: Science as a Vocation, Politics as a Vocation*, ed. David S. Owen, Tracy B. Strong and David Livingstone (New York: Hackett, 2004).

Wedeman, Andrew, *Double Paradox: Rapid Growth and Rising Corruption in China* (Ithaca, NY: Cornell University Press, 2012).

Westad, Odd Arne, *Restless Empire: China and the World since 1750* (London: Bodley Head, 2012).

World Bank and Development Research Centre of the State Council, *China 2030: Building a Modern, Harmonious, Creative Society* (Washington DC: World Bank, 2012). Available at http://www.worldbank.org/content/dam/Worldbank/document/China-2030-complete.pdf.

Wu Ming, *Xi Jinping Zhuan* [A biography of Xi Jinping] (Hong Kong: Hong Kong Culture and Arts Publishing, 2008).

Wu, Alfred M., 'Searching for fiscal responsibility: a critical review of the budget reform in China', *China: An International Journal* xii/1 (April 2014), pp. 87–107.

Xi Jinping, *The Governance of China* [English version] (Beijing: Foreign Languages Press, 2014).

Xiang Jiangyu, *Xi Jinping tuandui* [The groups of Xi Jinping] (Deer Park, NY: Mirror Books, 2013).

Yan Xuetong, *Ancient Chinese Thought, Modern Chinese Power* (Princeton, NJ, and Oxford: Princeton University Press, 2011).

Yeh, Emily T., *Taming Tibet: Landscape Transformation and the Gift of Chinese Development* (Ithaca, NY, and London: Cornell University Press, 2013).

Yu Jianrong, 'Social conflict in rural China', *China Security* iii/2 (spring 2007), pp. 2–17.

Yu Jie, *Zhongguo Jiaofu* [China's godfather] (Hong Kong and New York, NY: Open Books, 2014).

Zhang, Jianjun, *Marketization and Democracy in China* (London and New York: Routledge, 2008).

Zhou Tianyong, Wang Changjiang and Wang Anling, *Gong jian, Zhongguo zhengzhi tizhi gaige yanjiu bao gao, shi qi da hou* [Storm the fortress: a report on the reform of China's political system after the 17th Party congress] (Xinjiang: Xinjiang Production Corps Publication House, 2007).

INDEX